FOREIGN
INVESTMENT IN
LATIN AMERICA

Borzoi Books ON LATIN AMERICA

General Editor

LEWIS HANKE

COLUMBIA UNIVERSITY

FOREIGN
INVESTMENT IN
LATIN AMERICA

Cases and Attitudes

Edited with an Introduction by

Marvin D. Bernstein

STATE UNIVERSITY OF NEW YORK AT FREDONIA

ALFRED · A · KNOPF · *New York*

NOTE: *Documents 7, 15, and 16, as indicated by the source footnotes, were not heretofore available in English. These have been translated by Marvin D. Bernstein, who wishes to acknowledge with thanks the assistance he received from Ruth Engel and Susana Grun, students at the State University of New York at Fredonia, in preparing them.*

L. C. catalog card number: 66–10872

THIS IS A BORZOI BOOK,

PUBLISHED BY ALFRED A. KNOPF, INC.

FIRST EDITION

To My Wife
as a Token
for Her Understanding
and Patience

Contents

Contents

FOREIGN
INVESTMENT IN
LATIN AMERICA

INTRODUCTION

Investments for exploitation and development have been part of the history of Latin America from the very start of its contact with Europeans. Europeans swarmed over the new-found lands. Desires for land and the trappings of wealth, for personal glory and titles, for patriotically advancing the power and domain of the Nation and the Church, and for propagating the True Faith to the heathen, mingled with the wish to build cities and set up businesses for the profits of commerce and to exploit the wealth of the Indies. Columbus' first expedition attempted to blaze a new trade route to the East and establish commercial relations with the Great Khan in consonance with the aims of Europe's burgeoning bourgeois economy. His later voyages, and those of the captains who followed on his heels, were ventures seeking exploitable deposits of precious metals and gems, pearl fisheries, spice groves, slaves for sale abroad and land suitable for commercial farming. Two decades later an investment in an armed expedition paid off when Hernando Cortés overthrew the Aztec empire.

Spaniards and Portuguese laid out capital in lavish amounts to finance exploration and colonization. Some capital was European, but some came from fortunes already made in the New World by Europeans and reinvested with the hope of finding even greater El Dorados. Fernão de Noronha contracted with the Portuguese crown in 1503 for the right to set up *feitorias* (trading posts) for the cutting and export of brazilwood. The Portuguese settlements also became centers of commercial sugar production for export. Feitorias were soon scattered up and down the Brazilian coast as Portuguese, French, British, and Dutch capitalists vied in sending out expeditions. The Portuguese crown divided Brazil into huge *capitanias* and turned them over to noblemen, many of whom had done well in the India trade, to obtain settlers and foment economic development. Most of the *donatarios* who received land went bankrupt in the venture, but Europeans were settled in Brazil and they opened the land to produce dyewood, sugar, and cattle and made large investments in sugar mills, thus securing Brazil for Portugal.

Foreign capital played as important a role in the opening of Spanish America as in the Portuguese areas. Capital for Spanish America was organized in a number of ways: Crown money, heavy private investment by Spaniards, mixed ventures of Crown and private money, and even capital from non-Spanish companies. Charles V, Holy Roman Emperor and King of Spain, extended many of the privileges of trading and investing in the Spanish colonies to his Flemish, German, and Italian subjects. The Fuggers of Augsburg received trade privileges throughout the Spanish dominions in the New World, as well as the right to trade in the spices of the Moluccas by way of the Straits of Magellan. A Genoese house received the first contract to engage in the slave trade. And the German banking house of Welser, in concert with a Swiss house from Constance, energetically pursued the slave trade and attempted to colonize Venezuela in the 1530's.[1] Pedro de Mendoza formed a stock company to finance his conquest of the Río de la Plata and put himself and his brother on the payroll.

[1] Germán Arciniegas, *Germans in the Conquest of America* (New York: The Macmillan Co., 1943).

Foreign business interests were a major force in abetting revolutionary change in Latin America. The lure of new markets was irresistible to both Latin American and foreign merchants, particularly in the disrupted economic situation accompanying the Napoleonic Wars. Opportunities could not be passed up to end the Spanish and Portuguese national monopolies over the economic life of their colonies. Although British attempts to wrest the Viceroyalty of La Plata from Spain's grasp were repulsed by the *porteños* themselves, many of these very colonists petitioned the Viceroy to open Buenos Aires to British trade. Francisco de Miranda drew British support for his ill-starred attempts to foment revolutions in Venezuela, while Simón Bolívar found a most dependable group of foreign legionnaires among the British veterans of the Napoleonic Wars. Although the prospect of independence opened vistas of burgeoning economic benefits, direct foreign assistance in securing the independence of Spanish and Portuguese America was marginal.[2] After national freedom was established, however, diplomatic support of eager investors and traders followed quickly. (A case very much in point is the activities of the British traders and investors in Brazil. See Document 5.)

Once Latin America achieved independence, British investors responded with a flurry of speculation. (See Document 1.) Alexander von Humboldt, the great savant, found his works on Spanish America translated

[2] "In the great adventure of freedom no outside country came to their aid. The independence of the United States was obtained with the help of half Europe. . . . But no country declared war on Spain or Portugal in order to help Latin America emancipate itself. The wars of Europe indeed provided the opportunity. But from the European Governments it was long before even normal support was given." (C. K. Webster, *Britain and the Independence of Latin America* [Oxford: Oxford University Press, 1938], I, pp. 4–5.)

into English and used as prospectuses! Benjamin Disraeli practiced his art of persuasion early by penning a number of pamphlets for stock sellers. Investments in government bonds and mines, colonization schemes and ephemeral shipping and canal companies poured overseas to the former Spanish colonies. It is estimated that British mining associations formed in 1824–25 had an authorized capital of over £24 million, of which £3.5 million was paid in.[3] (For one investment that turned out poorly, see Document 2.) Latin American government bond issues floated in London between 1822 and 1825 raised from £19 million to £20 million. By 1880 it was estimated that British investments in Latin America came to over £123 million in government bonds and £56.4 million in enterprises including railways, public utilities, mines, banks and finance companies, real estate enterprises and shipping. This hectic outpouring of British wealth soon became as vexatious as it was imprudent. Defaults on government bonds started almost immediately, while returns from business enterprises were often most disappointing. (See Documents 4 and 5.) Brigandage and murder compounded the errors of poor management during the first decades of independence. By the 1880's, however, most of the British enterprises still in operation paid dividends and some enjoyed an excellent status.

The last quarter of the nineteenth and the beginning of the twentieth century saw large amounts of capital poured into Latin America from Great Britain, the United States, and the capital-exporting nations of western Europe. (See Document 1.) British investments rose from £85 million to £750 million between 1870 and 1914; fifty per cent of the total investment was made in

[3] J. F. Rippy, *British Investments in Latin America, 1822–1949* (Minneapolis: University of Minnesota Press, 1959), p. 24.

the last decade. These holdings were largely in government bonds, railways, public utilities, mines—Peruvian guano, Chilean nitrate, Mexican silver and nonferrous metals—and meat packing. French holdings grew rapidly after 1870. Despite an earlier difficult experience with Mexican government bonds—which led to the establishment of the ill-fated empire ruled by Maximilian—approximately 30 per cent of the French investment was in government securities. Large outflows of French funds began after 1880, increasing threefold between 1900 and 1913 to 6 billion francs ($1.2 billion). German capital bought government securities, financed port works and public utilities, operated plantations and mortgage banks. An estimated $900 million, 16 per cent of Germany's overseas holdings, were in Latin America, chiefly Argentina, Brazil, Chile, and Mexico.

Early nineteenth-century investments by United States capitalists are impossible to total.[4] By 1830 American capital was active in Mexico, Cuba, and Chile; by 1870 American money and skills had been invested at one time or another in every Latin American nation, although profits were meager. Railroads, international steamship lines, river boats, public utilities, and mines were the earlier objectives. In 1890 the total United States investment in Latin America came to $250 million—over half of it in Mexico. The list of enterprises was a varied one: mines, railroads, telephone exchanges, submarine cables, timber, sugar and banana plantations, asphalt, petroleum, public utilities, river transport, and ranch lands. By 1897, before the Spanish-American War, the American investment reached

---

[4] For general historical surveys of United States investments in Latin America, see J. Fred Rippy, *Globe and Hemisphere: Latin America's Place in the Postwar Foreign Relations of the United States* (Chicago: Henry Regnery Company, 1958), Chaps. I and II.

$320 million, about two-thirds of it in Mexico. Between the Spanish-American War and the year 1914, American investments grew from a not insignificant trickle to a large flow: United States holdings came to $1.6 billions, of which $352.6 million was in government bonds and securities of foreign-controlled corporations. Mining and petroleum, with about $580 million invested, represented the largest amount. Mexico's share was the largest, coming to $266.4 million in government bonds and portfolio investments—$202 million in mining and $110.4 million in railroads. Cuba followed with $265 million, mostly in sugar, and Chile came next with $180 million in mining. (The methods and effects of United States' activities in Cuba are reviewed in detail in Document 11.)

The loans and investments made during the latter half of the nineteenth century began to modernize the Latin American economy. Although still in a backward, pre-Industrial Revolution state, plagued by a shortage and neglect of public works and improvements, outdistanced materially by the rapidly advancing economies of the United States and Western Europe, certain areas began to display signs of betterment. Argentina, Uruguay, southern Brazil, central Chile, central Mexico, Cuba, and many of the national capitals, started to install electric power, lay paved streets, build sewers in the cities and railroads in the country. Many parts remained, as they are today, untouched by the comforts, conveniences, and power-driven appliances of the Industrial Revolution—but probably they were no more backward than many parts of central and southern Europe at the time. As a whole, Latin America became part of the world economy. The products of its mines and plantations provided the base of numerous manufacturing industries and fed millions of people in North

America and Europe. Much of this growth was the product of European and American capital concentrating on export industries—particularly mining and tropical foods—public utilities, and transportation. (A sobering look at the life and work of the trailblazers is provided by H. M. Tomlinson's sketch of railroad building in the Amazon, Document 10.) These enterprises yielded surer incomes by preparing commodities for sale in world markets or collecting tariffs on the use of public services. Little was done to satisfy internal markets or develop viable national economies. The export of raw materials paid for imports of manufactured goods and the use of the public services. These services, in fact, served to stimulate many nationally owned segments of the economy. Foreign-financed railroads not only opened remote areas to foreign capitalistic penetration, but provided outlets and incentives for local capital. Argentina, for example, was stirred by the building of railways and meat packing plants, the importation of barbed wire and steel windmills, the provision of fast refrigerator ships to develop her own Argentine-owned ranching industry. As a result, a close community of interest grew up between the Argentine upper class—rancher, businessman, professional, and government official—and British capitalists. Argentine newspapers praised British progress, and Argentine society aped British manners. Some Argentines saw this as a gigantic conspiracy to subject their nation culturally as well as economically to British domination, a conspiracy craftily hatched in London although difficult to document.[5] Defenders of Britain's policy of so-called

---

[5] This is the viewpoint of ex-President Arturo Frondizi, in his polemic *Petróleo y política* (Buenos Aires: Editorial Raigal, 1954). Frondizi also added allegations of a plot fostered by the United States against the political, economic and cultural independence of several other Latin American states.

"laissez-faire imperialism" have countered with the charge that Argentina at all times possessed the political power to change this relationship, but continued it because there were advantages for Argentina as well as Britain. (See Document 6.)

There is, however, another side to this story. In many instances the penetration of foreign capital was accompanied by a general political complacency and cooperation which led to sayings such as the Mexican remark during the regime of Porfirio Díaz, "Mexico is the mother of foreigners and the stepmother of Mexicans." Political chicanery and cooperation with dictators—and the buttressing of their power—could lead to lucrative concessions. (See Rómulo Betancourt's description of Venezuela under the tyrant Gómez, Document 7 and Bauer Paíz's description of Guatemala in Document 19.) "Dollar Diplomacy," the close association of United States businessmen and government officials to keep the area "safe," was a feature of Caribbean history from the Spanish–American War down to today. (See Documents 8 and 12.)

During World War I, American investments rose about 50 per cent while, with the exception of German holdings which were sold or confiscated, European capital remained at former levels because of the lack of new money. In the decade after 1919, United States investments in Latin America more than doubled, as capital was exported at a rate that reached some $200 million a year after 1925. Unfortunately, while some of the money borrowed by Latin American governments from United States sources at this time went into public works, large amounts did not add directly or indirectly to the borrowing country's productive capacity.[6]

[6] For the 1920 Latin American government bond scandals, see U.S. Senate, Committee on Finance, *Sale of Foreign Bonds or Securities in the United States* (Washington, D.C., 1932), and

Great Britain's investment in Latin America remained stable during the 1920's, new investment being offset by bond amortization, liquidation of unprofitable enterprises and the sale of assets to nationals or United States firms. Germany's holdings cannot be measured because of the lack of any official estimates. It is probable that German investments declined after 1914, but many owners became residents and German influence in chemicals, drugs, trade, and aviation continued. Inflation and continuing financial difficulties caused France's investment to fall off.

With the onset of the Great Depression, investments in Latin America declined drastically. Funds were repatriated, reinvestment and new investment dried up, holdings were considerably devalued to fit new monetary standards and last, but not least, the Latin American republics themselves adopted economic controls and nationalistic policies which effectively repulsed investors. Not until after 1945 did new capital enter Latin America, and most of that came from the United States.

Repatriation of investments marked the early postwar years. Following defaults and fractional settlements during the 1930's, the Latin American governments' treasuries filled with gold and dollars earned by selling foodstuffs and raw materials to the United Nations during the war. They now began to retire bonds at a rapid pace. Purchases of new Latin American government bonds by foreign nationals remained small. By the beginning of the 1950's, with the exception of Bolivia and Peru, outstanding government loans had been settled, often under prodding by the World Bank, which insisted that nations wishing Bank loans must first rehabilitate their international credit standing. In

Ilse Mintz, *Deterioration in the Quality of Foreign Bonds Issued in the United States* (New York: National Bureau of Economic Research, 1951).

addition, many Latin American nations began repurchasing economic assets owned abroad, particularly railways and public utilities.[7] (See Document 1.)

Direct investments by United States nationals, which slumped during the early 1930's and reached a plateau in 1936, began to increase in 1943. However, all figures concerning United States direct investments in Latin America must be viewed against the huge and fluctuating investments in Venezuelan petroleum.[8] Manufacturing investments—particularly in Mexico, Brazil, Colombia and Venezuela—were the next largest category, followed by mining and smelting—Peru, Chile, Mexico —and a diminishing amount invested in public utilities. Repatriations in the latter area were highlighted by Mexico's purchase of the Canadian-chartered Mexican Light and Power Company, and the rather noisy take-over of the properties of the International Telephone and Telegraph Company's properties by the government of the state of Rio Grande do Sul in Brazil in 1962. In late 1963 Argentina threatened to confiscate United States investment in her oil fields while Peru talked of nationalization. (See the letter of Raymond Vernon, Document 12.) These were minor annoyances, however, in relation to the billion dollars lost to the Cuban revolutionary government. Still, the total United States direct private investment in Latin America reached $8.657 billion in 1963, while its total assets and investments in the region came to $15.743 billion.

This vast outpouring of wealth into Latin America has

[7] A fine survey of this development is in Raymond F. Mikesell, *Foreign Investments in Latin America* (Washington, D.C.: The Pan-American Union, 1955).

[8] See the analysis of Leland L. Johnson, "U.S. Private Investment in Latin America Since the Rise of Castro," *Inter-American Economic Affairs*, XVIII (Winter, 1964), 53–75 and especially 56–60.

raised several questions and posed numerous problems. The questions concern the necessity and usefulness of these investments; the problems concern the effect of these investments upon Latin American life and these nations' relations with the outside world. As in all situations, close study but leads one to distrust pleas from either side and to note that whites offset blacks while great gray areas overshadow the picture. A Mexican version, c. 1938, was reported in *Fortune* magazine:

> . . . The total national income in "the treasure chest of the earth" is only $680,000,000 or $36 per capita. For this poverty and lost opportunity her economists blame the anomaly of two distinct economies that scarcely ever mesh but operate as if separated by different time horizons. There is the agrarian economy which is based on 70 per cent of the population and made up largely of shoeless, bedless, frijole-eating, plague-ridden peasants whose death rate is the world's highest next to Egypt's. There is the industrial economy, source of an estimated 85 per cent of the Republic's wealth, which is dominated by foreigners who export their profits to distant fatherlands. Of this second world the Mexicans have only small pieces; for example only 2 per cent of the mining industry, whose production last year was worth $143,000,000. But by taxation, by government-backed labor demands, and finally by expropriation, the Mexicans are jamming the profits from this second world into the medieval twilight of the first. And when the foreigners resist, the Mexicans get mad.[9]

Some twenty years later, in 1959, Robert L. Garner, head of the International Finance Corporation, defended foreign investors:

> There is also a fairly widely held view that though private enterprise can be useful it needs to be rather

[9] "Mexico in Revolution," *Fortune*, XVIII (October, 1938), 84.

strictly directed and controlled by government. Certainly no serious person today would dispute that governments have a responsibility to lay down broad rules of the game for private business. . . . But if an economy is to benefit from the vigor of individual effort and from the imagination and courage of the able man, government must not put him in shackles of bureaucratic regulation nor attempt to substitute the judgement of officials for his business judgement. I fear, and I think experience proves, that an economic system may get the worst of both worlds if it accepts private enterprise only under conditions which tie its hands and interfere with its ability to produce and grow.

One also frequently detects a distrust of private business in the minds of some well-meaning people because it enables certain individuals to make large profits. They see in this a social injustice. However, looked at from a practical standpoint, profits which arise from producing useful goods and services are a very big plus in an economy. Profits are the food without which economic life cannot sustain itself, much less expand. . . . Therefore, I wish to pay tribute to profits, which not only spur individuals to their best efforts, but are the sustenance on which economic life lives and grows, and from which are provided the public services essential to modern living.[1]

Where lies the truth? Perhaps the answer is akin to Maxim Gorki's thought that God does exist, but only for those who believe in Him. To reconcile the private enterprise views of the vice-president of American & Foreign Power, H. W. Balgooyen (Document 13) and the Marxian views of the Mexican economist, Pablo González Casanova (Document 15) is impossible.

[1] *Address at the 1959 Meeting of the Board of Governors of the International Finance Corporation* (Washington, D.C., Sept. 30, 1959), pp. 4–6. Also see the discussion by Emilio G. Collado, "Economic Development Through Private Enterprise," *Foreign Affairs*, XLI (July, 1963), 708–720.

To place the problem in proper perspective, we ought to begin with the question of why foreigners place their money overseas and why nations encourage and receive investments. The answer to the first question, it is generally agreed, is profits, immediate or future. Although a survey of the motivations of companies investing abroad, conducted by the University of Oregon, led Dr. J. N. Behrman to conclude that "the motives [are] complex and not singularly 'profit-directed',"[2] an examination of the motives actually given can lead to other conclusions. While only 20 out of 72 respondents answered, "Increased profits," only one answered "To raise living standards abroad," and the others reported such non-profit-oriented motives as: expanded foreign demand, nationalistic attitudes and restrictions on exports and imports, to obtain raw materials, lower costs abroad, diversification, and to maintain supplier relations with a customer. Working with his own esoteric definitions, Dr. Behrman remarked: "Though a wish to make a special contribution to the economic welfare of developing countries may seem at variance with the stereotyped motives of businessmen, there is a growing recognition of the role which private business can play in guiding the development of industrializing economies."[3] (Similar motives were appealed to by Dean Rusk in urging increased American investment abroad. See Document 14.) Dr. Behrman mentioned specifically the International Basic Economy Corporation founded by the Rockefeller Brothers to supply venture capital abroad, particularly in Latin America. A contrasting attitude is that of Dr. Robert S. Engler who in his study,

[2] Raymond F. Mikesell (ed.), *U.S. Private and Government Investment Abroad* (Eugene, Oregon: U. of Oregon Press, 1962), p. 88.
[3] *Ibid.*, p. 91.

The Politics of Oil,[4] notes that the IBEC extends loans and technical assistance out of obligation and foresight, building miniature welfare states, in Venezuela for example, based on the philosophy that it is easier to buy good will than to bully. In essence, the selection of motivations in the Oregon study takes little notice of any motive other than those bettering a company's economic position, which is, perhaps, as it should be, since corporations are founded and run to make profits, not to indulge in international welfare work with its political implications.[5]

Accepting the primacy of the profit motive in investments abroad, does the "invisible hand" guiding the foreign investor lead him to better the nation in which he invests?[6] (The pros and cons are weighed by Baer and Simonsen in Document 19.) The evidence seems to indicate that many areas are neglected by private capital and must be the focus of government-to-government loans to ensure balanced economic development. (See Document 14.) But then, why do nations allow, or even invite, foreign private capital to enter? Except for those who are blindly committed to damning foreigners under any and all circumstances, quite a few boons can be noted. Foreign investments have almost always aided the economic growth of the Latin American nations, creating jobs and stimulating business internally. (For

[4] New York: The Macmillan Company, 1961, pp. 184–185.

[5] For example, see Andrew Hacker, "Do Corporations Have a Social Duty?" *The New York Times Magazine* (Nov. 17, 1963), and Marvin D. Bernstein, "Foreign Investments and Mineral Resources: A Few Observations," *Inter-American Economic Affairs*, Vol. XIII, No. 3 (Winter, 1959), 33–49.

[6] A blunt analysis of this question is in Roberto Martínez Leclainche, "Ventajas y desventajas de las inversiones extranjeras," in *La intervención del estado en la economía* (Mexico: Instituto de Investigaciones Económicas, Escuela Nacional de Economía, Universidad Nacional Autónoma de México, 1955), pp. 55–65.

example, see the work of Sears, Roebuck in Document 9, and of European capital in financing Argentine credit purchases in Document 3.) While the underdeveloped nations of Latin America might be able to create their own capital by forced savings based upon reduced consumption—as was done by the Soviet Union and Red China and now by Castro's Cuba—the personal sacrifices and slow pace of development due to deprivation of foreign knowhow and techniques make the choice of this alternative singularly unattractive. Foreign-owned enterprises purchase power, use transport facilities and local supplies, and pay taxes. Investments in export industries, such as Peruvian mines or Venezuelan petroleum, even if designed to complement the economy of the investing nation, create foreign exchange income by opening markets developed by the investor. They bring in technological innovations and more efficient business methods which strengthen local industry, as with auto assembly plants in Brazil and Argentina. They also develop areas neglected or too complex for development by local capital or even governmental investment, such as chemical plants in Mexico. Foreign capital does raise the standard of living of the people and it can make the Latin American nations more self-sufficient and better able to take full advantage of their resources. Foreign-owned manufacturing industries whose product satisfies local demands remit profits to their home offices, but these remittances abroad are but a fraction of what would be spent abroad if the same merchandise were imported.[7] With

[7] An excellent exposition of this view is in John Fayerweather, *Facts and Fallacies of International Business* (New York: Holt, Rinehart & Winston, 1962), pp. 120–149. Also see S. Pizer and F. Cutler, *U.S. Investments in the Latin American Economy,* Part I: The Role of U.S. Companies (Washington, D.C.: Office of Business Economics, U.S. Department of Commerce, 1957).

capital borrowed abroad, governments can embark immediately on programs of public works, civic improvements and economic development in line with their own plans. At the very least, concrete benfits are left in the form of roads, power facilities, port facilities, etc.

Disadvantages, however, may also accrue to the debtor country from the entrance of foreign capital. Most important by far is that accepting a foreign investment imposes an obligation upon the underdeveloped nation which may well lead to diplomatic and political frictions. Despite Latin American governments espousing the Drago Doctrine (which holds that nations ought to eschew the use of force for the collection of private debts owned nationals by foreigners) and the Calvo Clause (which requires investors to renounce, under pain of forfeiture, any rights to appeal to their home governments concerning allegations of mistreatment by the host country), international law still supports the use of force by the home government of the investor to aid in the collection of debts and damage claims from the borrowing nation.[8] A modern version of "diplomatic" pressure is the threat to withdraw foreign aid funds when American capital is "mistreated." (See the U.S. Senate's reaction in Document 12.) Foreigners at times are accused of having more rights than Latin American nationals, for the latter must accept their government's actions with no appeal beyond their national courts, while foreigners, losing in these same courts, can appeal to their embassy and even request armed intervention to correct alleged wrongs. A related practice is called "Dollar Diplomacy": the government of a strong nation's deliberate encouragement of their

---

[8] See Donald R. Shea, *The Calvo Clause: A Problem of Inter-American and International Law and Diplomacy* (Minneapolis: The University of Minnesota Press, 1955).

capitalists to invest in a weaker nation in order to create a situation or an incident that would justify intervention and the establishment of a sphere of influence or a protectorate. (For example, see the accusations of Alfonso Bauer Paíz in Document 16.) It must be remembered that the dividing line between simple foreign investment and the manifold degrees of imperialism is not sharply defined. While foreign investment does not necessarily imply political domination—e.g., United States investments in Canada and Western Europe—when the host country is significantly weaker than the lender, political dependence may well follow economic dependence.[9]

In recent years several trends to offset this undesirable feature of international capital movements have appeared: the signing of a non-intervention treaty by the United States with the Latin American nations; a growing tendency on the part of international investors to accept voluntarily a Calvo Clause in their concessions and contracts; a reluctance on the part of the great powers to intervene to support economic demands by their nationals because of the possibility of a world war; the growing role of international agencies such as the International Bank for Reconstruction and Development in foreign lending; the appearance of companies with both nationals and foreigners as stockholders chartered in the host country and, therefore, beyond justifications for intervention,[1] and direct government-

[9] Sometimes the shoe ends up on the other foot, as when Mexico under the leadership of Benito Juárez expelled the foreign-imposed Emperor Maximilian and made his European sponsors—France, Great Britain and Spain—plead for reconciliation. See Alfred Tischendorf, *Great Britain and Mexico in the Era of Porfirio Díaz* (Durham, N.C.: Duke University Press, 1961), Chaps. I and II.

[1] Joint ventures, unfortunately, have not worked out as well as hoped, and the annual surveys of the U.S. Department of Com-

to-government loans which, paradoxically, are less subject to collection by force when in default than money owed private investors. However, government-to-government or international agency loans may lead to indirect intervention by pressures shaping development policies and by voting in international organizations.

Latin Americans are also sensitive to the aura of corruption that often surrounds the entrance of foreign capital. Foreign investors speak of the importance of their work and the hardships suffered (as with H. M. Tomlinson's English supply-keeper in Document 10), but Latin Americans talk of foreigners' use of money and power—threats, economic and military—to get what they want. Admittedly corruption and sharp business dealings, including bribery of venal officials and support of dastardly governments (Betancourt in Document 7 and Bauer Paíz in Document 16) are part of the Latin American political and economic scheme, but there is something particularly heinous when foreigners join the game and use their superior financial power. And add to it other inducements such as diplomatic recognition and the modern concomitants of military aid and development funds. Yet foreigners do have the value of providing scapegoats for local failures. (For examples of anti-foreign laws, see Document 17.)

Another major disadvantage of receiving large for-

---

merce indicates a steady decline in their number. Apparently the clash between the business methods and attitudes of Americans and Latins has been a major stumbling block. Some methods of circumventing laws that require joint ventures are to fragment local participation among many stockholders, or to include a bank or silent partner willing to put up part of the capital to meet the laws' requirements but to keep the actual control of the enterprise in the hands of the foreigners. The objection has been raised that it might be more advantageous for Latin American governments to permit foreign and national capital to freely enter into as many fields as the investors might wish, instead of inhibiting their activities by insisting that they team up.

eign investments is that they tie an underdeveloped nation's economy to the world's economic cycle without the country having any control over that cycle. In addition, many of these investments create one-crop economies, leaving the host nation economically helpless in relations with the world's markets.[2] Among the largest investments in Latin America, for example, are those in bananas, sugar cane, petroleum, and mining and smelting, which are tightly integrated with the United States and Western European economies. Their level of operation is determined, therefore, by the business cycle in these consuming areas. For day-to-day operations, it is the needs of the foreign areas and the orders of boards of directors in New York or London that establish the scale of operations in Venezuelan oil fields and Central American banana plantations. Business cycles are set in the industrialized areas, but the repercussions of their depressions are felt throughout the underdeveloped world. The development of alternate sources of supply, synthetics, or changes in manufacturing or consumption patterns, can strand the highly dependent economies of the host countries, as happened with Brazilian rubber, Chilean nitrates, and Cuban sugar. In fact, one of the contributing factors to many movements on the part of Latin American governments to expropriate foreign owned property is sparked by the desire to gain better control over certain sections of their own economy.

To offset these cycles, the governments of Chile and Mexico, for example, have taken the task of fixing production quotas out of the hands of the foreign mining companies and setting them domestically. Also,

[2] The debilitating effects of a one-crop economy based on foreign investment have been vividly sketched by Paul Blanshard in his study, *Democracy and Empire in the Caribbean* (New York: The Macmillan Company, 1947).

while foreign-owned export industries earn foreign exchange to pay for remittances abroad (e.g., Mexican chemicals) and manufacturing cuts the drain of foreign exchange for purchases abroad (e.g., Argentine and Brazilian rubber goods and tire plants), the industries developed by foreign capital for domestic consumption —public utilities and transportation—create the problem of finding foreign exchange to pay the remittances due the investors. Despite the advantages of industrialization, most Latin Americans are convinced that profit remittances drain their nations of capital. (See section on "Foreign Investment and Balance of Payments," Document 1.) Allied to this problem is the general question of the effect of absentee ownership upon the national economy, the balance of payments, and sentiments of nationalism.

Nationals of the host country frequently complain, with some justification, that their national wealth is being consumed abroad for others' comfort, and, in the case of mining, Peruvians, Chileans, and Mexicans complain that they are finally left with "holes in the ground." A complementary version of that cry is the question raised by the people of nations exporting raw materials and importing manufactured products. Chileans, for example, inquire: "Why do we export copper bars and import electric motors?" Careful and detailed economic explanations repeatedly fail to satisfy outraged nationalists.

Other effects of foreign investments appear as drawbacks to Latin American nations. Direct investments cannot be counted on, but vary in amount from year to year, and in a given year the profits remitted abroad to the investors may be greater than the new capital entering. While it is true that reinvested profits may offset this trend, the exchange difficulty still remains.

Brazil and Venezuela in particular suffer from these fluctuations. Foreign capital seeks out those economic activities that yield the highest profit, and as sanctioned by the business ethic, it neglects activities merely of social importance. Money granted or loaned on a government-to-government basis is necessary to offset this deficiency. (This weakness in private investment is well analyzed in Document 14.) Since many Latin American nations lack adequate planning facilities, the charge is often made—*post facto*—that foreign enterprises irrationally exploit and deplete natural resources, displace national enterprises, or limit the scope of national investments; leading nations, such as Mexico, strictly control the exploitation of their subsoil. Many activities, whether pursued by foreigners or nationals, will deplete national resources that might otherwise remain as "stuff" in the ground, but it does not inevitably follow that work will be irrational—except in so far as it is in any capitalist country, such as the United States itself— or that foreigners *must* drive out nationals. In fact, activities of foreigners often open new opportunities for nationals.

An oft-neglected consideration is that there are Latin American nations which do not want to "improve" and "progress." The powers-that-be, the controlling oligarchy, may wish to be left alone, to enjoy life as grandfather did. But when foreign capital enters, it becomes the destructive edge that exposes the decay of the old order and prepares the way for its death. Perhaps these changes are inevitable—today, in fact, the Alliance for Progress is dedicated to accelerating such changes—but they will just as inevitably lead to resentment and hostility by the representatives of the old order toward the meddling foreigners.

Psychological factors can appear as drawbacks too.

Governments of Latin American nations find that, when they borrow from developed nations or international agencies, the way the money is to be used is carefully scrutinized. The borrower, filled with the pride of nationalism, finds himself treated as a child while others decide whether the loan ought to be made or not and exactly how it is to be used. Final action depends upon criteria set by the creditors, whether these are acceptable or not to the Latin American nation. Latin Americans continually declaim against the Alliance for Progress for this very reason.

Can one, then, reach a conclusion concerning the aids and hindrances stemming from foreign investment in Latin America? Certainly the very complexity of the problem precludes a categorical statement. Foreign investors have aided and stimulated Latin American economic growth, although not always in the best manner. Foreigners have financed Latin American governments honestly as well as perpetrating or being parties to swindles, often with the connivance of venal officials and unstable governments. Foreigners have developed new (and often previously neglected) sources of wealth, found markets for Latin American products, and created numerous jobs; however, the products frequently deplete national resources, are exported to feed and supply alien economies, and take varying portions of the cream of the profits abroad. Foreign capital has accelerated the development of the Latin American economies, but it can be only a substitute for a more effective mobilization of domestic resources. In fact, it is quite possible that foreign capital may discourage domestic investment—where risks and the need for perseverence are involved, Latin Americans are prone to "let George do it"—it may compete with and even drive out of business economically weak national enterprises, and it may end up in areas which are not the best for effective national growth. (See Document 14.) At the very least, the nations of Latin America are committed to the support of many state-owned and state-operated enterprises and they often extend their control to rather rigid regulation of foreign capital—e.g. the extractive industries of Chile, Mexico and Venezuela—which must inevitably lead to misunderstanding and bad feelings between these governments and private investors. (See Documents 17 and 18 and footnote 1, page 14 above.) Foreign obligations impose the burden of financing debt service instead of financing the importation of capital goods; however, they make it possible to maintain a higher standard of living for the people during a period of industrialization. Still, it is claimed in rebuttal, foreign private capital is the magnet to attract the investment of indigenous private capital, which alone can come in large enough quantities to meet the needs of a developing Latin America. But foreign enterprises have brought advanced technologies and, at times, gunboats in their wake.

In the capitalist world, foreign investments appear to be as necessary as political parties in a modern democracy. And like political parties they can be well used or so abused as to make a mockery of their function. To claim, as do the proponents of Adam Smith's "Invisible Hand" or the followers of Dr. Pangloss, that all that occurs will be for the best is nonsense. Foreign capital has its benefits, but it also can be accompanied by drawbacks. For the partisan, there is ammunition enough in Latin American history and economics to make a convincing case for praising or condemning the role and uses of foreign investments. But citing cases in isolation can be unconvincing and at times harmful. Certainly, in retrospect, the progressive modernizing influences of foreign investments have been accompanied in many cases by jarring dislocations, political backlashes, and, at times, international incidents. It is better to recognize and appreciate the number and meaning of the multiplicity of facets to this problem. There is no universal formula or answer. Each case must be studied with its political as well as its economic implications in mind. Only then can situations be intelligently evaluated instead of being either peremptorily denounced or praised.

1

FACTS AND FIGURES

In many ways business secrets are more securely kept than military secrets. A few years ago, when the police broke up a wire-tapping syndicate in New York City, they found that its major source of income came from businessmen who wished to learn their competitors' prices and practices. Those who compile the totals of investments abroad carry on a frustrating task, since all the wiles of accountancy and legal definitions are called into play to hide and cover the actual amounts of money involved. In addition to the expected vagaries of definitions of value because of accountants' rationalizations, stock-market shifts, exchange-rate fluctuations, valuations for tax purposes, and the multitudinous ways of valuing shares of stock and the worth of enterprises, there is the fact that the investors themselves are not too certain of the size or value of their investment in world-wide corporations whose accounts are in flux and which may have money in several countries in interdependent accounts. Furthermore amortization, depreciation, depletion, reinvestment of foreign-earned profits, and repatriation of funds all complicate the picture. Only determined governments, with adequate staffs of trained economists armed with legal authority to compel compliance, can gather the data necessary for complete surveys. And most governments are reluctant to pry these figures out of a secretive and politically potent business community. Instead, they rely on estimates made by economists, financiers, and journalists of varying degrees of reliability and credibility. Too often axe grinding supersedes research. Ironically, the underdeveloped nations in which foreign enterprises invest are either technically unequipped to compile data concerning the finances of these enterprises and tend instead to indulge in propaganda outbursts, or else they adopt the attitude that discretion in these matters is best, since a prying government may be tagged as a government bent on expropriation.

The following selection, a report of the United Nations' Department of Economic and Social Affairs, brings together succinctly and in summary form much of the data and estimated totals concerning investments by all nations in Latin America down to 1955.

United Nations Department of Economic and Social Affairs

THE GROWTH
OF FOREIGN
INVESTMENTS
IN LATIN AMERICA

Over the protests of the United States, the Latin American nations in 1948 persuaded the United Nations to set up an agency called the Economic Committee for Latin America (ECLA) to study Latin American economic problems and recommend policies to aid economic growth. Under the direction of the Argentine economist, Dr. Raúl Prebisch, ECLA has done yeoman work in assembling data concerning Latin America's economic life and recommending remedial programs such as the organization of common market areas. In preparation for a meeting of the Inter-American Economic and Social Council of the Organization of American States in Rio de Janeiro,

From United Nations, Department of Economic and Social Affairs, *Foreign Capital in Latin America* (New York: United Nations, Department of Economic and Social Affairs, 1955), pp. 3–15. (Sales No. 54. II. G. 4.) Reprinted by permission of the United Nations Publications Board.

ECLA had a sister United Nations agency, the Department of Economic and Social Affairs, draw up a
study of foreign capital in the region. Chapter I of
that study contains a succinct history of the flow of
investments into Latin America since the achievement of independence.

The inflow of foreign capital became a distinctive feature of the economy of most countries of Latin America
in the second half of the nineteenth century. Until the
Second World War private investors were the source of
almost all such capital, which took the form of loans to
governments or private enterprises, or of equity capital.
The recent inflow of capital from governmental and international lending agencies has coincided with the reduced inflow of private capital into most countries of
the region since the 1920's and has partly been designed
to compensate for it.

The reduced amount of private capital imported into
the region has been traced to factors at work both
within and outside Latin America. Among those frequently mentioned are the laws, administrative regulations and other expressions of governmental policy of
capital-importing countries affecting the entry and operation of private foreign enterprises. The present
report is largely devoted to this subject. The following
record of foreign investment within the region attempts
to place presently applied governmental policies in their
historical perspective.

The Period Before the First World War

Before 1914 the international flow of capital to Latin
America proceeded in almost complete absence of governmental control in both the capital-exporting and the
capital-importing countries. Taxes in both these groups

of countries were low, and exchange control was non-existent. The legal framework within which foreign investments operated in Latin American countries was relatively simple and on the whole nondiscriminatory. Occasionally, special assurances were extended by the governments of capital-importing countries to investors, particularly in the form of a guaranteed yield on capital invested in railways and public utilities. As a major recipient of foreign funds, governments of course exerted a profound influence on the investment process, particularly if their part in encouraging railway construction is taken into account, and the stimulation of immigration through governmental action also helped to induce an inflow of capital. Otherwise, the only significant determination of the conditions under which private capital was invested was contained in concession contracts and franchises, applicable mainly to the extractive industries and public utilities.

The Early Capital Inflow

The liberation of the greater part of Latin America from colonial status during the early decades of the nineteenth century opened the area to international trade and investment. The servicing of foreign loans and the transfer of the yield of equity investment has naturally depended heavily on exports. The success or failure of foreign investments in Latin America has accordingly depended to a considerable extent on the development of exports. When markets for Latin American exports have been favorable, foreign investments have been attracted to the export sector, and the resulting economic expansion has in time attracted additional investments. This does not mean that foreign capital has been invested only in export industries; large sums have been absorbed by government borrowing or business activities, particularly public utilities.

From about 1820 to the outbreak of the First World War there were three main periods of capital flow into the region: a brief investment boom during the 1820's, a more sustained movement beginning in the 1860's, and a period of particularly large inflow during the decade before 1914. Throughout the period the main source of capital was the United Kingdom; toward the end of it, France, Germany, several other European countries and, in particular, the United States became important sources of funds.

The short-lived investment boom of the 1820's was concentrated largely in the United Provinces of the Río de la Plata, which formed the nucleus of Argentina. Capital was attracted to mining and to so-called immigration and land companies concerned with the opening up of the interior of the country for agricultural development. At the same time a relatively large loan was floated in the London market by Buenos Aires for the purpose of developing port and sanitary projects and other municipal facilities.

During this brief period investors were attracted to several other areas in the region. Bonds were issued in London by several of the newly established States, including Brazil, Chile, Colombia, Peru, and the Central American Federation. The funds raised were mainly intended to meet obligations resulting from the wars of liberation and also current governmental expenditure and only to a limited extent for public works directly or indirectly stimulating production. Somewhat later Haiti raised a loan in France to pay the first instalment of an indemnity due that country. The debt of the Central American Federation was divided in 1827 among Costa Rica, El Salvador, Guatemala, Honduras, and Nicaragua; in 1834 the new republics of Ecuador and Venezuela assumed parts of the external debt incurred earlier by Greater Colombia.

By the end of the 1820's all the governmental loans raised abroad had fallen into default and the bulk of the foreign investments in business ventures had failed. The collapse was due to a combination of fiscal difficulties, high interest rates, nonproductive uses of the loans, political instability and failure of the export trade to prosper to the extent anticipated. The failure of investments in Argentina, where the prospects had appeared very promising, was particularly striking.[1]

During the three decades following the 1820's the external financial relations of practically all the countries were characterized by recurrent defaults, conversions and funding of arrears of interest. Many of the old external loans, after conversion and adjustment, remained outstanding for almost a century; in some countries, such as Ecuador, they are still traceable in the external debt statistics. A large part of the early business investment was wiped out through bankruptcy or liquidation and left little trace in the following decades.

After the 1860's

An era of large-scale capital inflow into Latin America opened after the 1860's, and particularly after the 1890's, following the widespread effect on economic relations between Latin America and Europe of the development of cheap steel, ocean-going steamships,

[1] See H. S. Ferns, "The Beginnings of British Investment in Argentina," *Economic History Review*, Second series, Vol. IV, No. 3 (London, 1951). The study points out that, unlike several early loans to other Latin American countries, that to the United Provinces of the Río de la Plata was negotiated through a British brokerage firm of recognized standing (Barings') and that the proceeds were devoted to a constructive purpose, namely harbor development. The loan, nominally £1 million, was issued to the public at a 15 per cent discount; the brokers retained £150,000 as commission, and an additional amount of £130,000 was withheld as security against the payment of interest and sinking fund charges during the first two years. The effective interest rate would have been about 8½ per cent.

effective refrigeration, and new mining techniques. Latin America assumed a position in world trade which favored the attraction of foreign capital and facilitated the transfer of investment yields.

In addition to investments in mines and plantations, foreign capital found major outlets in the bonds and stocks of railways and port facilities, often privately owned, devoted primarily to getting primary products from the interior (for example the "coffee" railways of Brazil and Colombia and the "mineral" roads of Chile and Peru) and facilitating their shipment overseas. The same object was served by a substantial portion of the loans raised abroad by governments to finance railways and various public works. Considerable capital was also borrowed by governments to fund floating debts or to convert old external long-term debts into new ones.

The parallel growth of foreign trade and capital inflow in Latin America underwent rapid acceleration after the turn of the century. Spurred by rising prices of primary products, and facilitated by the cumulative effect of the technological developments referred to earlier, the volume of production and export of foodstuffs and raw materials increased rapidly. Perhaps the most rapid expansion occurred in the River Plate area, but Brazil and Chile also attracted large amounts of capital and joined with Argentina and Uruguay as the major centers of growth. In Central America and the Caribbean area foreign capital was attracted mainly to Mexico and Cuba after the turn of the century. The latter two countries were the only significant outlets for United States investments in the region before the First World War.

In the pattern of trade and investment that emerged about 1900, Latin American countries fell into two groups. The exports of the tropical countries and Chile

—countries which produced mineral and tropical agricultural goods—found their main market in the United States, but these countries depended largely on Europe (particularly the United Kingdom) for manufactured goods. On the other hand, the agricultural countries in the temperate zone, particularly Argentina, which engaged in agricultural production very similar to that of the United States, disposed of their exports largely in Europe but depended heavily on the United States for their imports of agricultural machinery, transport equipment, and similar manufactured goods. While the countries of the former group tended to develop export balances with the United States and import balances with the United Kingdom, the latter group tended to have an import balance with the United States and an export balance with the United Kingdom (and Europe in general). The Latin American countries accordingly became dependent upon triangular trade, and their balances of trade with the United States and Europe merged into a wider system of settlement comprising all the principal trading countries of the world.

In recent decades, the system referred to has been undermined by obstacles to the multilateral settlement of accounts. Trade has become increasingly bilateral; in addition, a heavy increase has taken place in two-way trade with the United States. Nevertheless, the factors determining the tendencies of bilateral trade balances referred to above are still at work and influence the payments position of the countries in question. Though the payments position of some of the tropical countries is far from strong, the large share of the United States in their merchandise exports is, by itself, a factor tending to facilitate the payment of foreign investment yields and hence to attract United States capital. The position of other countries in the region depends more heavily on a general improvement in the system of international payments.

The only available statistics indicating in a comprehensive manner the size and industrial composition of foreign investments in the region are those of the capital exporting countries. Their main features may be briefly reviewed.

United Kingdom Investments

United Kingdom investments in Latin America are estimated to have grown from some £85 million in 1870 to about £750 million in 1914. United Kingdom foreign investment generally appears to have been fairly sustained from the 1850's onward, except for a sharp drop in the 1870's and a mild retardation in the decade after 1893. There was a rapid upsurge in the decade before 1914, when an increase of over 50 per cent occurred in the total value of British investments overseas. Latin America appears to have shared in this general trend; the inflow of United Kingdom capital into Argentina and Brazil alone is estimated to have totalled over £200 million between 1907 and 1914.

In 1914 investments in Argentina and Brazil alone represented 60 per cent of total United Kingdom investments in Latin America. In that year United Kingdom investments in Latin America comprised about 20 per cent of United Kingdom investments overseas.

As in the case of United Kingdom foreign investments generally, the bulk of the capital was invested in bonds, issued mainly by railway companies (most of which were privately organized, though often with government guarantee), and by governments. According to one estimate, the distribution of the total in 1914 was as follows:

	Per cent
Railway securities	46
Bonds of national, state and municipal governments	31
Banks and shipping	3
Miscellaneous industries	20

A large proportion of the proceeds of the government loans was employed directly for productive purposes, particularly in the field of transportation and public utilities. While railways were by far the major object of foreign investment in the region, mining ventures and various agricultural enterprises also attracted foreign capital. Reference may be made to mining investments in Mexico and other countries along the Pacific Coast, the development of the Chilean nitrate industry, petroleum in Mexico and meat packing in the River Plate region.

French Investments

Among the early French investments in the region may be mentioned loans to the Governments of Haiti, Peru, and Mexico. After 1870, French investments in mining expanded rapidly in Colombia, Mexico, Venezuela, and elsewhere. But a really sustained flow of French capital to Latin America started only in the 1880's with the founding of French banks in several countries, loans to Argentina and Brazil, and some investments in railways. Among the ventures which attracted French capital was the unsuccessful attempt to construct a canal across Panama—then part of Colombia—which absorbed a nominal capital of over 2 billion francs ($400 million at the then prevailing rate of exchange).

After the turn of the century the outflow of French

capital to the region increased. It has been estimated that the nominal value of French investments in Latin America grew from 2 billion francs ($400 million) in 1900 to three times this figure in 1914, when it represented 13 per cent of total French investments overseas. . . .

Governmental obligations constituted about 30 per cent of the French investments in 1913. As in the case of United Kingdom investments, the largest single non-governmental outlet was railways. Other investments in private enterprises, representing some 40 per cent of the total, were divided about equally among four groups: real estate, including agriculture; banking and finance; mining and commerce, manufacturing and public utilities.

German Investments

The inflow of German capital to Latin America became sizable after 1900, though Argentina had obtained some capital from Germany at the end of the 1880's. Among the main outlets for funds were governmental obligations in Argentina, Brazil, Mexico, Chile and Venezuela. German capital was attracted to port works and public utilities, but not to railways to the same extent as United Kingdom and French capital. German mining activities were limited; on the other hand, business investments were significant in mortgage banks and plantations.

By 1914 German investments in the region were estimated at 3.8 billion marks (about $900 million), or 16 per cent of total German investments overseas.[2] They

[2] J. F. Rippy, in "German Investments in Latin America," University of Chicago, *Journal of Business,* April, 1948, estimates the value of German investments in Latin America in 1918 at $677 million, including those held by German residents in the region.

were located chiefly in Argentina, Brazil, Chile and Mexico, with minor holdings in Guatemala, Peru, Venezuela and elsewhere.

United States Investments

Before the late 1890's United States investments overseas were negligible, and those in Latin America were limited to gold-mining ventures and railways in Mexico and minor holdings elsewhere. Although the United States remained a net debtor on international capital account until the First World War, an increasing amount of funds from that country found its way into Latin America after the Spanish-American War in 1898. In contrast with European investments in the region, those of the United States were largely confined to equity investments in private business ventures, mainly public utilities and enterprises producing for export to the United States.

[United States] investments were concentrated in neighboring countries, at first in Mexico and later in Cuba. By 1914 they amounted to $1.6 billion or 45 per cent of estimated United Kingdom investments in the region. In that year direct investments are estimated to have comprised about 80 per cent of United States holdings in Latin America.

Many of the early investments in agriculture, mining and petroleum extraction represented an extension of the activities of existing United States enterprises producing the same commodities at home or seeking a source of materials for processing in the United States. The investments in agriculture were made mostly in sugar production in Cuba and the banana trade in the Caribbean area. For a time, gold and silver production, chiefly in Mexico, dominated the mining ventures, but in the years before the war industrial minerals, notably copper, became more important and accounted for larger investments in Chile and Mexico. Most of the investment in petroleum was located in Mexico; smaller amounts were devoted to exploration for petroleum in Colombia, Peru and Venezuela. Railway investments were significant in Cuba, Mexico and several other Central American countries. Investments in public utilities were concentrated in Cuba and Mexico. Investments in distribution (including, presumably, distribution of imported merchandise) were confined largely to a few of the more developed countries.

Other Investments

Latin America also received significant amounts of capital from Belgium for investment in railways and utilities in Argentina and Brazil, from the Netherlands for governmental loans and petroleum investments in Mexico, from Portugal for investment in Brazilian government bonds, and smaller amounts from Switzerland and other European countries. If these are estimated at $1 billion, the total (nominal) value of foreign investments in Latin America in 1914 may be put at about $8.5 billion, or about one fifth of worldwide long-term foreign investments, distributed as follows:

	Billions of dollars
United Kingdom	3.7
United States	1.7
France	1.2
Germany	0.9
Other countries	1.0

Since the estimates of the holdings of the several creditor countries vary considerably in definition, it is evident that the total can be regarded only as a rough approximation. As to the distribution among debtor countries, it appears fairly certain that one third of the total was located in Argentina, almost a fourth in Brazil, a similar amount in Mexico and the remainder largely in Cuba, Chile, Uruguay, and Peru.

The Interwar Period

The First World War brought about a transformation in international creditor–debtor relations, but Latin America was less affected than most other regions. The inflow of capital from Europe practically ceased, but little reduction of European investments occurred in the course of the war—except through the sale or confiscation of German holdings or the acquisition of Latin American citizenship by their owners. In consequence, however, of the drop in Europe's exports during the war several countries, notably Argentina, accumulated an export surplus that was financed through short-term credits to European countries and continued to grow for several years after the war. The United Kingdom resumed lending to Latin America on a reduced scale in the 1920's—especially evidenced if allowance is made for the increase in prices—and little new capital entered from other western European countries.

An inflow of capital from the United States occurred during the war and paved the way for the major expansion of United States investments in the region during the 1920's. In a few countries the wartime reduction of imports from Europe provided an incentive to industrialization, and the resulting economic changes increased the scope for investments through branches and subsidiaries of manufacturing enterprises in the United States. Governments became eager to borrow abroad as domestic economic activities expanded, stimulated partly by high prices received for exports.

Conditions in the United States were likewise favorable to an increased outflow of capital. Savings in the United States were at a high level, and there had not yet developed the strong counter-attraction of yields on domestic investments which tended to divert interest from foreign securities towards the end of the 1920's. The quantum of exports from Latin America to the rest of the world rose by more than three fourths between 1913 and 1928, increasing substantially the capacity of the region to meet the service of additional investments.

Between 1914 and 1919 the dollar value of United States investments in Latin America increased by about one half and in the decade after 1919 it more than doubled. In contrast with the shrinkage in value in the 1930's that reflected mainly financial adjustments, most of the growth from 1914 to 1929 was the counterpart of an inflow of capital.

Some idea of the significance of the capital inflow to the recipient countries may be derived from a comparison with imports. During 1925 to 1929 the average annual inflow to Latin America of long-term capital from the United States (after deduction of amortization and redemption payments but including reinvested earnings) was $200 million, equivalent to 42 per cent of the merchandise imports (f.o.b.) from that country. Capital inflow from all sources was equivalent to 13 per cent of the region's total imports and 9 per cent of imports of goods and services, including net outward payments on account of interest and dividends on foreign capital.

Latin America absorbed 24 per cent of the new capital issues floated for foreign account in the United States during 1924 to 1928, the period of greatest outflow. The region's share in new United States direct investments abroad was considerably greater—44 per cent during the period 1925 to 1929. While direct evidence is lacking, the inflow of capital from the United States during this brief period appears to have exceeded that from the United Kingdom during the peak period of 1904 to 1914, even allowing for the rise in prices that had occurred.

Flotation of Securities in the United States

A very large part (perhaps as much as 80 per cent) of the increase in United States investments in Latin America between 1919 and 1930 was in the form of publicly floated bonds of governments and the bonds and stocks of private corporations. During the early part of the 1920's the chief governmental borrowers were Argentina, Brazil, Chile, Colombia, and Cuba, countries in which this type of external financing had previously been undertaken by both United Kingdom and United States capital.[3] As the foreign investment "boom" progressed, other countries entered the United States capital market, and by the end of the decade, fourteen of the twenty countries had floated new dollar bonds. Corporate issues of both bonds and stocks were substantial in Cuba, mainly by sugar enterprises, and Chile, mainly for the exploitation of copper and nitrate resources.

The net nominal capital obtained through securities floated in the United States amounted to $2.2 billion in the decade 1920 to 1929. The flotation of new issues came to an end in 1930; during the remainder of the 1930's the only flotations were for the refunding of Argentine issues.

The only governments that did not enter the United

[3] Before the First World War, some $400 million of Latin American securities had been floated in the United States; from 1914 to 1919, inclusive, underwriting of such securities (net of refunding) was $316 million.

States capital market were those of Ecuador, Honduras, Mexico, Nicaragua, Paraguay and Venezuela. The credit of Ecuador and Mexico was impaired by earlier defaults. Venezuela, with the aid of royalties on petroleum production, was retiring its external public debt, which was extinguished by the end of 1930.

The average yield (at prices offered to the public) of new Latin American dollar bonds ranged from 8.0 per cent in 1921 to 6.3 per cent in 1928 and remained consistently about 40 per cent above the yield on high-grade domestic bonds in the United States. On the average, during the 1920's the price of bonds to the investor was 97 per cent of par, while the Latin American borrower received 93 per cent of the nominal value, the difference of 4 per cent representing the bankers' commission. Argentina, Cuba, the Dominican Republic and Uruguay received a higher percentage; others received less.

Of the proceeds of the governmental bond issues, a substantial amount financed the construction of productive public works, but part was used in ways that did not add directly or indirectly to the borrowing country's productive capacity. The laxity of the standards of United States lending abroad in the 1920's has been the subject of widespread investigation. It may be useful to distinguish between the question whether the proceeds of loans to Latin American countries were as efficiently used as they might have been and the question whether Latin America had the capacity to meet its foreign obligations in the face of events in the 1930's. Whether the countries of the region could have continued to meet their external debt service at the level of foreign exchange receipts prevailing on the eve of the depression of the 1930's—with or without a continued inflow of capital—became largely irrelevant in face of the drop in prices and volume of primary products exported and the simultaneous drying up of capital inflow from abroad. It is estimated that in order to meet its external obligations during 1934 to 1938, Latin America would have had to reduce its 1925 to 1929 volume of imports by no less than 60 per cent. The countries chose the alternative of defaulting on their external debt; by the end of 1935, 85 per cent of Latin American dollar bonds were in default as compared with 52 per cent of European and 3 per cent of Canadian dollar bonds. The value of dollar bonds held in the United States was subsequently reduced sharply by repatriation (often at market prices well below nominal values) and by adjustments, which are discussed below.

United States Direct Investments

The growth of United States direct investments and of portfolio investments in Latin America proceeded in more or less parallel fashion. This was a reflection mainly of developments in South America; in the rest of the region the expansion was confined largely to direct investments. To a greater extent than in the case of the United Kingdom, the expansion of United States business investments abroad took the form of branches or wholly owned subsidiaries of existing enterprises in the capital exporting country. Part of the expansion of such investments was financed by the public flotation of securities, but a considerable amount of the capital was obtained in the first instance from earnings of the parent enterprise in the United States. This was true particularly of investments in manufacturing and in the extractive industries.

During the first decade of the period 1914 to 1929 the bulk of the investments went into agriculture—especially sugar production—and minerals, including petroleum extraction. The most significant development during 1924 to 1929 was the expansion of public utilities, largely electric power, and manufacturing. Investments in manufacturing were mainly limited to Argentina, Brazil, Cuba, and Uruguay, and a large part consisted of processing of agricultural products for export. Petroleum investments expanded during the entire period, but the emphasis shifted from Mexico mainly to Colombia and Venezuela. The effect of these developments was an increasing concentration of direct investments in South America, particularly during the latter half of the 1920's.

Investments of Other Countries

The nominal value of United Kingdom investments in Latin America appears to have remained roughly unchanged during the 1920's. In consequence of the international position of the United Kingdom, the outflow of capital to Latin America was much smaller than before the war and appears to have been counterbalanced by the amortization of bonds, the sale of assets to nationals in the region and outside, particularly in the United States, and the liquidation of unprofitable ventures.

New flotations in London of publicly offered Latin American securities from 1924 to 1930, inclusive, absorbed about £132 million ($650 million). Among the uses made of the new sterling loans may be mentioned the funding of floating government debt and, particularly in Brazil, financing the storage of primary products with a view to preventing a drop in prices.

A shift occurred in the geographic distribution of United Kingdom holdings. There was a decline in the holdings in Mexico, reflecting the acknowledgment of long-defaulted governmental obligations and sale of some properties to United States enterprises, and in

Chile, where United States firms became dominant in nitrate and copper production. United Kingdom investors shared in the expansion of petroleum production in Venezuela and increased their holdings in Argentina and Brazil slightly. While not absorbing any significant amount of new capital, railway securities (both shares and debentures) continued to be preponderant.

Railway investments together with governmental obligations and public utilities comprised 85 per cent of the total in South America, which was distributed in 1930 as follows:

	Per cent
Railways	55
Governmental obligations	21
Public utilities	8
Mines	1
Miscellaneous	15

If market, rather than nominal, values had been employed, the share of railways would probably appear lower; during the 1920's about one-fourth of the securities, including a large portion of railway securities, returned no yield to shareholders.

The extent of investments in Latin America owned by non-resident Germans both before and after the First World War is subject to considerable uncertainty, in the absence of any official estimates by either creditor or debtor countries. Some decline in such investments occurred as the result of the war, and the shift of the owners from non-resident to resident status no doubt continued during the 1920's and 1930's. Among the fields in which important German holdings remained were chemical and drug production and distribution, and other types of manufacturing (with much additional manufacturing activity controlled by German residents), as well as trade and aviation.

The depreciation of the French franc caused Latin American franc obligations to drop sharply in value and led to an accelerated repatriation of such securities. France ceased to be an important source of new funds and there was little change in French business investments in the region. Other European creditor countries maintained or slightly increased their holdings in Latin America during the inter-war period. Belgian investments, estimated at about $350 million, were mainly in public utilities in Argentina. Portuguese investments in Brazil, largely in sterling bonds of the Government, equalled about $300 million. About two thirds of the holdings of the Netherlands, totaling $200 million, were absorbed by petroleum enterprises in the Netherlands West Indies, Mexico, and Venezuela; minor amounts were in manufacturing and governmental obligations. Spanish and Swiss investments, located chiefly in Argentina, amounted to about $60 million each and were concentrated in government obligations and utilities. Substantial investments were made by Italians in Argentina, Brazil, Chile, Peru, and Uruguay, but the extent to which their owners remained nonresident is uncertain.

The investments of countries other than European countries and the United States were few and relatively small. Canadian investments amounted to at least $200 million, chiefly in the form of banking and insurance, mining, and utility enterprises in Brazil and Mexico. Several companies operating in Latin America and incorporated in Canada were largely Canadian in name only, the Canadian parent firm being owned mainly in the United States.

Governmental Measures

During the 1920's there was little change in the policies of Latin American governments concerning foreign capital. Unrestricted entry remained the rule, full convertibility of currencies prevailed and, except for those operating under concessions, foreign enterprises were not subject to any special regime. Taxes and royalties remained low.

In the capital-exporting countries, freedom of capital exports remained the dominant policy. Some restraint was exercised by the United States Government, mainly with a view to blocking the flow of funds to certain countries. In March 1922 issuers of foreign bonds to be sold to the public were requested to ascertain the attitude of the State Department toward the issue in question, but it was explicitly stated that the Government would not pass on the economic merits of foreign loans. The policy applied only to securities offered publicly and not to direct investments. The application of this policy resulted in the withholding of approval of a few issues of countries in the Caribbean area. In the early 1930's this official scrutiny was abandoned. Another feature of United States policy during the interwar period was embodied in treaties with Cuba, the Dominican Republic, and Haiti, providing that new borrowing undertaken by the Governments of these countries required the consent of the United States. This arrangement was a sequel to events which had led to the presence of United States troops in the latter two countries for the announced purpose of safeguarding United States interests.

The United Kingdom maintained control of capital exports during the First World War but relaxed its restrictions soon afterwards and abolished them in 1921. Official control over new public foreign security issues was reintroduced, however, in the 1930's.

The onset of the world depression in the 1930's led to several changes in the policies of the Latin American countries. Following widespread defaults on external government bonds, action was taken over a period which did not end until the early 1950's to adjust obligations through such steps as funding, reducing or canceling arrears of interest, scaling down interest rates and extending the period of amortization. Some governments, as noted above, adopted the policy of repatriating their external debt at the low market prices prevailing.

The governments of the creditor countries, particularly the United Kingdom and the United States, played a limited role in connection with the adjustment of defaulted obligations. The United States Government took the initiative in establishing a private body known as the Foreign Bondholders' Protective Council, Inc., a counterpart of which had existed in the United Kingdom since 1868 under the name of the Council of the Corporation of Foreign Bondholders. The function of these bodies was to consult with foreign governments with a view to reaching a settlement that could be commended to investors, who remained free to assent or not. In the case of Argentina, the United Kingdom in the 1930's also negotiated certain trade and payments agreements which facilitated the servicing of sterling obligations.

The most important development affecting business investments in the region was the introduction of exchange control by many countries to alleviate the pressure on the balance of payments. A related development that affected certain types of foreign enterprise was the increasing practice of licensing imports. Another trend was the tightening of restrictions on the entry of foreign nationals for gainful employment, partly in response to slackness in local labor markets.

So-called "saturation laws," limiting the expansion of investment in specified industries, also had their origin in several countries during the depression. Except in Brazil and Mexico, however, legislation excluding foreign investment as such from specific sectors of the economy was not generally adopted during the 1930's, nor was there substantial formal limitation on the extent of foreign participation in local enterprises. Furthermore, the outstanding action against foreign enterprises during this period, the expropriation of oil properties in Mexico in 1938, was not occasioned primarily by events related to the depression.

The Period After the Second World War

During the postwar period, the almost complete absence of foreign private capital entering Latin America in the form of portfolio investment that characterized the 1930's has persisted. The nominal value of externally held governmental debt has been substantially reduced in many countries. In addition, the governments of several countries have repurchased important foreign business investments, notably United Kingdom holdings in Argentina.

The inflow of private capital has consisted largely of direct investments by United States enterprises, at first chiefly in petroleum, but since 1950 increasingly in manufacturing and the extraction of minerals other than petroleum. The growth of investments has resulted to a considerable extent from the reinvestment of earnings of existing enterprises. The inflow of private capital from western Europe has been small, but it has served to introduce new enterprise and technology in a few countries. Several countries have obtained substantial amounts of foreign capital from governmental sources, particularly the Export-Import Bank of Washington and the International Bank for Reconstruction and Development.

Repatriation of Investments

By 1945, a large part of the external bonded debt of Latin American countries had been repatriated through purchases in the open market by individuals, and also by governments, with cash from sinking funds and other sources. During the postwar period this process continued, particularly with respect to sterling bonds. A further reduction in external debt resulted not only from normal amortization but also from the direct scaling down of the nominal value of external government bonds in several countries, notably Brazil and Mexico. In addition, a substantial amount of foreign-owned securities in business enterprises in Latin America was repurchased.

Between 1930 and 1945 the nominal value of publicly offered Latin American dollar bonds held by United States residents dropped by $1.1 billion or 70 per cent. Following the war, repatriation continued at a slower pace, but a larger portion of the bonds was formally redeemed by the debtor governments. Of about $2.1 billion of dollar bonds outstanding in 1930, only $767 million remained at the end of 1952.[4] At the end of 1952, less than half of the Latin American dollar bonds

[4] The figure for 1952 includes Mexican securities amounting to $200 million. Under debt adjustment plans of 1942 and 1946 to 1950, however, the Mexican Government had reduced the nominal value of its external debt in dollars, sterling and pesos from about $440 million to $81 million, all denominated in dollars. The difference between the two figures is accounted for by unassented securities, that is, securities whose owners did not accept settlements offered by governments.

outstanding were held in the United States, and their market value was below $200 million. A similar reduction occurred in Latin American sterling bonds; by the end of 1951 the amount had dropped to about £111 million as compared with over £300 million in 1939. United Kingdom residents at the end of 1951 held only £57 million in the sterling bonds of Latin American governments and municipalities.

The pattern of debt reduction varied considerably among the countries concerned. The entire external debt of the Dominican Republic and Haiti was retired by regular amortization and redemption at par. Argentina repurchased a large part of its external debt at close to par and redeemed the rest at par. In many other cases the repurchase of external obligations was effected at a considerable discount from nominal value, ranging to as low as 10 per cent of par. In Brazil the principal of a number of bonds was scaled down by 20 to 50 per cent, and in Mexico a reduction of 80 per cent in the nominal value was effected by a debt settlement plan.

After 1945 a substantial repurchase of business investments in Latin America also occurred. This affected mainly United Kingdom investments in Argentina and Brazil.[5] Including the repatriation of sterling bonds, the net withdrawal of investments in Latin America owned

[5] The most important investments affected and the payments involved were as follows:

Argentina: 1946, French-owned railways, 5,500 million French francs; 1947, telephone and telegraph companies owned in the United States, $99 million; 1948, railways owned in the United Kingdom, £150 million.

Brazil: 1948, railways owned in the United Kingdom, £15 million payment completed in 1951.

Mexico: 1946 to 1950, settlement for expropriation of oil properties owned in the United States, $9 million; settlement for expropriation of landholdings owned in the United States, $12.5 million.

Uruguay: Payment of $41 million made in 1949 and 1950 on account of the following, owned in the United Kingdom: 1947, tramways; 1948, railways; 1949, waterworks.

by United Kingdom residents involved cash payments, from 1946 to 1951 inclusive, of about £227 million for securities with a nominal value of £353 million. Net payment to the United States from 1946 to 1950 on account of amortization of privately held bonds and repurchase of dollar bonds and other private long-term assets is estimated at $361 million.

External Debt Settlements

By the end of 1952, the defaulted foreign obligations of Latin American governments had been reduced to a relatively small amount, affecting only a few countries. Of the $24 million of contractual interest falling due on dollar bonds in 1952 only $9 million was unpaid, mostly obligations of Bolivia and Peru.

With respect to the termination of defaults, the countries in the region may be classified into three groups.[6] Argentina, the Dominican Republic and Haiti met most of their contractual debt service obligations and subsequently retired all publicly held external debt at or close to par. A second group of countries offered settlements of defaulted obligations calling for interest rate reductions (ranging from 10 to 70 per cent of the nominal rate), and for longer maturities, but no change in the principal amount. In most cases a partial payment of accrued interest was offered, usually in the form of additional bonds. Most of the settlements were offered after negotiations with the United Kingdom and United States councils of bondholders and were recommended for acceptance by the councils.[7] A third group of settlements involved substantial reductions in both the nomi-

[6] A fourth group was made up of countries—Honduras, Nicaragua, Paraguay and Venezuela—with no dollar bonds and few or no sterling bonds outstanding by the end of the 1930's.

[7] Settlements of this type were put into effect by Brazil, Chile, Colombia, Cuba, Guatemala, El Salvador, Panama, Peru, and Uruguay.

nal value of the bonds and in the interest rate. The most important example of this type was the settlement of Mexico's external debt. Brazil also offered holders of its dollar bonds a large reduction in principal with a partial cash settlement as an alternative to a reduction of interest rates and extension of maturities.

In several cases the International Bank for Reconstruction and Development has stressed the importance of eliminating remaining defaults in connection with the consideration of loans to the countries concerned.

United States Direct Investments

According to an official United States census, the value of United States direct investments in Latin America remained practically unchanged between 1936 and 1943. In several countries a decline occurred, offset largely by a growth in Venezuela. Between 1943 and 1950, however, direct investments increased by about 70 per cent, reaching a total of $4.7 billion. By the end of 1953 the total value of such investments had reached $6.0 billion. Much of this growth occurred during a period of sharply rising prices and the real increase may, therefore, have been less; on the other hand, it should be noted that the assets are computed at their book value (usually depreciated original cost), which in most cases is less than current replacement cost.

In 1950, 55 per cent of United States investments in the region were in subsidiaries, organized under the laws of the country of operation, and the remainder in branches. In all, some 2,000 separate business units were involved, of which about 600 were established between 1946 and 1950. The bulk of the investment was concentrated, however, in a relatively few large enterprises.

The countries experiencing the largest increases in the

value of direct investments between 1943 and 1952 were, in the order of importance, Venezuela, Brazil, Chile, Panama, Mexico, Cuba, Peru and Colombia. The growth of investments in Panama, however, reflects mainly the registration in that country of foreign-owned tankers. The largest increase in investments occurred in petroleum production, including refining and distribution, followed by manufacturing and mining and smelting. Public utilities, the second most important category of outstanding investments, underwent little change and even declined in several countries. Large capital outlays were made by several foreign-owned public utility enterprises in Brazil and Mexico but were financed to a considerable extent by loans from the Export-Import Bank or the International Bank for Reconstruction and Development.

Total investment in manufacturing more than doubled between 1943 and 1950, equaling the rate of growth of the petroleum industry. The expansion was substantial, however, only in Brazil and Mexico, though a large relative increase occurred in manufacturing investments in Colombia and Venezuela.[8] At the end of 1950 chemical production absorbed the largest proportion of investments in manufacturing, followed by food processing, motor vehicles, electrical equipment, and rubber products.

The book value of United States direct investments in Latin America as a whole increased on an average by about $400 million annually between 1947 and 1952.

[8] The estimates of investments in manufacturing exclude petroleum refining and processing and also the processing of ores by integrated enterprises classified under mining and smelting. Manufacturing investments in selected countries were as follows in 1943 and 1950, respectively (in millions of dollars): Argentina, 101 and 161; Brazil, 66 and 285; Colombia, 6 and 25; Mexico, 22 and 133; Peru, 6 and 16; Venezuela, 1 and 24.

Year-to-year fluctuations in the total were substantial, however, both in the capital outflow as recorded in the balance of payments and in reinvested earnings of subsidiaries. Part of these fluctuations were due to intercompany transactions and to temporary blockings of earnings awaiting transfer in certain countries. The increase reached a peak of $580 million in 1952 and dropped to $275 million in 1953. In 1950 and 1951 the rate of investment in the petroleum industry dropped off, but it recovered somewhat in 1952, though part of this represented undistributed earnings of tanker subsidiaries in Panama. A growth of investment in manufacturing and mining of $552 million during the two-year period, 1950 and 1951, partly offset the decline in petroleum investments. In 1953, however, the inflow of capital for manufacturing in Brazil and Mexico, the two main recipients of such funds, dropped considerably.

A large part of the expansion of direct investments in recent years has been financed by retained earnings of the enterprises concerned. Thus, during 1949 to 1952, about 60 per cent of the increase in United States direct investments in Latin American enterprises was financed from reinvested earnings of subsidiaries. In the case of branches, the increase in investments is treated in the accounts as an inflow of fresh capital, whether or not the amount represents retained earnings. In recent years (1950 to 1953) branch earnings have substantially exceeded capital outflows to branches; the capital outlays of branches as a whole may thus be regarded as entirely financed from retained earnings. Taking this into account, it may be estimated that the proportion of total capital outlays financed from retained earnings was well above 60 per cent.

In a number of subsidiaries in Latin America controlled in the United States, nonresidents of the latter have some financial participation. In 1950 this participation, mainly by residents of the countries concerned, represented 10 per cent of the investment in such subsidiaries. Participation by capital not originating in the United States is found largely in manufacturing and public utilities (13 and 15 per cent of total investment, respectively) and is higher in the case of enterprises organized since 1945. It appears to be concentrated in Brazil and Mexico.

Capital from Governmental Sources

By the end of 1953 the International Bank for Reconstruction and Development had authorized loans of $426 million to Latin American countries. Most of the loans have been for the expansion of electric power facilities, transportation absorbing the next largest amount. In the two years, 1952 and 1953, loans to the area were about 30 per cent of the total authorized by the Bank. Disbursements from such loans were about $60 million in 1952 and $50 million in 1953.

Disbursements from grants and credits by the United States Government have thus far exceeded those by the International Bank for Reconstruction and Development. From 1934 to the end of 1953, the United States Export-Import Bank of Washington authorized credits to Latin American countries of $1,603 million (after reduction of cancellations); $1,296 million was disbursed of which $438 million was repaid. The largest disbursements were made in Brazil, followed by Mexico, Chile, Argentina, and Colombia. A substantial part of the credits authorized for Argentina ($97 million in 1950) and Brazil ($300 million in 1953) served to finance commercial arrears on account of United States exports. Large amounts of Export-Import Bank loans have financed equipment for highway construction, transportation, electric power development and miscellaneous industrial activities. The range of projects financed by the Export-Import Bank has been broader than that of the International Bank for Reconstruction and Development.

Investment Yields

The income earned on United States direct investments in Latin America during recent years has been much larger than during the late 1920's, the last previous period of comparable prosperity. In 1950, for example, such income exceeded $700 million; a roughly comparable figure for the period 1925 to 1929 is $150 million to $200 million per annum.[9] Part of the increase reflects growth in the value of the investments, but a more important factor is the increased rate of return in recent years, owing partly to a higher proportion of investment in mineral extraction and manufacturing. Earnings on total direct investments in Latin America ranged from 11.2 per cent of book value in 1945 to 21.0 per cent in 1948 and 20.5 per cent in 1951, the last year for which comprehensive figures are available. In 1929 the estimated rate of return on all United States direct investments overseas was about 6 per cent of book value, and investments in Latin America appear to have yielded about the same rate of return.[1]

During the postwar period, as in the past, the return

---

[9] Earnings refer to all income accruing to the investor, net of Latin American taxes, but before United States taxes, including amounts reinvested or blocked by exchange restrictions.

[1] According to an estimate by the Department of Commerce relating to 1930, the return on direct investments in Latin America, excluding reinvested earnings, was $121 million, or about 4 per cent of book value (United States Department of Commerce, *Trade Information Bulletin No. 761*, Washington, 1931). Excluded from this calculation were investments of about $500 million in sugar production which yielded no return.

on direct investments in Latin America has varied considerably according to the industry and country concerned. The highest yields have been earned in the petroleum industry (averaging 31.1 per cent during 1948 to 1951) and in distribution (an average of 28.1 per cent during 1948 to 1951). While public utilities have always yielded a relatively low rate of return, the rate during recent years (2.9 per cent on an average during 1948 to 1951) has been particularly depressed by the failure of rates to keep pace with rising costs. It should be kept in mind that figures of this kind afford only a rough measure of the profitability of the investments in question, particularly since the return is computed as a percentage of book values which frequently have not been adequately adjusted to the replacement cost of fixed assets at the prevailing price level.

In view of the many factors that have reduced the incentive to invest abroad during the postwar period, particular interest is attached to a comparison between yields on investments in Latin America and in the United States. Such a comparison is subject to many qualifications, but the data indicate that the spread between the return on United States investments at home and in Latin America has recently been relatively slight. The average yield on investments in Latin America as a whole has exceeded that in the United States in every year during the period 1948 to 1951 by a margin ranging from 4 to 9 percentage points. The rate of return on investments in Latin America, however, is weighted heavily by the profits of the petroleum industry, which accounted in 1950 for about half the income received and for about 30 per cent of total investments. A comparison of rates of return on investments in manufacturing in the two regions indicates a narrower spread, except in 1951; in 1950 the United States domestic rate of return, in fact, exceeded that on United States investments in Latin America, though by a narrow margin. While the spread between the rates of return may be regarded as narrow in view of the current risks attaching to investment abroad, it is of interest that in the late 1920's, when a substantial outflow of capital for direct investment occurred, the average rate of return on direct investments in Latin America appears to have been considerably below that on domestic investments in the United States. At that time, however, a much larger portion of foreign capital in Latin America was invested in public utilities, which, while less profitable, were considered less risky.

In the above comparisons, Latin American profits are measured net of Latin American taxes on business incomes, and United States profits net of corresponding United States taxes. Since income received in the United States from foreign investments is subject, roughly speaking, to a corporate income tax equivalent to the difference between United States tax liabilities and taxes on business income paid abroad, the question arises whether this tax liability reduced the margin between the rate of return on foreign and domestic investment. It appears that net United States tax liability on account of income earned on foreign direct investments in Latin America is small in most instances.

This situation results from several features of United States laws relating to the taxation of income from overseas. First, a credit is generally provided against income taxes paid abroad, which have been increasing in recent years. Second, reinvested earnings of foreign subsidiaries are not subject to United States taxes. Third, foreign income of enterprises operating through so-called Western Hemisphere corporations is taxed at a specially low rate. Finally, special depletion allowances reduce the United States tax liability of enterprises engaged in petroleum production and other extractive industries.

Thus, in 1950 the net United States tax liability of United States enterprises on income of $905 million from direct investments in Latin America is estimated to have been only $16.4 million. In that year $251 million, or 28 per cent of the income received from such investments, was paid to Latin American countries as income taxes. There was considerable variation in the percentages among countries and industries, with mining and petroleum production recording the highest average rate. Furthermore, such calculations may conceal wide variations in the tax liabilities of individual firms.

A comparison of the effective yields of Latin American dollar bonds with yields of domestic bonds in the United States has limited significance in view of current inactivity in portfolio investments. The yields returned on Latin American dollar bonds cannot be taken as an indication of rates at which countries could borrow substantial fresh capital should they so desire. Nevertheless, it is of interest that since 1945 the market value of such securities has risen substantially as the result of the settlement of defaults and other factors. Yields on Latin American dollar bonds remain, however, about two to three times those of United States government securities of comparable maturity, and slightly less in relation to dollar bonds of the International Bank for Reconstruction and Development and of prime industrial corporations in the United States.

Foreign Investment and the Balance of Payments

The relationship between foreign investments and the balance of payments is complex and often indirect. Nevertheless, some aspects of this relationship may be illuminated by statistics relating to the postwar period.

Given the reduction in external debt and the repurchase of certain foreign investments, on the one hand,

and the postwar rise in prices, on the other, the portion of Latin America's receipts of foreign exchange from current transactions that is absorbed by transferred investment yields—which may be called the investment service ratio—would be expected to drop in most countries. In some countries the tendency has probably been reinforced by currency depreciation and multiple exchange rates. For Latin America as a whole, the ratio was 12 per cent in 1950 compared with 27 per cent from 1925 to 1929. Comparable figures for income transferred to the United States and exports to the United States were 19 per cent in 1952, 22 per cent in 1949, and 30 per cent in 1925 to 1929. The decline in the ratio with respect to the United States would have been much greater but for the large earnings on petroleum investments in Venezuela.

The drop in the investment service ratio was particularly sharp in Argentina, Bolivia, Cuba, Mexico, and Peru. In Costa Rica, however, the ratio moved contrary to the general trend, and little change occurred in Venezuela, where both export proceeds and investment income increased substantially. Information is limited concerning the extent to which the ratio would have been higher in certain countries had the transfer of earnings not been restricted by exchange control and other restrictions, but this factor appears to have been important during a few years in several countries, particularly Argentina and Brazil.[2]

During the second half of the 1920's, the annual

[2] According to a sample tabulation of United States subsidiaries in Argentina, net profits rose in 1947 and 1948; but in consequence of the tightening of exchange restrictions, dividends remitted dropped from $11.3 million in the first half of 1947 to $7.3 million in the second half of the year and $0.1 million in the second half of 1948. (See United States Department of Commerce, *The Balance of International Payments of the United States, 1946–1948*, p. 98.)

investment income paid abroad by Latin America ($600 million) was about three times as great as the capital inflow. Investment income paid to the United States was $300 million, against a capital inflow from that country of $200 million. A trade surplus served to meet the balance on these accounts and also on account of shipping and other invisible transactions.

The tendency of investment income paid abroad to exceed the inflow of capital has become more pronounced in recent years. In this respect, however, both 1949 and 1950 must be regarded as abnormal, in view of the large-scale repatriation of British investments, on the one hand, and the unusually large inflow of capital into the petroleum industry, on the other. In 1952, perhaps a more typical year, the margin between the inflow of private and public capital from the United States and the payment of investment income to that country was $336 million, compared with an average of about $100 million in 1925 to 1929. During 1946 to 1951, the margin was largest, in absolute terms, in Venezuela and Cuba and varied widely from year to year.

Unless the rate of capital inflow increases substantially or the average yield on outstanding investments declines, the margin between investment income paid abroad and the receipt of foreign capital will, of course, increase with an increase in the stock of foreign capital. Comparisons of particular items in the balance of payments are of limited significance, however, in judging the effect of foreign investments on a country's balance of payments, on its capacity to meet the service of additional foreign investments or on its economic development generally. Even a more refined analysis of the net flow of foreign exchange due to the operations of foreign enterprises—taking into account exports by such enterprises or the reduction in imports due to their activities—would be inconclusive. The basic questions are how a given amount and composition of foreign investments affect the country's output and international payments position, and how at the same time other internal and external forces are influencing the country's economic situation.

It follows that a tolerable relation between outward payments on account of investment yields and receipts on current account may vary widely from country to country, and that the capacity to absorb additional capital from abroad for purposes of economic development will also vary, depending on many factors, of which the potential expansion of export proceeds may be considered particularly important.

II

CASE STUDIES

Totals of investments have a certain bloodless quality about them that mocks the life they conceal. Behind the arrays of figures and screens of tables lie stories of people and the enterprises they organized, the hopes and plans they nurtured, the methods they used, the hardships—financial and physical—they suffered, and the effect of their investments, work and machinations on the country in which they invested and even on the international economy. Investments do not come forth like grapeshot from a cannon. They represent, each one, an individual scheme and a hope—absolutely selfish or mingled with altruism. But as investments become large and numerous, they affect national structures, national policies and international economic and political relations. Economics and investments are not the only determinants of international relations, but in many cases they enter as important or even decisive factors.

The following selections were chosen to illustrate the experiences and work of foreign investors in Latin America. Romero and Neifeld report on two enterprises with opposite fates: Romero writes of Real del Monte (1824–48), a failure, which began with large amounts of enthusiasm and money only to founder on the reality of

Mexico; and as counter, Neifeld discusses PLANIKA (1961), a modern Argentine Eldorado, one of the prizes in the lottery of foreign investment. British businessmen and investors literally swarmed into Latin American ventures during the century following independence. D. C. M. Platt explores the tragic story of the investors who, with hopes of high profits, sank millions of pounds sterling into Latin American government bonds, were literally mulcted of their money, and yet came back again for more of the same. In contrast, the British who worked in Brazil found a most lucrative combination of investment and trade opportunities with success in one field spurring on success in the other. The interesting case of British-Argentine relations during the late nineteenth and early twentieth centuries is examined by Henry S. Ferns. The question at issue is whether British investments in key sectors of the Argentine economy subjected that nation to "laissez-faire imperialism" and made it a part of the "informal Empire" subordinate to Britain's desires. If this were the case, then any large investment, no matter how devoid of political interference by the investors' home government, would constitute a form of the detested imperialism. Rómulo Betancourt and Robert F. Smith write at length on the sordid side of foreign investments—viz. oil politics in Venezuela and sugar politics in Cuba. In the former, oil companies connived in corruption and supported dictatorship as the price of retaining their concessions. In Cuba, American economic interests, rallying alongside the military and the Navy, reduced the island to a protectorate tied to the American economy, and more recently, used their influence to try to frustrate attempts at social and economic reform. Whether Castroism is a viable answer for the Cubans is a moot question, but throughout Latin America United States policy toward

Cuba is used as anti-Yanqui propaganda. As counterpoint, the next selection concerns an enterprise with the "new look," a broader vision than profits alone, a mode of operation which includes stimulating economic and social development for the host country. The philosophy and work of Sears, Roebuck & Company is described with earnest patience by John F. Gallagher, a Sears executive. The final selection, from H. M. Tomlinson's classic travel book, *The Sea and the Jungle,* focuses on the small "mere mortals" who carry out the job being paid for by the foreign investors. The sacrifice and self-sacrifice of these men—natives as well as transient strangers—imparts a picture of the quiet heroism of the agents of distant capitalists.

In sum a picture emerges of successes and failures, sordid skulduggery and government intervention, and "enlightened capitalism" and governmental desires to control investments in order to avoid political clashes. Some investors entered with the expectation of manipulating the local scene to their advantage; some entered in good faith, accepting the country, its social structure and way of doing business as facts to which they must adapt themselves. Some investors, as in Argentina, took full advantage of a safe, profitable climate to work with the powers-that-be and pour their capital into any enterprises essential for Argentine economic growth— only to be ungraciously accused in later days of perverting the development of the national economy and reducing the Argentine state to economic vassalage. While some agents of foreign capital lived high on the hog—oil executives are generally singled out as examples—others poured out their health and life's blood to help construct the utilities and public works that provided the foundations for contemporary growth.

2

Matías Romero

BRITISH INVESTORS AND THE REAL DEL MONTE MINE: MEXICO, 1824-1848

Matías Romero, a Mexican statesman of the latter half of the nineteenth century, worked tirelessly to attract American investors to Mexican opportunities. As a hard-working Secretary of the Treasury after the fall of Maximilian's Empire, he started the Mexican Republic on the road to the financial stability which became the hallmark of Mexico, under Díaz. While Ambassador to the United States, he wrote incessantly about his native land. In the following selection Romero succinctly outlines the rise and fall of one of the early great British enterprises that were founded more on enthusiasm than good business sense. A contributing factor was the lack of ability on the part of the men sent to manage many of these enterprises. Military and naval veterans of the Napoleonic Wars, their talents on battlefield and quarterdeck were often better suited to pursuing Mexican brigands than to directing business enterprises.

It would be interesting to refer briefly to the ups and downs of one of the mining enterprises of Mexico—the

From Matías Romero, *Coffee and India-Rubber Culture in Mexico, Preceded by Geographical and Statistical Notes on Mexico* (New York: G. P. Putnam's Sons, 1898), pp. 15-17.

Real del Monte—as a typical case which exemplifies what has happened with many other of our mines, namely, that sometimes they yield large profits, and soon afterwards they cause tremendous losses. The Real del Monte is located about three miles from Pachuca, a large mining center and the capital of the State of Hidalgo, distant about sixty miles northeast of the City of Mexico.

In 1739, a Biscayan, by the name of Don Pedro José Romero de Terreros, came from Santander and settled in Querétaro. He acquired a fortune of $60,000 in a small store in 1749, closed up his affairs, and started to return to his native land. On reaching Pachuca he met an old mining friend, Don José Alejandro Bustamante, who called his attention to the Real del Monte. In company with Bustamante he staked out the Biscaina, Santa Brígida, and Guadalupe mines and began to get the water out, but they soon exhausted their united funds. However, they succeeded in raising money in the City of Mexico on hard terms and drained their properties by a tunnel, which started at Morán, on the northern slope of the mountains, and, running 9000 feet through hard porphyry rock, struck the vein at a depth of 600 feet. This was accomplished a few years later in 1759. Bustamante by this time had died, but Terreros continued the work. On striking the vein he drained it, and in 1760 began the erection of the Hacienda de Regla, to work the rich ore he was taking out. He took out $15,000,000 at a small cost, repaid his advances, built and presented to the King of Spain a man-of-war and 4700 bars of silver, for which he was created Conde de Regla. He lived in grand style in the City of Mexico, and built a palatial residence on Cadena Street.

He died in 1781, and was succeeded by his son, the second Conde, who from 1774 to 1783 struggled with the water, which, as depth was attained, was very severe; according to Ward, twenty-eight horse-whims[1] were employed in the drainage at great expense and unsuccessfully. However, they had gotten down to 324 feet below the Morán adit on the Biscaina vein in the Guadalupe and Santa Teresa shafts. The production was $400,000 per year, drainage costing $250,000 per year, and sinking was abandoned, and the work was confined to drifting above water level.

From 1801 to 1809, $300,000 per year was taken out, but the cost of extraction was severe. Humboldt visited the property, and in 1810 the war of independence broke out, and all operations were suspended. Meanwhile the water rose and the Morán tunnel caved in, and so allowed the water to rise to an enormous height, and the district went to rack and ruin.

In 1822 the Conde's administrator, Don Ignacio Castelazo, made a report, and by his Italian mining friend, Rivafinoli, sent it to the Conde, who was living in England.

That country was only too anxious to reap for themselves some of the spoils that Spain had gleaned from Mexican mines. Here was their opportunity, many became interested, and the celebrated mining expert of that day, Mr. John Taylor, the founder of the present London firm now so heavily interested in South Africa, Taylor Bros., was sent to make an examination, and in 1824 the English Real del Monte Company was formed on the following terms:—The company leased the mines and haciendas for twenty-one years: 1st. The capital invested was to be returned from the products of the mines with interest; 2d. The Conde was then to have one-half of the remaining proceeds yearly; 3d. Meanwhile he was to receive $16,000 per year as an

[1] Mine hoists worked by horses turning a large drum. (Ed.)

advance against his portion or anticipated profits. In case of failure of this third clause the lease would be cancelled and everything revert to the Conde. As the outlay amounted to over $5,000,000 and no profit ensued, it amounted to a rent of $16,000 per year.

In 1824 Captain Vetch, of the Royal Engineers, was sent out as manager. He brought three ships filled with one thousand tons of machinery, pumps, etc., and after untold trials in transportation and erection, finally got them to their destination. All this was done by English engineers, machinists, miners, and workmen, nearly all Cornishmen, under the direction of Colonel Colquhoun, a Peninsular veteran, who finally died of yellow fever with over fifty of his men. After unheard-of troubles they got everything by 1826 safely landed in the Real del Monte. The magnitude of the task may be understood when the almost roadless condition of the country is considered, and the bringing up of the machinery from the coast was a splendid example of British tenacity and pluck.

Captain Vetch had now cleaned out the Morán adit and the Dolores shaft, and the machinery was at once erected. The stock now rose from $500 to $8000 per share. The Conde had, in the meanwhile, borrowed money from the company and made the twenty-one-year lease perpetual, the annual rent of $16,000 remaining in force.

By 1829 Captain Vetch had grappled with the water question, and with an annual cost of $30,000 had accomplished what the first Count had paid $250,000 for, and extracted metal 324 feet below the Moran adit.

Captain Tindall, R.N., succeeded Captain Vetch, and a new shaft (1830) was commenced on the Santa Teresa and called the Terreros shaft. It was 1140 feet to the vein and was started at four points, and was connected in 1834 by drifts run from several levels, and then raised and sunk on. The work came out as true as if it had been done from the surface, thanks to the correctness of the plans of the English mine surveyors.

A 54-inch engine was erected, and with it they sank to 720 feet below the Morán adit. At this point water overpowered them. This was in 1838, and Captain John Rule, who had succeeded Captain Tindall, put in a 75-inch engine at Dolores, and removed the 54-inch one to Acosta. Captain Rule enjoyed a salary of £10,000 per year, and all other payments were in proportion. He struck two bunches of rich ore, one on the Santa Brígida, near Acosta, and the other on La Biscaina, near Dolores. From these two and one at Torreros they had produced $10,481,475 at a cost of $15,381,633 or nearly $5,000,000 loss in twenty-three years. By 1846 the stock had fallen to $12.50 from $8000 a share.

In 1848, Mr. J. H. Buchan arrived, representing the English stockholders. He found water in the mines and increasing; a heavy debt of $5,000,000 bearing a tremendous interest; no money on hand and no ore. So in October, 1848, by order of the bondholders he turned over the business to a Mexican company—the present one—composed of Manuel Escandón, Antonio and Nicanor Beístegui, Mr. Mackintosh, and others for the paltry sum of $130,000. The haciendas, stock, and ores on hand were worth millions, but the English company could not dispose of them.

This was the end of the famous English Real del Monte Company. Their Mexican successors reduced expenses, completed the adit from Omotitlán commenced by the first Conde, which, running 13,500 feet, cut the mines 1110 deeper and struck immediately the *bonanza* in the Rosario, which tradition says had previously been discovered and covered up by Captain Rule.

3

M. R. Neifeld

EUROPE'S FUNDS
BACK COMPANY
IN SOUTH AMERICA

While no full accounting is possible, many students
of foreign investments in Latin America believe that
more money has been lost in unsuccessful ventures
than was ever taken out in profits. Yet, there are
bonanzas for some, and regular profits for others who
arrive well financed and well prepared for the fray.
For most enterprises, however, life is touch and go,
with bankruptcy grinning in the offing. But stories of
bonanzas and high profit rates crop up with enough
regularity to keep investors coming. The following
report appeared in *The American Banker* for April
25, 1962.

Sales finance companies in Latin America have to wres-
tle with unusual problems to finance their operations.

From M. R. Neifeld, "Europe's Funds Back Company in
South America," *The American Banker*, Vol. CXXVII, No. 80
(April 25, 1962), pp. 1, 35. Reprinted by permission of the pub-
lisher.

Most of these problems do not plague sales finance companies operating in the United States. In Latin America capital is scarce and all business firms suffer from lack of sufficient cash. Bank rates are high. There is criticism that the automobile business is attracting too much of the available capital to the detriment of other sectors of the economy. National pride is sensitive to penetration of foreign capital. The price level is under insistent inflationary pressure. Returns to investors have to be correspondingly high.

A close-up view of these problems peculiar to operating in Latin America is available in the experience of the wholly owned finance subsidiary of Industrias Kaiser Argentina, S.A. (IKA) manufacturers of the complete Jeep line, Renault Dauphine, Kaiser Bergantin and Kaiser Corobela. Beginning in 1962, IKA will also manufacture Ramblers under a licensing arrangement with American Motors of Detroit.

The full name of this affiliated finance company is Permanente S.A. Comercial y Financiera, or Permanente for short. It is also known as "PLANIKA."

Local pride is soothed by inviting nationals to become stockholders. Common stockholders expect 20% to 25% return. Preferred stockholders have to be offered issues that carry 15% cumulative dividend rates. To escape censure for siphoning off too much capital from other projects, most borrowed funds are obtained abroad.

"Permanente" started in business in March, 1960. On June 30, 1961, end of its first full fiscal year, it was the largest sales finance company in South America. In United States currency, share capital in round numbers at the beginning of the fiscal year amounted to $1 million. At the end of the year share capital had been increased to $3.6 million, of which $600,000 was common and $3 million was preferred.

During the year, 9,500 cars were financed and receivables outstanding at year-end were $20 million. It is estimated that early in 1962 there will be 20,000 accounts on the books, and monthly collections on these will generate enough cash inflow to finance new monthly volume.

Of the borrowed funds used in the business, one quarter were peso loans and three quarters were foreign funds, mainly dollars, borrowed in Europe. All foreign borrowings are protected by the purchase of forward foreign exchange.

Long-term funds are not available. Foreign borrowings are limited to 180 days. Occasionally, it may be possible to purchase 270-day futures, but this market dried up during 1961. Peso borrowings are also short-term: mainly 6-month money, with only 10% of local borrowings running 9 to 12 months.

Normal bank rates are 12%. Allowing for fees and charges the cost of peso borrowing is 18% per annum. Foreign money costs 10% with a 1% commission to dealers. As maturities are 180 days, the dealer cost is 2% a year. Bank fees to buy futures are 3% to 4%. The overall cost of money is some 24%, against an over-all return of some 33%. Provision for income tax is some 38% of net operating profit.

"Permanente" uses the sum-of-the-months digits system of accounting. In the face of high money costs—and even though the business was new and had not yet reached the turnover point—a net profit after taxes for the first year was just under 32% of average invested capital.

How was this possible?

A clue is suggested when we note that revenue for the year was disbursed as follows:

Salaries	2.0%
Operating expenses	8.6
Taxes	19.2
Cost of borrowed money	47.8
Total expenses	77.6
Net profit	22.4
	100.0

This remarkable record is due to the character of the operation.

During the fiscal year "Permanente" did business with some 200 dealers who account for 86% of total sales of the 260 IKA dealers. One office, located in Buenos Aires, handled all the business.

. . .

Average cost per car to dealer during the year was approximately $3,300. On "flooring" a dealer is required to pay $1,200 before delivery of any unit. Units are floored for a maximum of 90 days. Floor-plan receivables on June 30 were 2.1% of retail receivables and there were none past due.

Payments on retail paper are made to the dealer who remits twice a month. He remits whether the customer pays or not. Spot checks are made one day a week.

Of some 9,500 contracts on the books June 30, there were 7 past due 1-to-15 days, 4 past due 15-to-30 days, and none past due over 30 days. There were no repossessions and no losses. This trend had been maintained throughout the year and continued throughout the latest available figures in the second year.

About two thirds of all new cars are financed. Dealers carry some of the paper themselves or obtain some credit from the First National Bank of Boston, which has recently begun to extend credit to dealers. In turn, "Permanente" finances about two thirds of the cars that are financed, or something over one out of three of all new cars. At the present moment this means between 1500 and 1600 new cars financed a month, and outstanding receivables in excess of $30 million at Sept. 30, 1961.

"Permanente" discovered a finance vacuum. There were no other substantial finance companies around. Small local companies find it difficult to tap foreign money markets and the scarcity of local capital prevents progress. A Ford finance affiliate is only now being organized. "Permanente" is larger than all the others put together.

Among other reasons, this accounts for the rapid profitable growth of "Permanente" in the face of unusual obstacles, with which my own and other companies in the United States do not have to cope.

There are similar opportunities in other places in Latin America—but any finance company not a factory affiliate would have to consider seriously the effect of persistent inflation when earnings on invested funds are repatriated.

4

D. C. M. Platt

BRITISH BONDHOLDERS
IN NINETEENTH CENTURY
LATIN AMERICA:
INJURY AND REMEDY

"Once burned, twice shy," is an ancient piece of folk wisdom. But among investors seeking high returns for a small capital outlay, it seems to be forgotten. During much of the nineteenth century, the bonds of the newly emancipated Latin American republics enjoyed a favored place in the affections of British bondbuyers, despite their miserable record of interest payments and redemptions. D. C. M. Platt of St. Anthony's College, Oxford, has made a most interesting study of this facet of economic and diplomatic history. Pointing out that chicanery and greed marked the actions of all parties in this game, Mr. Platt goes on to show that it was a dangerous game: bondholders, failing to influence

From D. C. M. Platt, "British Bondholders in Nineteenth Century Latin America—Injury and Remedy," *Inter-American Economic Affairs*, Vol. XIV, No. 3 (Winter, 1960), pp. 3–43. Reprinted by permission of the publisher.

"public opinion," the Latin American law courts, or appeals to the long-run best interests of the heads of the Latin American states, repeatedly called for intervention by their home governments to retrieve their money. While the British government never denied its right to intervene to protect the rights of its nationals, it usually forebore as a matter of expediency.

———

While the work of Mr. Rippy has given some conception of the scope of British investment in nineteenth-century Latin America, there appears, as yet, to be some need for an explanation of the motives for investment, the means by which investment was induced, and the methods employed to seek redress once disaster was apparent. It is with a view to fulfilling this need that the present paper has been written; for the intention is not to reinforce already established figures, but to emphasize the facts and events behind the figures, and the motives which created those figures. The Spanish Republics provided an obvious outlet for Victorian England's surplus capital, and the figure of £23 million worth of the produce and manufactures of Great Britain exported to Latin America in 1900—£3 million more than the total British exports to the United States—provides an indication of the manufacturing interests at stake. Latin America, throughout the nineteenth century, supplied an invaluable market for British goods, which at first commanded a virtual monopoly. The confidence inspired by the size of the market, and by the promising natural resources of the Continent, stimulated investment in Government loans. It was this investment which constituted the major item on the debit side of Britain's balance sheet for Latin America, for though commerce and industry had their failures, there was probably nowhere the same universal degree of disaster as that experienced by the British holder of Latin American government bonds. Of the four Loans investigated by the Select Committee on Loans to Foreign States (appointed by the House of Commons in 1875), those of Honduras, having reached their highest point in November, 1868, of 93.5, fell by December, 1874, to 6.5; the Santo Domingo loans reached their lowest point at 6, the Costa Rican at 19, and the Paraguayan, having risen to 97, fell in just over two years to 11.5. Moreover, even by 1900, Argentina, Colombia, Guatemala, Honduras, and the Dominican Republic were still in default, with a total principal outstanding of over £31 million, and arrears of interest of £14½ million. Depreciation and default on such a scale brought hardship to a number of innocent bondholders, but it is important to see the situation in the correct context. It was not solely the fault of the "rascally republics," nor that of their sinister diplomats; the fault lay as much with the London agents and with their dupes, the original investors. The Select Committee on Loans, in fact, reached this conclusion when they reported that, though they did not feel it their duty to apportion blame in the transactions they had investigated—"to a great extent they agree in the opinion of the Secretary to the Honduras Legation, that 'the fault of the failure falls with equal force upon all who have interests, rights, claims, complaints, or any participation whatever in these matters. It is a kind of *original sin*, which reaches even the most innocent who have had anything to do with this undertaking.'"

. . .

Despite the findings of the Select Committee, the accusation of rascality is even now largely confined to the Latin Americans—the English bondholders being described as the innocent victims of a monstrous fraud. And the accusation is not entirely unfounded, for there was considerable justice in the English complaints. In the first place, Latin American Governments tended to give preferential treatment to national interests over international obligations. The British Chargé d'Affaires at Lima, in a note to Señor Castilla, July 1, 1839, complained characteristically that very many millions of the home debt had been redeemed, whilst the dividends on the Anglo-Peruvian Loan had been in arrears since the 15th of October, 1825, and he urged the Peruvian Government to put "an end to so odious a distinction between the home and foreign debts, the continuance of which is manifestly incompatible with good faith and national honor." Moreover, it was not uncommon for a Latin American Government to claim, as did Señor Mosquera for New Granada in 1840, that the foreign debt, though sacred, was subordinate to a national duty of higher category—that of a State's self-preservation and existence. Or, alternatively, a new Constitution might be accepted after a revolution, which would omit the customary article guaranteeing the foreign debt. And there was always the excuse of the physical impossibility of meeting international obligations. Señor D. Portales wrote to Vice Consul White, July 12, 1830, that only an absolute impossibility could justify the delay of the Chilean Government in the discharge of its obligations to the creditors of the State, but that it was evident that that situation now existed; and he asked, somewhat plaintively, whether it was in the Government's power "to avoid imperious circumstances."

Deceit and corruption were far from unusual at the issue of loans, and Latin American governments had the uncomfortable habit of disowning the actions of their predecessors. Sir Henry James, moving the appointment of the Select Committee on Foreign Loans, noted "a system that has sprung up comparatively of late years, of bankrupt States, knowing themselves to be in a state of complete bankruptcy, recklessly coming into this English market, and endeavoring to obtain from English creditors money which it is clear that those States can never repay." And in raising this money, later to be disowned scornfully as being obviously beyond the capacity of the State to repay, false information might be given by Latin American diplomats. It is clear from the evidence given before the Select Committee by Mr. R. Foster (of Messrs. Knowles and Foster, contractors for the Costa Rican 7% Loan of 1872) that the exaggerated statements of the prospectus were based largely on the information supplied by Señor Alvarado. The Select Committee, commenting on this habit, remarked that:

> By means of exaggerated statements in the prospectus the public have been induced to believe that the material wealth of the contracting State formed a sufficient security for the repayment of the money borrowed. . . . Much evil has been caused by the misstatements and suppressions to be found in the prospectus.

Latin American diplomats themselves were not above personal corruption. Captain Bedford Pim, R.N., M.P., accused M. Herran, the Minister Plenipotentiary of Honduras in Paris, and M. Pelletier, his son-in-law (and Honduras Consul-General), of refusing to agree to the loan which he, as special commissioner for Honduras, was attempting to launch, unless he took care that they had £40,000 and £16,000 respectively. Yet, once the loan had been issued and the Government overthrown, it was quite conceivable that the next Government might disown it. Wheaton (*International Law,* ed. 1863,

p. 41) gave the opinion that: "As to public debts—
whether due to or from the revolutionized State—a
mere change in the form of government, or in the person of the ruler, does not affect their obligation." Vattel,
dealing with the subject of dishonest agents remarked:

> Que l'argent emprunté ait tourné au profit de l'État,
> ou qu'il ait été dissipé en folles dépenses, ce n'est pas
> l'affaire de celui qui l'a prêté. Il a confié son bien à
> la nation; elle doit le lui rendre. Tant pis pour elle, si
> elle a remis le soin de ses affaires en mauvaises mains.

But this did not stop Ecuador claiming (1869) that,
since the Convention with the foreign bondholders was
"the fruit of the most frightful corruption," and had
been entered into without considering the Government's
manifest inability to pay in face of other obligations, she
was entitled to suspend payment on her External Debt.

The practices of Latin American Governments *after*
the loans had been raised, however, gave rise to the
most acid comment. Certain funds or resources were
invariably hypothecated as the security for loans raised
on the London market. Not only were these often
worthless in themselves—the "valuable refuse metals of
the mines of Tarapaca" allocated by the Peruvian Government for the redemption of the home and foreign
debt were described by the British Chargé d'Affaires,
on Feb. 18, 1840, as "utterly valueless rubbish (*basura*),
not worth the conveyance to England, and . . . not the
property of the State to dispose of"—but they were di-
verted to different interests whilst still legally the property of the bondholders. . . .

A further development . . . was the arbitrary reduction of customs duties or tariffs specifically hypothecated to the bondholders. Under the Arrangement of

1895 the Guatemalan Bondholders were given the special and "irrevocable" security of a fixed duty of six shillings per quintal on the export of coffee. Yet in 1898, in direct violation of its contract with the Bondholders, the Government arbitrarily reduced the tax to one third of the above amount.

Still more provoking was the practice of scaling down External Debts by a succession of unfavorable Settlements forced on the bondholders *faute de mieux*. Ecuador (1855–6) reduced the principal and accrued interest on her Debt by 40 per cent, and in 1892 she again scaled it down by nearly 80 per cent. In 1898 she set about diminishing the remainder by a further 70 per cent. The Ecuador Committee of the Corporation of Foreign Bondholders pointed out that: "This means that £100 originally borrowed, with interest due and not paid to date, would at present be represented by about £3. 12s. or, leaving out the question of interest, by about £11 of Bonds, valued on the market at less than 25 percent of their normal value." . . .

An ironical twist was given to this arbitrary reduction in value of Latin American bonds by the arguments advanced by the Honduras Government Commission (appointed to consider a proposed agreement between the Government and the bondholders' representatives, Messrs. Bain and Turner). The Commission seriously proposed that since the old Bondholders, who had paid high prices for the loans, had already disappeared and the present holders had purchased them at the price of 2 per cent, then the Honduras Government was only obliged to consider £107,971 (i.e. 2%) as its External Debt, out of the original £5,398,570! . . . As Palmerston wrote of Portugal, April 10, 1841, the Government "has been profiting by its own wrong, and has been cancelling part of its debt at a low rate of value artificially created by its own want of good faith."

Settlements were sometimes offered on positively insulting terms, and could only have been intended further to delay genuine negotiations. Dr. Angel Ugarte, the Agent of the Honduras Government at the negotiations of 1903, proposed a settlement which meant, the Council of Foreign Bondholders told him (in a letter date January 5, 1904), that "a holder of £100 of Honduras Bonds, with arrears of interest of £300, should accept in exchange therefore £6 of New Four per Cent. Bonds, worth at 40 the insignificant sum of £2. 8s."

The final resort of the more dishonest of the Latin American Governments was either to call despairingly for more immigration, or to apply to London for a new loan to pay off the interest on the old. Señor Malo of Ecuador urged Consul Cope, January 24, 1850, to inform the English creditors that the only means of obtaining the repayment of their loan was to encourage European immigration, thus leading to an appreciation in value of the inexhaustible Ecuadorian waste lands. For he appreciated the truth of Alberdi's dictum that— "En America, gobernar es poblar." As for the practice of applying for new loans, Palmerston warned Venezuela, July 25, 1848, that "the plan of paying the interest of one loan raised in England, by applying to that purpose the principal of a new loan, also to be raised in England, is one which cannot give satisfaction in that country; nor is it calculated to inspire confidence in the pecuniary resources or in the good faith of Venezuela." His admonition, unfortunately, had little effect, and the Republics continued, with varying degrees of success, to call good money after bad.

. . .

Clearly the behavior of the Latin American States was reprehensible, but there was another aspect which emerged more reluctantly in contemporary British journalism. There was, after all, some justice in the complaint of the Costa Rican Minister of Finance (1895) that, since the Republic only received about a third of the money for which it had made itself liable, she felt that "she should not in justice be called upon to assume the whole responsibility for a matter in which she has been notoriously defrauded." And the defrauders were *not* exclusively Latin American politicians and diplomats; indeed, the most successful were the London financiers. The eminence and apparent respectability of some of the names associated with these outrageous enterprises might justifiably cause some surprise. Latin American Governments and British bondholders presented irresistible opportunities for successful exploitation, and financiers of every degree surrendered to the temptation.

The most immediately noticeable features of these Latin American Loan negotiations were the harsh terms of the contracts, the huge profits of the loan contractors and the minimal financial results secured by the Republics. English contractors were not above taking advantage of a dangerous revolutionary situation to impose particularly harsh terms on a failing regime. Government bonds, given in place of wages to army officers, could be bought on the open market at a fraction of their face value, whereupon the purchaser would lay claim to the total face value, threatening diplomatic intervention if the claim were denied. The Montgomery, Nicod and Co. incident is a case in point. The Company had entered into a contract with the Mexican Government in 1840, at a time of serious internal difficulties, by which they were to appear as creditors of the

Republic to the amount of $2 million at 12% interest, while 17% of the receipts of the maritime customs were to be pledged exclusively for repayment, so soon as obligations were paid off. The Mexican Government later contested the contract, and Montgomery, Nicod and Co., true to form, obtained the assistance of H. M. Government. But, as M. Murphy, the Mexican Minister in London, explained to Aberdeen (14 October, 1843):

Sur les deux millions de piastres qu'ils réclament à l'intérêt de 12 pour cent par an, 45 pour cent ont été livrés en espèces, partie en monnaie de cuivre et partie en argent, et 55 pour cent en crédits achetés à vil prix sur la place à la veuve nécessitéuse et à l'invalide affamé.

In other words, Montgomery, Nicod and Co. were claiming $2 million at 12% for a loan which had probably cost them not more than $1 million.

Similarly, harsh bargains were concluded by loan contractors in cases of particular need. The Honduras Government had set its heart on an Inter-Oceanic railway, linking the Atlantic and the Pacific, which was to bring vast wealth, so it hoped, to a chronically impoverished State. With this in mind it had issued the Loans of 1867, 1869 and 1870, had become indebted in respect of principal in a sum of approximately six million pounds, and, in return, was pledged to pay £695,-700 annually, in periods varying from 15 to 17 years. Yet all it ever received was an abandoned section of line 53 miles long. The remainder of the six million had vanished along the way, and the Report of the Select Committee indicated the direction when analysing the disposal of a £2 million section of the total Loan. After computing Mr. Lefevre's receipts by various sharp practices in the course of issuing the Loans, the Committee concludes:

. . . out of this portion of the loan of 1869, and the loan of 1870, Mr. Lefevre has received in cash, or by the remission of his contracts £955,398.[1]

Of the remainder of the proceeds of these loans, the Honduras Government received £58,930; the trustees were paid £16,374; the engineer, £6,675, and the expenses of the loan amounted to £30,112. Messrs. Bischoffsheim and Goldschmidt received £47,000 for what purpose is not shown, out of which they returned £23,701, and a sum of £10,000 for commission; £6,000 was expended in the purchase of federal stock . . . only £217,232 was paid to the railway contractors.

Risks were high in Latin American finance, but were they high enough to justify such returns? It is arguable that the result of such extortion was the very collapse against which such high returns were demanded.

The character of the loan contractors is indicated not only by the extortion which they practised against the republics, but also by the infamous methods by which they deceived the British investor. A Latin American Republic, attempting to float a loan on the London market, usually met with some difficulty in finding either a respectable contractor or a guaranteed result. This difficulty was solved by the practice of giving a loan to a contractor or to a syndicate at, say, 64 which was then brought out with a flourish at 80 on the open market. The contractor would either take the loan "firm" (i.e. undertake to provide the 64% come what may, no matter what response the loan had achieved), or, in even more dubious cases, obtain an undertaking that the Government would buy the stock unsold at 80

[1] Charles Lefevre already possessed a criminal record. He was sentenced to two years' imprisonment after conviction in Paris on a breach of trust (*abus de confiance*), 22 May, 1856. (See *Report from the Select Committee on Loans to Foreign States*, Parliamentary Papers, 1875, XI, 15).

or above. In any case vital information was withheld from the public, for a loan issued at 64 obviously promised less than one issued at 80. Moreover, the contractors, normally organised as a syndicate for the sake of spreading the risk, were able to make very substantial sums of money if they could raise the issue price to 80 or above. Admittedly they normally ran the risk of having to take up a certain proportion of the loan which they had guaranteed if it should fail to find a market. The Erlanger syndicate on the Costa Rican 7 per cent loan of 1872 undertook, in return for a commission of 5 per cent, to take up £800,000, however the market responded. But the risk was well rewarded, and in the case of the Paraguayan 8% Public Works Loan of 1871 for a nominal amount of £1,000,000, the contractors, Waring Bros., having taken the loan at 64, appear from Mr. Grant's evidence to have received a total profit, after paying all expenses, commissions, etc., of rather over £100,000.

The profit, however, depended on the contractor's ability to raise the price of the loan above his own taking price. Several rather neat, if ethically unacceptable, devices were employed to ensure this satisfactory result—a process which went under the name of "making the market," and which, as Baron Emile Erlanger pointed out (April 22, 1875), in justification of his own behavior with regard to the Costa Rican Loan of 1872, was common practice in the loans of almost every European Government, including France (whose loans at that period were always extremely popular). Thus the contractors, holding the loan at 64, set to work in the period between advertising the loan and its allotment. As the Select Committee noted: "Although no scrip is in existence, they contrive by purchases and concerted dealings on the Stock Exchange to raise the loan to a premium, and this premium is maintained at any cost till the period of allotment is over." These purchases were called "buying back"—i.e. the syndicate, seeing the price of the loan declining, brought back a certain amount, creating a demand which raised the price once more. . . .

. . .

"Buying back" was intended to create "fictitious premiums" which in turn had two purposes; first, to induce the public to believe that the loan was a good investment, and, secondly, to induce the public to believe that they would, if they obtained an allotment of the stock, realize that premium.

The intention was to create the impression that the public was so keen on owning the stock that they were prepared to pay a little extra in order to be sure of getting the share of the allotment they wanted, rather than run the risk of having to pay more for it once the loan had been allotted. Moreover, many people subscribed to a loan purely with the idea of realizing the profit created by the difference between the fixed rate at which the loan was quoted (e.g. 80) and the premium it was fetching on the market (e.g. 88). If they received an allotment, they would then stand to make an immediate clear profit of 8. Meanwhile, of course, the syndicate had applied for, and obtained, a quotation of the loan on the Stock Exchange, and the flotation was completed. The purchasers (i.e. the syndicate or contractors) now became sellers, and if possible maintained the premium until they had sold out. But in fact they had already enjoyed such favorable terms that the stock could be sold at a discount on 80 and still yield a substantial profit. The only remedy the Select Committee could suggest was that the buying back authorization (i.e. from the Government to the loan contractor) should be published in the form of a statutory declaration before the Stock Exchange gave a settling day. It was realized that, in the face of Stock Exchange opposition, it would be impossible to apply the only complete remedy—i.e. the prohibition by law of all dealings before allotment.

There were occasions when, even in spite of these manipulations, the public seemed reluctant to take up a loan. It was possible then to ensure that a favorable piece of news reached London before the allotment—the arrival of two cargoes of mahogany directed to the bankers for the payment of back interest on a previous loan, a hint of accelerated amortization, or the announcement of extra drawings, over and above the prescribed. In the case of the Honduras Loan of 1870, Mr. Lefevre managed to dispose of a larger quantity of bonds by advertising, in the *Investor's Monthly Manual,* two additional 2% drawings of £50,000 apiece *beyond* the annual drawing of 3% (£75,000) mentioned in the prospectus.

Most surprising of all is the allegation, emerging in the evidence of the Select Committee and never adequately disproved, that London financiers were concerned with the direct bribery of Latin American politicians and diplomats. Messrs. Knowles and Foster, one of the loan contractors giving evidence, handed in a translation of President Guardia's message to the Costa Rican Congress. Not only did President Guardia, who was obviously making an apologia in face of serious accusations of dishonesty, confess to having received "as an act of pure generosity, following the custom established for these negotiations," the sum of £100,000 from Mr. Henry Meiggs, the American contractor for the railroad, but he went on to reveal that £60,000 had

been placed at his disposal in the name of the contract-
ing house, Messrs. Emile Erlanger and Co., "in order
that I might divide them among my friends and other
members of the Cabinet." Baron Erlanger, of course,
totally denied this allegation, but he gave no satisfactory explanation for the President's conduct, and the
reputation of the financiers was further compromised by
the Honduras bribery allegations. Mr. George Hatfield
Gossip, one-time clerk of Mr. Lefevre, in answer to the
questions of Sir Henry James, reported that £4,000
worth of diamonds had been sent by Lefevre to
Madame Gutierrez (the wife of the Honduras Minister)
because "Mr. Lefevre was of the opinion that she had
great influence over her husband, and that she could
induce him to sign the agreements which Mr. Lefevre
wished to be signed." He also remembered £10,000
having been sent to President Medina in Honduras "as a
recognition of the services he had rendered in connection with the promotion of the railway." But it should
be remarked that Mr. Gossip had a grievance against
Mr. Lefevre, who had, according to him, grossly under-
paid him, treated him unfairly, and finally dispensed
with his services. He also appears (or at least, so the
members of the Committee evidently thought) to have
been conducting a private blackmailing campaign
against the people involved, notably Lefevre, Messrs.
Bischoffsheim and Goldschmidt (the bankers), and
Señor Gutierrez—and his lack of success may well have
led to spiteful exaggeration.

Yet, in spite of the revelations of the Select Committee, opinion among financiers and stock brokers inter-
viewed was virtually unanimously opposed to remedial
legislation . . . on grounds ranging from possible damage to London's position as the centre for foreign
Government Loans to resentment at "too much of the

nursing system." The existing situation was too lucrative to be dispensed with. The Stock Exchange had nothing to gain and a great deal to lose by tightening its regulations, and the bankers, themselves interested in the profitable flotation of loans rather than the holding of Latin American Government bonds, were in very much the same position. The recommendations of the Select Committee in effect left things very much as they were.

. . .

To a certain extent, then, the excuse of fraud advanced by the Latin American Governments is tenable, and it becomes more so when the avarice and stupidity of the British bondholder is revealed. There certainly seems little reason, at this distance, to compel one victim of a fraud to reimburse, out of his own private funds, the losses of another. The British bondholders paid the price of their ignorance, as did the Republics, and it was a handful of politicians, diplomats, financiers, stockbrokers and speculators who reaped the rich harvest.

The small British investor remained, throughout this period, subject to the most elementary swindles. Utterly ignorant of conditions in Latin America, and with only just enough knowledge of the 'Change to make a fool of himself, he invested his savings in the most unlikely ventures, and then wept bitterly when they failed to yield the expected fabulous returns. . . .

Knowing nothing of the realities or falsehoods behind the convincing blandishments which poured from the Stock Exchange, the small investor depended to a great extent on the reputation of the banking house issuing the loan, on the mythical security offered by the admission of the loan to a quotation by the Stock Exchange

Committee, or on the reception which the Stock Exchange seemed to be giving the loan before allotment (i.e. the premium it achieved). Most of the Brazilian and Chilean issues were introduced to the public by the Rothschilds, while the Argentine loans were the responsibility of the Barings, the Murrietas, J. S. Morgan and Co., Morton, Rose & Co., Stern Brothers, and the River Plate Trust. . . . But what the small investor did not realize was that the banking houses often held no stake whatsoever in the loans they issued, and, since they collected their commission and insurance charges *before* handing the public's money over to the foreign Government, stood to gain whether the loan was good or bad. Mr. William Shaw, M.P., asked Mr. William McKewan, joint General Manager of the London and County Bank (bankers for the Honduras Loan of 1867) whether he had made any investigations as to the character of the loan, or the security, before taking it. The answer was in the negative, and Mr. McKewan admitted that they took the Loan purely as a matter of their business as bankers. He also admitted, in reply to a question from Sir Charles Russell, M.P., that the name of his bank "would have given some confidence to the undertaking."

. . .

The ultimate remedy of the bondholders lay in the powerful intervention of their own, sympathetic, or allied Governments. Frequent attempts were made to gain security for a loan or arrangement by linking it with the names of foreign Governments, or by writing into a contract the safeguard of guaranteed foreign intervention. The Council of Foreign Bondholders, in the negotiations for the settlement of the Guatemalan External Debt in the last quarter of 1901, insisted that the Guatemalan Minister in London should accept a clause based on the formula used in the Chinese Imperial Railway 5% Loan of 1898, by which the arrangement should be notified to the Governments of the countries interested as constituting a binding engagement on the Guatemalan Government, and a memorandum should be endorsed on the bonds that one or more of such Governments took note thereof. Of course, "taking note" did not mean armed intervention, but there was something of an implied guarantee. But it was not only the bondholders who were interested in such an implied guarantee. There were occasions when Latin American Governments themselves found a guarantee useful. Señor Guzmán Blanco made a proposal to the foreign creditors of Venezuela, the sixth Article of which ran as follows:

> The Government of Venezula anxious that the Bonds of Venezuela should be re-quoted on the Exchange of Europe at a price which shall be the true Index of its Credit is disposed to celebrate with the Government of Her Britannic Majesty a diplomatic Act by which all possible Guarantees shall be agreed on, both for the most punctual collection and application of the Funds which the Republic binds itself for the payment of the Interest and Sinking Fund of the National Debt.

In other words, the British Government was to be used as a peg on which to hang the credit of Venezuela. Salisbury, hardly surprisingly, refused to accept such a proposition on the grounds, as he told M. Rojas, that "H.M.G. did not find it possible to enter into the arrangements suggested as it might involve them in responsibilities which it would not be in accordance with the interests of this country to undertake. . . ."

Bondholders were on occasion able to bring in Allied intervention on a large scale to safeguard their rights. Britain, Spain and France actually signed a Convention,

31st of October, 1861, agreeing to enforce the bondholders' rights against Mexico, though Britain came
later to an independent arrangement. Britain, Germany,
France, Belgium and Italy applied pressure and threats
of armed intervention to Guatemala in 1901 on behalf
of the holders of the £1,600,000 External Debt, and
were successful in arriving at a Settlement. And there
was the notorious incident of joint British, German and
Italian intervention in Venezuela, December 1902,
which had as one of its objects the Settlement of the
bondholders' grievances. Apart from these, there are
any number of examples of minor protests and block-
ades, reflected, for example, in Mr. Samuel G. Inman's
remarks (1921) on the U.S. assumption of a protectorate
over both Santo Domingo and Haiti, "in order to save
them from a foreign foreclosure" . . . because it was
claimed that these countries were likely to be seized by
European countries for nonpayment of debt.[2] . . .

The bondholders found their richest source for diplomatic intervention, naturally enough, in the British
Government, but the British Government remained traditionally reluctant to intervene by force of arms. H.
Edward Nettles, commenting on the attitude of the
British Government toward intervention for the bondholders, appears to assume, mistakenly, that it was
based exclusively on Palmerston's Circular of January
1848 (i.e. "that it is for the British Government entirely
a question of discretion and by no means a question of
international right, whether they should or should not
make this matter the subject of diplomatic negotiation"). Mr. Nettles refers to the endorsement of
Palmerston's dictum by Russell, Salisbury, Balfour, "and

[2] "The Monroe Doctrine and Hispanic America," *Hispanic
American Historical Review,* Vol. VI (1921), p. 647.

other leading heads of the foreign office," and affirms that "our final conclusion, from the attitude of both writers and statesmen, should be that the leading nations reserve the right to intervene with armed force in extreme cases, for the collection of public debts." But the opinions of Canning, Aberdeen and Bryce, spanning the century, combine to give a very different impression. Canning, while Secretary of State for Foreign Affairs (1824), replying to the request of Robert Cairncross, Esq., that H. M. Government should make a representation to the Government of Spain, remarked that he did not consider it "as any part of the duty of the Government to interfere in any way to procure the repayment of loans made by British Subjects to Foreign Powers, States, or Individuals." Aberdeen, though not so consistent in practice, or so categorical in his denial, informed William Ewing, Esq. (representing the holders of South American and Mexican bonds) that "the grievances of which you complain arise out of speculations of a purely private nature, for the success of which His Majesty's Government are in no way responsible, and upon which they cannot, as matter of right, claim to exercise any authoritative interference with foreign States." He added (1842) that "Her Majesty's Government would not be justified in taking any measures to compel foreign Governments to pay interest on loans which have not been formally guaranteed by Great Britain." Mr. James Bryce, Parliamentary Secretary for Foreign Affairs (1886) and President of the Board of Trade (1894–5), writing to Dr. Manuel A. Montes de Oca, June 15, 1903, remarked that he agreed with Dr. Drago that civil debts owed by a State to the private citizens of another State should not be taken as the basis for military and naval operations against a State. A State may properly make observations or friendly remonstrances to another State in defense of civil debts or other claims of its citizens, and can try to come to an arrangement of its claims by diplomatic means. But there is a big and dangerous difference between this and compulsory action. ". . . Britain's normal, if not absolutely invariable practice has been to take coercive military or naval measures, or threaten them, in defence of her citizens, only when these were wronged by the seizure of their property or by personal injuries." Even Palmerston, with some inconsistency, had informed Sir J. T. Lee on September 27, 1839, that "Her Majesty's Government cannot exercise any interference with Foreign Governments on the subject of loans voluntarily made by British subjects to Foreign Powers."

The fact was that the British Government never held a consistent policy towards bondholders. But it remained throughout the nineteenth century extremely reluctant to employ force on their behalf, though it was quite prepared to enter into friendly negotiations with foreign Governments, or even to address stern, threatening Notes. . . .

. . .

An estimate of the extent of the injury received or of the total effectiveness of the remedy has not been attempted here. But the complaints of the bondholders, the counter-complaints of the Republics, and the remedies available for the deluded investors should at least become a little clearer. Some idea of the magnitude of the problem, even as late as 1903, can be gathered from a speech given by Sir Charles Fremantle in which he estimated that the amount of the debts of Spanish American Republics, known on the London Stock Exchange, was some £200,000,000, of which at that time between £50,000,000 and £60,000,000 were still in default.[3] Yet by 1905 the worst was over. A renewed boom in speculation and investment in Latin American securities was under way, and between 1901 and 1905 Colombian bonds rose 215%; Costa Rican, 223%; Guatemalan, 200%; Honduran, 160%; Nicaraguan, 37%; Paraguayan, 120%; Uruguayan, 45% and Venezuelan, 97%. By the end of 1905 hopeful negotiations were proceeding for the settlement of the Costa Rican Debt and Buenos Ayres Cedulas, and only Honduras and Guatemala remained obstinately in default.

[3] *The Economist* (June 20, 1903), p. 1097.

5

Alan K. Manchester

BRITISH PREËMINENCE IN BRAZIL

Brazilian history has long been a neglected field of study in the United States. It has been said, despairingly and not facetiously, that the American Brazilianologists could hold professional meetings in a very small room. Dean Alan K. Manchester of Duke University has been one of the outstanding American students of Brazilian development, and his book, *British Preëminence in Brazil*, is regarded as a classic. Dr. Manchester has painstakingly traced the course of Brazilian history in the nineteenth century to delineate that nation's struggle to throw off the tutelage of Europe. Great Britain, as leader of the European nations with interests in Brazil, occupied a unique and privileged position, buttressed by treaties and tradition, which enabled it to dominate Brazil's commerce and economic development. Although the Brazilians successfully nullified the political privileges enjoyed by foreigners—including extraterritoriality—their economic life during the

From Alan K. Manchester, *British Preëminence in Brazil* (Chapel Hill, N.C.: University of North Carolina Press, 1933), pp. 337–340, 312–328. Reprinted by permission of the publisher.

nineteenth century remained dominated by foreign merchants and foreign capital, of which the British held first place by a wide margin.

The foundations of British preëminence in Portuguese America were laid before Brazil became a nation, for the line of continuity may be traced to the Anglo-Portuguese treaties of 1642–'54–'61. By those agreements practices which had become recognized by custom and by the decrees of Portuguese kings were legalized, and additional privileges in Portuguese economic life demanded by English merchants were guaranteed to them. . . . So valuable to Englishmen were the commercial relations which developed after 1703 that Portugal outrivaled France in the esteem of the British merchant and industrial class. Consequently, by the middle of the eighteenth century English penetration developed to such a degree that Portugal became the economic vassal of its ally. To the British merchant, the principal factor in this Anglo–Portuguese exchange was the colony of Brazil, for the mother country served as the *entrepôt* for the streams of merchandise which flowed from England to the Portuguese colonies and from these colonies back to England.

The industrial revolution in Great Britain, which was coincident with the effort of the Marquez de Pombal to free his country from its economic vassalage, almost severed the connection between the two allies, but raw cotton from Brazil and the wars with France re-established the intimate relations which had been threatened with dissolution. When the invasion of the French forced D. João to flee to Rio under the protection of England, the opportunity came for Great Britain to transfer its old privileges and preëminent position in

Portugal to the colony itself. Strangford, by his treaty in 1810, succeeded in this task beyond the expectations of the London court.

From 1808 to 1821 the relations between the two countries were conducted on the traditional European basis, although the Portuguese court was residing in the colony. During these thirteen years English penetration into Brazil assumed formidable proportions, for, encouraged by the special privileges, immunities, and guaranties specified to them by treaty, British capital and enterprise were enticed into the huge colony, ripe for exploitation. When the cry of independence was raised in 1822, these interests had become so important that Great Britain forced the revolting colony to accept as binding upon itself the obligations which Portugal had incurred by the treaty of 1810, despite the fact that Brazil had renounced the authority of the government which had negotiated that agreement. This transfer of the traditional English privileges so long enjoyed in Portugal to the independent empire of Brazil was completed by the commercial treaty of 1827, by which the new state paid a debt due Great Britain for its services in securing the entrance of the empire into the family of European nations.

Two currents of interest threatened to disrupt the transfer of traditional British privileges in Portugal to the new state. One was the desire of the Rio court to absorb the north bank of the Plate River, but under British mediation the question was settled in 1828 without fundamentally disturbing Anglo-Brazilian relations. The other problem, the suppression of the slave traffic, was far more serious and proved impossible of solution during the formative period of the empire, although Great Britain succeeded in forcing Brazil to sign agreements which nominally abolished the slave trade under conditions which would enable the English to employ their cruisers to enforce the prohibition. . . . The fact that the empire in 1827 acceded to the demands of England in regard to the slave trade is evidence of the preëminence of Britain in Brazil, but persistence in those demands constantly threatened during the first three quarters of the century to destroy the good relations which existed between the two governments.

Between 1825 and 1827 British preëminence in Brazil reached its zenith. In shipping, commerce, and investments Great Britain enjoyed the paramount position among foreign powers interested in Brazil, and politically the London Office was beginning to exercise a virtual protectorate over the empire. Yet the twenty years following 1827 witnessed a steady decline in the political influence exerted by Great Britain over Brazil. Friction which arose from England's efforts to suppress the slave trade embittered Anglo-Brazilian relations and led to a revolt by the South American nation against the traditional position of Great Britain in Portuguese affairs. . . .

The revolt against British preëminence in the political affairs of Brazil was carried to a successful conclusion in the two decades following 1845. By 1850 the imperial government, which in the first quarter of the century had been forced to yield to the commanding diplomacy of British agents, was stabilized, confident of its future, and divorced from the old idea of maintaining close relations with the European powers. Irritated by forty years of friction arising mainly from the slave trade controversy, and aided by the marked national and economic development of the empire, Brazil was able to throw off its political subjection to Great Britain. In 1860 it was strong enough to sustain its revolt; thereafter friendly relations were to exist between the two governments, but the thread of political control by

England in territory possessed by the Portuguese race was definitely broken in Brazil.

A different phase of this revolt against British preëminence was revealed in the efforts exerted by the South American empire to free itself from the extraterritorial privileges, consular concessions, and economic favors imposed by England during the period from 1808 to 1827. The aim of the Brazilians was not to eliminate British interests from their foreign commerce, capital investments, and domestic enterprises, but to open their country to the competition of all other nations, and thus to make the paramount position of England dependent not on special favors but on economic superiority over rivals. That objective was attained by the middle of the century.

Yet Great Britain was able to maintain its position of economic supremacy in Brazilian shipping, markets, and investments throughout the nineteenth century. The traditional privileges, won in Portugal centuries earlier and transferred to South America between 1808 and 1827, were abolished at the expiration of the treaty in 1844 without altering England's preëminence in Brazilian economic life. During the period when the trade of the Portuguese empire was a monopoly of the mother country, these special privileges had played a useful part in opening colonial possessions to British trade and their continuation in the early years of the independence of Brazil had guaranteed a low import tax during the transition period and at the same time had prevented the granting to other foreign powers special favors adverse to British interests. By the middle of the century, however, their usefulness was past, for in open competition Great Britain was superior to any rival.

. . .

Statistics for the early period of the empire are uncertain or nonexistent, but there is no doubt that in 1827 England was the greatest foreign supplier of the markets of Brazil. In the number of ships entering the port of Rio, where more than half of the imports of the empire was landed, Great Britain was far in the lead. . . . No figures are available as to the amount of foreign capital invested in the empire in 1827, but it is more than probable that British investments exceeded those of other foreign powers.[1]

Yet competition began at once. For coincident with their recognition of the independence of the empire, France, the United States, the Hanseatic Cities, Holland, and Sweden initiated the long struggle which eventually was to result in the successful rivaling of Britain's favored position. In the early period France was most active despite very serious handicaps which resulted in part from French colonial laws and in part from lack of capital and industrial development. Due to this competition the number of British ships entering Rio in 1837 fell to 110, whereas French vessels numbered sixty-eight and American ships (in 1836) almost equalled the British with 102.

This competition proved futile, however, as long as the market in which it occurred remained comparatively stationary in the value of goods imported. That condition existed from 1827 to 1850 due to the disturbed conditions of the last years of the reign of D. Pedro I and the internal disorder of the period of the Regency and of the first years of the rule of the second Pedro. During that period, Great Britain not only maintained a

[1] The only foreign loan contracted by the empire had been floated in London and the economic penetration of the preceding twenty years would indicate an influx of British capital.

fairly level average of exports to Brazil but even increased its annual sales slightly. . . . Thus there was little chance for the rise of a successful rival. . . . In 1835 the value of all exports from the British Islands to Brazil was £2,553,203. . . . The total value of imports from the empire into the British Islands was £1,479,588.

As these figures show, British sales to Brazil greatly exceeded British purchases. In 1842, whereas over fifty-one per cent of the total importations received at the port of Rio came from Great Britain and its possessions, only twenty per cent of the exportations were destined for English ports. As explained to Henry Ellis by the Rio merchants, this unbalanced trade was completed in a triangular exchange. Goods were sent by consignment to Brazil on long term credit, the only kind of credit under which Brazilian buyers could operate. After selling his articles, the British merchant loaned the proceeds of his sales to non-British foreign merchants, taking bills of exchange on London in return. These non-British agents used the money so obtained to buy Brazilian articles for shipment to their respective countries, where English purchases equalized the bills of exchange drawn on London. Thus by means of British capital Brazilian trade with Sweden, Denmark, Hamburg, Trieste, and other places was helped materially.

Moreover in 1843 approximately three eighths of the sugar, one half of the coffee, and five eighths of the cotton exported from Pernambuco, Bahia, and Rio de Janeiro were shipped on British accounts although, except for cotton, very little of these products was actually landed in England. Of the coffee shipped from Rio, for example, over three hundred and fifty thousand sacks were sent to the United States alone whereas the British Isles took less than two hundred thousand. . . .

Thus although less than one fifth of the total coffee export was shipped to England, one half of the crop, by the estimate of Henry Ellis, ordinarily was handled through British accounts. Consequently in the evaluation of Anglo-Brazilian economic relations, there must be added to the actual commercial interchange carried on between the empire and Great Britain the participation of British agents and capital in the trade of Brazil with other foreign powers.

No less commanding was England's position in the investment field in 1842. Of the internal funded debt British subjects held over eight times as large a share as citizens of all other foreign powers combined.[2] In addition, all foreign loans since the declaration of independence had been floated in London, a new loan of £732,600 being secured in 1843.[3] As to the value of British capital employed in private enterprise in Brazil, there are no figures available for the 'forties, but in shipping England still maintained its lead, although the United States was a close rival.

The cessation of the commercial treaty in 1844 did not alter England's preëminent position in Brazilian economic life. . . . The merchants themselves placed slight importance on the continuation of the treaty if they could be assured of equality of treatment with other foreign agents, and the percentage of British goods in the import values of the empire in 1854

[2] The internal debt amounted to approximately 38.134:419$000 (read thirty-eight thousand, one hundred thirty-four contos, four hundred nineteen milreis). Of this British subjects held 8.491:000$000 and subjects of all other foreign nations only 979:000$000 (Bivar, "Chronica do Anno de 1842," *Revista do Inst. Hist. e Geog. Bras.*, Vol. V [1843], pp. 385–386).

[3] Four loans were contracted between 1824 and 1843; namely, £3,686,200 (1824), £769,200 (1829), £411,200 (1839), and £732,000 (1843). See Liberato de Castro Carreira, *Historia Financeira e Orçamentaria do Imperio do Brazil*, p. 656.

revealed no loss by England of the preëminent position maintained prior to the expiration of the treaty.

During the period when the trade of the Portuguese empire was a monopoly of the mother country, these special privileges had played a useful part in opening colonial possessions to British trade, while their continuation in the early years of the independence of Brazil had guaranteed a low import tax during the critical transition period and at the same time had prevented the granting to other foreign powers of special favors adverse to British interests. Their usefulness, however, was past, for as long as all competitors were placed on a basis of equality and Brazil continued to be essentially an agricultural country, the economic superiority of England would guarantee its preëminent position in the markets of the South American nation. . . .

The year 1850 marked a turning point in Brazilian economic development. The centralization of power in the hands of D. Pedro II, who began his personal rule two years earlier, the restoration of order after the revolutions of the preceding twenty years, and the extension of the authority of the national government to the provinces introduced a period of economic expansion which in turn increased the purchasing power of the empire. The federal income, which had grown from twenty to forty thousand contos of reis between 1838 and 1850, leaped to one hundred thousand contos in 1858. Deficits ceased, Brazilian credit abroad became more firmly established,[4] and import taxes trebled between 1836 and 1856—an increase which was due in

[4] The loan of 1839 was contracted for 76 per cent, that of 1842 at 85 per cent, that of 1852 at 95 per cent, that of 1858 at 95½ per cent, and that of 1859 for 100 per cent. The interest rate was lowered from 5 per cent, which hitherto had been charged on all loans, to 4½ per cent for the 1853 and 1858 loans (Castro Carreira, *Historia Financeira*, p. 656).

part to the higher rates imposed when the commercial treaty with England expired, and in part to the fifty per cent rise in the value of goods brought in. In the same period exports more than doubled.

In the years immediately following 1850 commercial and industrial corporations began to be organized for the first time; the Bank of Brazil was founded with numerous state and private banks appearing immediately after the authorization of the national banks; the first telegraph line began operation in Rio with extensions to various points in the provinces, and the first railroad was inaugurated. Although the preëminence of north Brazil in the production of articles for export still continued, the south was rising to importance as the province of São Paulo began its striking development. Sugar, cotton, cacao, coffee, hides, and tobacco with two new articles, rubber and maté, were the chief exports of the country just as in the first quarter of the century; it was in the quantity of production of these articles that 1850 differed from 1827.

In social life as well as in economic development of the empire, the year 1850 marks a transition from the customs and manners of the first half of the century. The political independence gained in 1825 did not produce an immediate revolution in the social and economic life of Brazil, for the succeeding twenty years revealed slight differences in the conditions which had existed prior to the formation of the empire. But by 1850 with stability and order came prosperity and a striking economic development which in turn reacted on the social life and national consciousness of the Brazilians.

These changes made the empire a more desirable market than before, with the result that England encountered severer competition in this traditional field of interest. Partly as a reply to the threat of other nations and partly as the natural result of the increased purchasing power of the Brazilians, England increased its activity in the empire. In 1851 the first mail steamboat line to England was inaugurated by a special convention signed by the two governments. The Royal Mail Steam Packet Line was granted the contract, two thirds of the expenses to be paid by the British and one third by the Brazilian government. Special exemptions from port taxes and quarantine laws were specified and the postage rates agreed upon. The vessels which carried the mail averaged eight hundred tons burden.[5] The advantages accruing to England from the arrangement were visible immediately, for, in the opinion of the British legation at Rio, the inauguration of this steampacket line was a strong contributing factor in the sudden growth of British exports which occurred after 1850.

As an indication of the trend of international relations existing between Brazil and foreign powers the number of consuls maintained by other countries in the empire and by the Rio government abroad is suggestive. In 1853 England outranked all other nations with the exception of Portugal in the number of consuls serving in Brazil while the Rio government maintained its greatest number of representatives in Great Britain and its possessions. . . . Great Britain as the greatest supplier of the South American country received a large

[5] Brazil, *Relatorio dos Negocios Extrangeiros,* 1851, Notes 8–16, and 1852, p. x. The first concession granted to any steamship company was conceded to France by an agreement closed November 21, 1843. France was to maintain a steamship line for travelers and official correspondence with regular sailings. The vessels were to be French warships moved by steam. A monthly service from St. Nazaire by Lisbon, Cape Verde, Pernambuco, and Bahia to Rio was specified (Rocha Pombo, *Historia do Brazil,* IX, p. 451, note 3).

body of Brazilian consuls within its territory in order to furnish the necessary invoices, whereas Portugal and Spain, and later Italy and Germany, required a large representation in Brazil to care for the emigrants who settled there and to supply invoices for purchases. The United States as the greatest buyer of all foreign countries maintained an increasing number of consuls.

These figures are also indicative of the growth of British exports to Brazil. In 1835 the value of goods sent to the empire from Great Britain was a little over two and one-half million pounds sterling; by 1854-5, exports doubled in value; by 1863-4 they were forty-one per cent over the 1854-5 figure; by 1874-5 they were fifteen per cent above the value of the previous decade; by 1905 a decrease occurred when the average exports from England fell to the 1854-5 period, but by 1912, just prior to the World War, British sales to Brazil not only recovered from the depression of the early years of the twentieth century but reached the highest figure ever attained. Thus Great Britain, although it was the leading supplier of Brazil in the early period with a relative high value of exports, succeeded in increasing its sales six hundred per cent between 1835 and 1912.

To accompany this growth in exports, British enterprise in Brazil was intensified after 1850. Although the first railroad inaugurated in the empire was constructed by Brazilians with national capital,[6] English capital and

6 An English engineer, Thomas Cochrane, secured a contract with the Rio government in 1840 to construct a railroad from Rio to the province of São Paulo, but he was unable to initiate construction. In 1855 a national company operating under the supervision of the government began construction of the line which today links the cities of Rio de Janeiro and São Paulo. The first to operate was a short line from Rio to Petropolis, where the mountain palace of the emperor was located, constructed without guarantee by a famous Brazilian engineer, Irineu Evangelista de Souza, later Visconde de Mauá. The first section of the Rio—

agents were a large factor in the expansion of railroad building which occurred during the last half of the nineteenth century. In 1856 a company was incorporated in London with British capital to construct a line from Santos up the mountain to the city of São Paulo and down to Jundiahy, a town which lies at the point where the vast inner plateau joins the mountains.[7] The first railways in Pernambuco[8] and Bahia[9] were constructed by English companies. In the case of the Pernambuco line all the plant, materials, and labor were imported from England; costly and complete locomotive workshops were constructed with a staff from Great Britain; and the road was administered by British subjects. A telegraph line built along the right of way was opened to public use.[1]

São Paulo project was inaugurated in May, 1854 (Rocha Pombo, *Historia do Brazil*, IX, pp. 444–446). It soon became the most important railroad of Brazil and has continued to hold that position.

[7] This road was a remarkable engineering feat, as the abrupt rise from the port of Santos to the summit of the ridge necessitated the use of a cable section for the severest part of the incline. It still serves as the funnel through which the imports and exports of the state of São Paulo pass. Financially, it has been extremely successful. The line from Santos to Jundiahy was in operation by 1867 (Rocha Pombo, *Historia do Brazil*, IX, p. 447).

[8] Capital £1,200,000 with an increase of £485,000 later. The line extended from Recife to São Francisco. It was inaugurated 1875 (*ibid.*, p. 448, note 1).

[9] From Bahia to São Fancisco (*ibid.*, note 2).

[1] The Brazilian government guaranteed seven per cent on the capital invested. The line which was inaugurated in November, 1862, made a profit of less than £3,500 during 1862–3. The 77½ English miles of road and the workshops, stock, etc., cost £1,800,000 (Great Britain, *Commercial Reports, Consular,* 1863–4, pp. 49–51). As the line did not pay, the company obtained authorization to continue this first stretch of 77½ miles to São Francisco, 230 additional miles, in an effort to secure increased traffic. The government guaranteed £350,000 yearly for construction although it had already paid a sum equal to the original cost of the road as a result of the seven per cent guaranty (*ibid.*, 1877 [4–5], p. 1185).

In the province of São Paulo railroad expansion was rapid and profitable. By 1877, ten years after the line was open to traffic, the Santos–Jundiahy road not only dispensed with the government guaranty of seven per cent but returned a profit to the government in excess of the specified returns to the company. By connections with other lines a continuous road penetrated 170 miles into the interior with numerous offshoots to the most productive sections. In 1877 between seven and eight hundred miles of line were either in operation or under construction or survey. All lines seemed prosperous.

The greatest activity in railroad construction occurred in the provinces of Pernambuco, Bahia, Rio de Janeiro, Minas Geraes, and São Paulo, although lines were built in other sections. The extent to which Great Britain contributed to that phase of economic life is indicated by the estimate compiled by Acting Consul General Rhind in 1901. In railway enterprises throughout the republic there was invested, according to his figures, about thirty million pounds sterling of British capital.

It was not only in railroad construction and management that British enterprise was manifested in the years following 1850.[2] In 1863 an English company was installing gas works to light the city of Pará while a Manchester firm under the direction of British engineers was completing a similar plant in the city of Pernambuco. A reservoir and connections had just been completed in the latter place at a cost that was below the estimate and the enterprise was yielding fifteen per cent profit. . . . Several years later a drydock cut from solid

[2] The first mail steamship line inaugurated by England in 1851 was followed by the Liverpool, Brazil, and River Plate Steam Packet Company, the Pacific Steam Navigation Company, the London, Belgium, Brazil, and River Plate Steam Packet Company, the Lamport and Holt Company, and others (Great Britain, *Commercial Reports, Consular*, 1870, p. 242).

rock and large enough to accommodate the largest vessels afloat was constructed and operated in the Rio harbor by an English company.

In 1875, at the invitation of the Brazilian government, a group of British engineers, headed by Sir John Haupshaw, visited Pernambuco and other ports of the country with a view to suggesting plans for improvements, while English contractors were building a magnificent bridge to connect the mainland on which part of the city of Pernambuco was situated. That region was a special center of English interest: for more than half a century the greater part of the commerce of that port had been carried on by the English; large British import and export houses prospered there; two English telegraph companies, the Western Brazilian and the Brazilian Submarine, had stations there; two English banks maintained branches in the city; a long railroad constructed with British money joined the capital to the interior; regular steamship lines picked up a sizable volume of business at the port; the light, gas, and sewerage works were in the hands of an English company, and many millions of pounds sterling were invested there. The tramways were owned and operated by the British and a steam cotton press was under British control.

The drainage contract not only for the city of Rio but for outlying districts was secured by one Joseph Hancox, an engineer who had acquired a favorable reputation in the country by his public improvements work.[3] In Bahia two English companies, one of which had already constructed the "stupendous" bridge which con-

---

[3] Great Britain, *Commercial Reports, Consular,* 1878 [4–5], pp. 1415–1416. This enterprise was successful. By 1895 nearly two millions sterling, all English, had been invested in the sewerage project (Great Britain, *Commercial Reports, Consular and Diplomatic,* 1895, Report No. 1531).

nected the two sections of the city, secured concessions from the imperial government to construct eight sugar factories when Brazil endeavored to rejuvenate that historic business. By the law of 1875 the government had authorized a guaranty of six and seven per cent on capital, not to exceed three millions sterling, which was to be invested in sugar factories throughout the northern and central provinces. By 1884 fifty factories with a capital of £2,965,000 were set up under this plan while eleven more without guaranty were in operation. Most of the capital employed in these enterprises was British.

In the São Paulo region the British were equally prominent. In the words of one of the chief local authorities, the Brazilian might be jealous of the foreigner but he could "not do without the English." The São Paulo Railway from Santos to Jundiahy, the Cities Improvement Company of the capital supplying gas, water, and tramways, the Western and Brazilian Telegraph, the English banks, all were owned and administered by British subjects and all were prospering. By one estimate over six million pounds sterling of English capital were invested in São Paulo by 1888, while by another estimate over twelve millions were employed in the state in 1890. The strong financial and commercial position acquired by the English in São Paulo was due, in the opinion of the consul, to the fact that they were the first to develop its resources. The marvelous prosperity noticeable in 1890 from the seacoast to the interior had its inception "with the advent of the English merchant, engineer, and capitalist."

As might be surmised, British banks were numerous in Brazil. The London and Brazilian Bank with a capital of a million and a half sterling, all British, was established at Rio in February, 1863, with branches in Bahia, Pernambuco, Santos, and Rio Grande do Sul. During the first year it did business to the amount of more than two million sterling. At the same time the Brazilian and Portuguese Bank was incorporated, with headquarters in London, its million sterling capital being all English. By 1913 the assets of the British banks operating in Brazil constituted almost thirty per cent of the total assets of all banks, national and foreign, and over fifty-seven per cent of the assets of all foreign banks operating in Brazil.[4]

The opportunities which the growth of Brazil offered to British economic interests are seen in the report of Consul Cowper in 1884. After describing the prosperous trade which had begun to pass through Santos to and from the interior of São Paulo, the consul predicted that this embryonic trade was but the first flow of the sap from a few incisions which would become channels of incalculable commerce. To reach and utilize the regions of future wealth two things were required: first, a solid and abundant immigration and, second, the resources of foreign industries and civilization. The first would be supplied from Germany, Italy, and Spain; the second, which comprised the principal factors of development of a new country, would be derived from England. Many thousands of miles of railroads would have to be built and immense supplies of rails, rolling stock, and supplies furnished; new lands would be brought under cultivation and agricultural interests promoted; new industries requiring the most improved machinery would be started; and many thousands of pounds sterling would be required to carry out urban improvements and rural developments. This activity had its basis in

[4] Brazil, Ministry of Agriculture, Industry and Commerce, *What Brazil Buys and Sells,* pp. 98–99. The figures are: assets of British banks $304,620,000 (gold dollars); all foreign banks $532,548,000; total assets of all banks, $1,047,956,000.

gold, coal, and iron—factors of which Great Britain possessed a virtual monopoly. As long as England controlled these three factors, its supremacy in Brazil would remain unrivaled.

But the consul warned his government that already the United States had entered a thin wedge by furnishing some of the new railroads with rolling stock, while American farm machinery was beginning to attract notice. The British manufacturer should break that entering wedge by supplying the market with the most suitable materials of that nature before the Americans obtained too strong a leverage, for once lost, a trade was exceedingly difficult to regain.

The consul was right, for Britain's strength lay in its abundant capital and excellent manufacturing ability. As long as England commanded the necessary capital to be invested in this virgin field, maintained its leadership in the manufacturing of those articles which Brazil needed but did not make, and controlled the foreign shipping business of the South American nation, its preëminent position in Brazilian economic life would remain intact. But, as the consul intimated, that position was not to be maintained without a struggle, for since the founding of the empire other nations had attempted to rival England's favored place and, as the century wore on, that competition grew more keen.

6

H. S. Ferns

BRITAIN AND ARGENTINA: LAISSEZ-FAIRE IMPERIALISM?

An oft repeated defense of the actions of investing nations is that they are not engaged in imperialism when they have not annexed the region in which they are investing. In answer, H. S. Ferns, a British scholar at the University of Manchester, advanced the concept of "laissez-faire imperialism" and "informal empire" in an article in 1953. He contended that control of key enterprises and domination of foreign trade can securely attach the recipient nation to the investing nation's financial control and direction, thus making it into a sphere of influence. Britain's role in Argentina was cited as an example. Ferns, however, has reconsidered his thesis and, writing in 1960, he presented a series of arguments to show that the ties were made with the voluntary acquiescence of the Argentine government, were never pushed into the political sphere, and resulted in advantages as great for Argentina as for Britain.

. . . These prosperous years [1900–1914] witnessed a considerable relaxation of political tension within Ar-

From H. S. Ferns, *Britain and Argentina in the Nineteenth Century* (Oxford: The Clarendon Press, 1960), pp. 486–491. Reprinted by permission of The Clarendon Press, Oxford.

gentina. The armed forces as a factor in politics appeared to be fading out and the institutions and political habits of representative democracy to be gaining in strength. There was little direct political tension between Britain and Argentina, but indirectly Argentina eyed Britain with suspicion. The pressure of the financial interests to use force in the collection of debts and other claims, which Salisbury had resisted during the Baring Crisis, was successful in 1902 in the case of Venezuela, and Britain joined with Germany and Italy in blockading Venezuelan ports. Argentina reacted sharply to this unwise proceeding. The Drago Doctrine was given to the world by the Argentine Foreign Minister. For the first time since the brief romance of 1846 the United States and Argentina found themselves effectively on the same side politically. But even the Venezuelan *contretemps* was obliterated from the public conscience by the flood of prosperity.

The long-standing ambivalence of the Argentine community to foreign enterprise was not effaced by an age of abundance nor by favorable terms of trade. Professor Eteocle Lorini, in his study of the Argentine public debt, voiced a very common view: "All the industrial, commercial, agricultural, and mining companies which furnish our Argentine statistics bear the foreign mark *limited;* so that one ends by getting the impression that one is studying a purely English colony, for one finds *limited* upon all species of manufactures; *limited* after the statement of capitals; all undertakings are *limited;* insurance is *limited;* the circulation and distribution of Argentine wealth is *limited.*" Lorini acknowledged that capital investment increased employment, raised land values, and increased production, but he advised his countrymen to save and invest on their own account in order to create a "national capital" which would reduce dependence upon international finance. Thoughts of this kind take us back to the 1850's when the business men and politicians of Buenos Aires Province were projecting a development based on their own accumulation and forward to the 1950's when Perón was seeking to emancipate Argentina from foreign influences. Were they worth uttering then and are they worth examining now?

Speculation on the subject of British enterprise in Argentina carries us to the heart of Anglo-Argentine relationship, both as it has existed historically and as it exists at the present time. The term "imperialism" is widely used in Argentina and elsewhere in discussing the connection between the two countries. Argentina has never belonged to the British Empire, of course; but Argentina is, or was, part of Britain's informal empire. Argentina is within a British sphere of influence. Britain exercises great influence in Argentina. Britain exploits Argentina. So the argument runs, and the argument is widely believed, and attitudes affecting action derive from it.

There is a case for the large British investment in Argentina, and there is one against it. The evidence suggests, however, that neither case has been sufficiently related to the facts.

Can the term imperialism be applied to Anglo-Argentine relations? If we accept the proposition that imperialism embraces the fact of control through the use of political power, then the verdict for Britain is unquestionably "Not Guilty." The only complete attempt made by Britain to establish political power in the River Plate failed, and out of that failure developed a policy which specifically recognized that political power exercised in and over Argentina or any other country in South America was an ineffective means of achieving the

British objective of a beneficial commercial and financial relationship. The Anglo-Argentine political equation, which recognized Britain and Argentina as independent variables, was not derived from the liberal idealism of Canning, but from the material facts learned on the field of battle and discernible to anyone familiar with the character of the terrain and people of Argentina. During the nineteenth century there was no alteration in the Anglo-Argentine equation, and there is no reason for supposing it is any different today than it was a century and a half ago.

This political equation is the equation from which all equations in the sphere of economics have been derived. The Argentine Government has always possessed the power to forbid, to encourage, or to shape the economic relations of Argentina with other communities, including the British community. The British Government has never had the power to oblige Argentina to pay a debt, to pay a dividend, or to export or import any commodity whatever. The only occasion when the British Government went beyond talk in dealing with Argentina, during the troubled time of General Rosas, they were defeated and they formally admitted that they were defeated. When powerful financial interests urged the use of political power to influence Argentine economic policy in 1891, the British Foreign Secretary privately and publicly repudiated such a suggestion. Every crisis in the economic and financial relations of Britain and Argentina has been resolved in economic and financial terms—by a weighing of advantages and disadvantages by both parties—and not by the intrusion of political power. Of course, British commercial and financial interests have exercised great influence in Argentina; but so have Argentine interests exercised great influence in Britain. Any agricultural landlord or farmer in Britain between the years 1890 and 1939 could argue that Argentina was a factor in their fate, and a very adverse one. Derelict fields in Cambridgeshire existed in part because fields in the Argentine Republic were heavy with cheap cereals, and Argentine *estancieros* have wintered on the Riviera while herdsmen in Shropshire went bankrupt. These are facts which make nonsense of myths about British imperialism and Argentina as a semi-colony of a great and powerful state.

One may deplore the consequences for Argentina, and likewise the consequences for Britain, of the kind of relationship worked out by the Argentine landed and commercial interests in conjunction with the financial, industrial, and commercial interests of Great Britain, but when one starts deploring let no one blame an abstraction called Britain or another one called Argentina. If, over a long span of time, Argentina has possessed a weak and narrowly based industrial structure compared with that of the United States or even Canada, this has been due to the concentration of effort in Argentina upon agricultural and pastoral enterprise and upon the production of pastoral and agricultural commodities. Political power and/or decisive influence upon policy in Argentina has belonged until recent times to the interests with most to gain by such a concentration.

The dominant interests in Argentina sought out the foreign capitalists in the first instance; the foreign capitalists did not invade Argentina, and in the beginning and for many years after the investment process commenced European investors were reluctant to supply Argentina with as much purchasing power as the Argentine Government required. That the European investors invested anything depended partly upon the guarantees given by the Argentine authorities, partly upon the direct responsibility for payment undertaken by the state, and partly upon the existence in Argentina of a British business community capable of organizing in a practical way enterprises like railways and meat-freezing plants. Contrary to common belief the British investor received help and protection from the Argentine Government, not the British Government. When the British Government finally felt obliged to assist British investors in Argentina, it did so not by sending an expeditionary force to the River Plate, but by underwriting the Bank of England, which in turn underwrote the private and joint-stock banks, which in their turn underwrote the firm of Baring Brothers.

There is still much work to be done before any convincing answer can be given to the question: who benefited most from economic development in Argentina? The evidence in hand, however, suggests some tentative answers. Some foreign interests benefited greatly; for example, the shareholders of some of the banks; some railway shareholders and investors in meat-processing and cold-storage enterprises and some mercantile establishments. But the overall profits of British investors were sufficiently low to prompt the hypothesis that the great interests of Argentina did not dominate the fields occupied so largely by British enterprise because the returns were greater in the fields dominated by Argentinos. The appreciation of land values and the profits of pastoral enterprise, commercial agriculture, and sharecropping seem to have been the best sources of wealth in the years from 1860 to 1914. The political power, the social knowledge, the entrenched position of native Argentinos gave them a tremendous advantage in this field. The system of education, handicapped in its scope by niggardly state expenditure and in its content by the influence of the Roman Catholic Church, further ordained that native Argentinos were ill equipped to take control of enterprises requiring great technical knowledge and habits of exact application to managerial responsibilities. Thus foreigners, and particularly the British, dominated in the less rewarding and more demanding fields of endeavor.

There seems to be considerable evidence during the period we have studied that the permanent wage worker both urban and rural benefited least from the developments we have described. If this is so, why was immigration so abundant? Economic opportunities, not wage rates, seem to be the predominant inducement to immigrants. Argentine wages in the long run seem to have been rather better than wages in Italy and Spain, from whence the majority of immigrants came, but much inferior to wage rates in the United States, Canada, or Australia. But economic opportunities seem to have been roughly alike. Indeed, in Argentina the prizes open to people possessed of peasant shrewdness in buying and selling were, perhaps, greater than elsewhere. For a man with only a strong back and a willingness to work, Argentina was, perhaps, a slight improvement on his homeland, but not a place of rich rewards.

Among the beneficiaries of Argentine expansion before 1914 we must not neglect mention of the English wage working class. Some benefited from employment opportunities created by manufacturing for the Argentine market. A much wider mass benefited as consumers from the cheap food products flowing in increasing flood from the River Plate. If the Englishman of that age was the biggest meat eater in Europe it was partly due to the fact that Argentina was the cheapest producer of beef in the world.

The Anglo-Argentine connection, with the benefits and disadvantages which we have described as they existed in the years between the Boer War and World War I, was a phase in the life of growing communities and not a system which can be recreated. The passage of time and the changing social composition of the Argentine community revealed weaknesses and altered the objectives of economic activity. One of the leading staples of Argentine international trade—cereals—was marketed under conditions of nearly perfect competition. So long as the over-all factors in the world market kept up cereal prices in relation to the prices of manufactured goods, the Argentine economy functioned without crippling frustrations. When the over-all factors in the world market began to alter this relationship between cereal prices and the prices of manufactured goods, Argentina began to discover the limitations and defects of concentration on food production.

7

Rómulo Betancourt

VENEZUELA: POLITICS AND PETROLEUM

Venezuela's outstanding literary figure and statesman, Rómulo Betancourt, has spent years of his life
in exile from his native land. As a leader of *Acción
Democrática* (Democratic Action), he saw his country struggle to rise after the death of the dictator
Juan Vicente Gómez, only to fall again under a more
modern but still ruthless military autocrat, Leonardo
Pérez Jiménez. When an uprising overthrew that
regime, Betancourt returned to his homeland and
became its first freely elected president.

While exiled in Mexico, Betancourt wrote a study
of the role of petroleum in the politics and history of
his country. His story illustrates the seamier side of
foreign investment: the skulduggery and corruption,
the overpowering effect upon a nation of foreign
domination of a major segment of its economy.
Through Betancourt's eyes we see successful business
enterprise whose very success leads to a reaction of

From Rómulo Betancourt, *Venezuela: Política y petróleo* (Mexico: Fondo de Cultura Económica, 1956), pp. 25–32, 231, 233–
234, 725. Reprinted by permission of the publisher.

hate and fear. He claims that by pursuing their ends as good profit-seeking businessmen, adapting themselves to the "political realities" of the country, working hard to pay as little in taxes as possible while cutting costs and maximizing profits, foreign investors have led Venezuela to a point at which she finds herself in thrall to a few giant corporations. In his analysis her economy becomes distorted by an absolute reliance on petroleum—the nation is converted into a "petroleum factory"—and the country depends on petroleum for its revenues, its jobs and the overwhelming bulk of its export trade. Foreigners determine the output of petroleum and hence control, indirectly, the national economy and government finances. And all is based on a non-renewable resource which once gone can never be replaced. In the frenzy of new wealth, progress is unbalanced: modern technology operates in the oil fields and oxen help till the corn fields; super-turnpike highways radiate from the capital and dirt roads traverse the countryside; oil-field workers live well (and oil company executives—foreigners and upper-class Venezuelans—live in the style of southern California), while evil-smelling poverty-ridden slums crowd the hills around the capital and ramshackle huts dot the countryside; exports run to hundreds of millions of dollars (90 per cent petroleum) and produce the highest per capita G.N.P. in Latin America, while the nation remains one third illiterate and half barefoot. A maddening paradox: progress and poverty.

In later years, when Betancourt himself became President of Venezuela, he embarked on a policy of "sowing the oil"—using the government's royalties from oil exploitation to launch a program to improve the social and economic status of the Venezuelan peasant and lower class worker, and to build up the nation's heavy industry. In the latter category is the complex of petrochemical plants at Morón near the

Maracaibo oilfields and a steel center at Coroní on the Orinoco near the iron mines operated by the United States and Bethlehem steel companies.

The Dance of Concessions

It was not until 1909, after the failure of the Venezuelan company "Petrolia" and the stormy attempt at exploiting asphalt, that the Venezuelan Government granted a foreign company the first contract to exploit hydrocarbons.

In December, 1909, the Executive signed a contract with John Allen Tregelles, who represented The Venezuela Development Company Ltd., for the exploration and exploitation of an enormous area. . . .

This first Company, hunting for "light petroleum," was not successful. In the course of the four years following its establishment in Venezuela, it registered claims to various deposits in the States in which it operated. But it did not drill a well, and the *Ministerio de Fomento* voided the contract for non-compliance.

Meanwhile, in the course of the first decade of the 1900's, the Executive granted numerous concessions to individuals closely connected to the governing regime. These contracts, which still exist, were all drawn up in the year 1907. On the 28th of February of that year, Andrés Jorge Vigas contracted for the exploitation of the petroleum deposits in the Colón District of the State of Zulia. On the 28th of February, the Executive contracted with Antonio Aranguren—the same man who was in prison during the years 1950–53, for presumed complicity in the assassination of Delgado Chalbaud—

for the deposits of the Maracaibo and Bolívar Districts of the same State. The Zamora and Acosta Districts of the State of Falcón, and the Silva District of the State of Lara, were "conceded" to Francisco Jiménez Arráiz, on the 3rd of July. And on the 22nd of July following, the deposits of the Buchivacoa District of the State of Falcón were granted to Bernabé Planas.

These concessions, obtained by Venezuelan citizens, passed in later years into the hands of foreign enterprises. In the period between the making of those grants and their transference, a United States company located with an expert eye the lands that it desired. This was the Bermúdez Company, an affiliate founded by the General Asphalt Company in order to launch into the hunt for concessions.

The Bermúdez Company was not unaware of the air of hostility that surrounded it. Public opinion was against it because the Castro Administration had given great publicity to the criminal intrigues of its twin sister, the New York and Bermúdez Company. It therefore resorted to an expedient, so as to obtain concessions without troublesome frictions: it utilized Dr. Rafael Max Valladares as a front.

On July 14, 1910, Dr. Valladares signed a contract with the Executive, by which he acquired the right to explore and exploit the zones that the Tregelles contract had reserved for the State—that is, those of the Peninsula of Paria, the Benítez District of the State of Sucre and the Pedernales Municipality, and the islands adjacent to the Delta Amacuro Territory. The taxes to be paid were the same as had been agreed upon in the contract with Tregelles, but the term of the concession was increased to 47 years. Four days after signing that contract, the figurehead turned it over to the Bermúdez Company.

Two years later—on January 2, 1912—Valladares signed a second contract with the Federal Executive. The concessionaire now obtained the right to explore and exploit the subsoil of the States of Sucre, Monagas, Anzoátegui, Nueva Esparta, Trujillo, Mérida, Zulia, Lara, Falcón, Carabobo and Yaracuy. The area covered by that monstrous concession was about 27 million hectares (about 68 million acres). The conditions stipulated were: one bolívar per hectare as surface tax; a royalty, or *regalía,* of two bolívares per metric ton of crude mineral produced, and 50 per cent of the import tax which the refined products paid. Two days after signing that contract, Dr. Valladares ceded it to another affiliate of General Asphalt, this time camouflaged behind the label: The Caribbean Petroleum Company.

The Valladares concession, traveling on rails well greased by bribery and corruption, was granted with the rapidity of a *blitzkrieg:* ten days sufficed for the application to become a contract. Of no avail were the objections formulated by the Director of Mines, J. M. Espíndola, and a member of the so-called Federal Council of Government, Dr. Leopoldo Baptista. Dr. Baptista foresaw that the concession would be turned over to a foreign enterprise; as we have already seen, that was just what was done.

This concession was granted in violation of express legal dispositions. Under the norms of the Law of Mines of 1910, in effect at that moment, the maximum extent of lots that could be granted for exploration was 800 hectares, while the Valladares concession covered 27 million hectares, located in twelve States of the Republic. It conceded in one stroke lands of the nation and of individuals, empty lands and lands held by communal villages—all the explorable land in the twelve States. This was done by an executive act which surpassed what might have occurred to the wildest and most anti-Venezuelan imagination.

The grant of that concession, which constituted one of the most scandalous take-overs of the international petroleum industry, stirred up a mounting wave of protests—not so much on the part of Venezuelans (who at that time were still ignorant of the wealth that had been squandered and were already under the fist of what would come to be the most implacable dictatorship suffered until then by the country), but by the foreign competitors of the beneficiaries of that fabulous deal, who were themselves foreigners. . . .

This Venezuelan version of the United States "Teapot Dome" scandal, which covered the Harding administration with unpopularity, did not end here. The Valladares contract, by way of a liberal distribution of checks among venal functionaries, was renewed in 1922 before the end of its stipulated life; this new term was extended until 1943. . . .

The English Take the Lead

This extraordinary lode of concessions to which we have been referring—which by the end of a few years had brought forth torrents of petroleum and astronomical numbers of pounds sterling and dollars to the concession holders—fell originally into hands of citizens of the United States. It remained there only a short while. United States capitalism, taken as a whole, did not yet have a bright vision of the future of petroleum. Its surplus capital did not flow toward the markets and productive zones of raw materials of Latin America in the same proportions as it would after the United States emerged triumphant from the first World War. In Venezuela, as in other countries of Latin America, the agents of Royal–Dutch Shell hastened to seize positions before their American counterparts did so.

Sir Henry Deterding's men "smelled" the enormous wealth of the concessions illegally obtained by the Caribbean Petroleum Company. This company had already exploited, at a juicy profit, the first "commercial" well brought into Venezuela: the "Mene Grande" (1914). Its shares had risen 200 per cent in value. In view of that, Royal–Dutch hurried to make the vast and rich concession its own. It acquired the Caribbean Company, paying its original organizers $1,500,000 at the time of executing the operation and assuring them a participation, or royalty, of 8 per cent, payable in cash on the gross production of the active wells and of those which might be drilled in the future.

England prepared to enjoy the profits from the new fount of the coveted fuel which it had brought into the world. Warned by the experts, she hoped that she would be able to clear the road of possible legal difficulties. And thus it was that the *Procurador General* of the Nation introduced, on the 19th of June, 1912, a plea before the *Corte Federal y de Casación*. This pointed out the conflict existing between articles 8 and 10, 40 and 42 of the Code of Mines then in force, and the 2nd guarantee of article 20 of the National Constitution and articles 462 and 467 of the Civil Code. The High Court did not take long in issuing its opinion. It decided, 8 days after the introduction of the plea, to declare unconstitutional articles 40 and 42 of the Code of Mines, which accorded one third of the liquid product obtained from the exploitation of the subsoil to the owner of the surface. The happy beneficiaries of the mineral wealth of a country that was in a state of defenselessness were not bargaining, upon the issuance of that judgment, but working with a complacent partner: the dictatorial governing clique. They had been freed of any obligation to divide the product of the wells with the private owners of the land, the occupants of the national territory, or the lessors of the village communal holdings, since the articles, [that had been] suppressed with a stroke of the pen, had favored all those natural or juridical persons. And if it is true that in the long run the best interest of the nation has coincided with the decision of the High Court on June 27, 1912 (since in the end it is the nation as a whole that ought to be benefited by the petroleum, and not individuals or isolated corporations), it is no less true that the front-starters in the hunt for concessions exercised their subtle influence with one definite objective: to be in a position to deal with only one master, who was yielding and venal.

The road now clear, the caravan of the auctioneers of the Venezuelan subsoil sped voraciously along it. Royal–Dutch Shell organized in 1913 another affiliate with a declared capital of £1 million. This new subsidiary of the Anglo–Dutch interests was baptized with the name of Venezuela Oil Concessions, Ltd. Its first large-scale operation in Venezuela was the acquisition, from Bolívar Concessions Ltd., of the right to explore and exploit the oil concessions of the Bolívar and Maracaibo Districts in the State of Zulia. The contract acquired by this company was drawn up in the most liberal terms by the concessionaire: term of duration of 50 years beginning in 1907 and the option of renewal of that term for another half century. The taxes were scarcely one bolívar per hectare, for the surface tax, and a royalty, or "participation," of two bolívares per metric ton of oil produced. The concession covered more than 3,000 square miles of land, so productive that for decades the Venezuela Oil Concessions, Ltd. was the largest single producer.

In the same year 1913, Royal–Dutch organized in London another affiliate: the Colon Development Company. This company acquired from Andrés Jorge Vigas an extensive concession, which covered about 840,000 hectares. That concession is located to the southeast of Lake Maracaibo in zones lying between Venezuela and Colombia, and covering entirely the Colón District of the State of Zulia. Colon Development Ltd. controlled, from the beginning of its activities in Venezuela, 75 per cent of the so-called Vigas Concession. The other 25 per cent was held by the Carib Syndicate, a company organized by the famous banker John Pierpont Morgan in 1915 in the State of New York. When the Colon Oil Corporation (another creature of the Royal–Dutch Shell) acquired the stock of the Colon Development Company, the Carib Syndicate received 550,000 shares of the new company.

While powerful foreign interests were securing for themselves a solid predominance over the principal fount of Venezuelan wealth, there were occurring in the political life of the nation events that would determine its course for many years. . . .

[Juan Vicente] Gómez and his courtiers put into execution a rapid and expeditious plan on all fronts. Taking advantage of an imbroglio at the time—the so-called "French Protocol"—they dissolved the Federal Council of Government and its members were obliged to take the road to exile. . . .

The end of the conspiracy against the country forged by Gómez and his courtiers was the meeting in Caracas, in those same days of 1914 in which were fired the first cannon shots of the first World War, of a so-called Congress of Plenipotentiaries. It was a very peculiar Constituent Assembly, with all its members chosen by a tropical version of the Grand Elector of Saxony: Gómez. As a result, this group elected him Chief of the

Army, and Dr. Victorino Márquez Bustillos, a man of his clan, Provisional President; immediately afterward, the Constitution underwent a matching reform. Two years later, another Congress—also designated "of the finger" by Gómez, who used to carry out those *elections* by running [his finger] down the list of his unquestioned friends without taking the trouble to solicit anybody's presence at the ballot boxes—gave the color of legality to the usurpation of power. Gómez was then elected Constitutional President for the period 1915–22. . . .

This period of incubation of one of the most primitive despotisms that any Hispanic American people have ever suffered did not halt the "Saraband of the Concessions." The British, who were then operating without a competitor in sight, had learned in the Middle East that the sheiks of Arabia and the shahs of Persia were most docile to the foreigner who enriched them and helped them, at the very same time when they were being most implacable toward the "natives" who fought against them.

Proof of this is the fact that, following the private enterprises of the City, there was launched on the Venezuelan subsoil an overindulged daughter of the government of His Britannic Majesty, nourished with pounds sterling of state origin: the British Controlled Oilfield.

The British Admiralty saw, with complacent eyes, how the trust of Sir Henry had set its feet solidly in Venezuelan territory. But it did not miss the usefulness of also taking, directly, its part of that country, when it was being sold at such a low price. The strategic importance of Venezuela, because of its nearness to the Panama Canal, could not pass unnoticed by the chiefs of the British Navy. That is why they started the British Controlled Oilfield—a company directly controlled by the Crown—to conquer for them too a portion of the petroliferous Venezuelan subsoil, in accordance with the concealed objective of bringing economic strategy together with military strategy. "The concessions of the British Controlled Oilfield are always on the coast, or very close to the sea, which is a considerable advantage," wrote Pierre l'Espagnol de la Tramery, in his book *World Struggle for Oil* (1923).

In 1918 there was organized and registered in the Dominion of Canada the "Venezuelan" affiliate of the British Controlled Oilfield, Ltd., with a declared capital of 27.5 million dollars.

The British, hardly established in Venezuela, covered the entire country with a vast network of their affiliates. Thus, just as Hollywood has its "Man of 100 Faces," that Company hid its name behind numerous veils, which they called Antonio Díaz Oilfield, Ltd., Aragua Exploration Company, Ltd., Bolívar Exploration Company, Ltd., Lara Exploration Company, Ltd., Pedernales Oilfield Ltd., Tucupita Oilfield, Ltd., Central Area Exploration Company, Ltd. (20 per cent of the stock) and American British Company, in which a royalty was reserved.

Concerning the impact of the arrival in Venezuela of that company set up by the British government, Ludwell Denny writes:

> In the period from 1918 to 1920, the British Controlled Oilfield, under the direction of the British Government, monopolized in Venezuela as much territory as it could. It included a great area, which it kept unexplored, to the east of the Delta of the Orinoco. Of more importance was its acquisition of the Buchivacoa Concession, which covered 15,000 square miles. Being essentially a political company, without experience as a producer, the British Controlled Oilfield has spent much

money without succeeding in extracting any profit from its extensive zones. It has sought, for that, the sure method of permitting Standard [Oil] to test and develop the eastern part of its concession on a base of 12½%, with cautious terms and other conditions. The western sector of Buchivacoa was exploited slowly and inefficiently by the British Controlled Oilfield.

The concessions of the British, years after having initiated their activities (1932), covered 3,000 square miles in the State of Falcón, in the region of the northwest coast of the country, and some 15,000 square miles in the Delta of the Orinoco, in a zone which for some decades the directors of the Empire have wanted to take hold of. This is the site where the Orinoco—one of the greatest fluvial arteries of America—empties into the ocean. It is the center of the immense Amazon basin and is located close to British Guiana and the British Antillian island of Trinidad. Its strategic importance— in terms of commercial and military strategy—does not have to be underlined.

In the six years between 1912 and 1918, British imperialism solidly sunk its drill bits and reserved to itself strategically utilizable zones the length and breadth of Venezuela.

. . .

The Modern Myth of El Dorado

The Gómez dictatorship and the pseudo-democratic governments of the decade following 1935 took the responsibility of diffusing an Eden-like version of our country for export purposes. "Venezuela *smells of gold,*" said a certain Baron of Royal–Dutch Shell, the Baron Rothschild. And in an Hispano-America with its public finances compromised and its economic activity developing at a slow pace, our country appeared to be an impressive exception. We were not weighted down with external debts; the internal debt was at a minimum; the fiscal budgets closed annually with a cumulative surplus, and it was presumed the length and breadth of America that the Venezuelan people were enjoying a delighted and happy life.

Nothing was further from the truth than that idyllic picture. Venezuela was one of those Latin American nations that balanced technical backwardness with overwhelming oppression for its wretched, uneducated and abandoned population.

. . .

The Social Drama of Venezuela in Numbers

The national census of 1941 X-rayed the social drama of Venezuela in numbers that caught its essence.

Of 2 million inhabitants over 15 years of age, 1,300,-000, 75 per cent of the adult population, were illiterate. Of a school population which totaled 780,000 children, only 264,000, or 35 per cent, went to school. Of 678,000 dwellings, over 60 per cent—more than 400,000—were houses of straw and sticks with a dirt floor. Only 2.8 per cent of the inhabitants were supplied with running water; 36.8 per cent used water taken from wells, and 29.8 per cent river water. The economically active population was scarcely 1,200,000 people, a figure equal to 32.2 per cent of the total population, and in a way appreciably less than that in other Latin American countries (Colombia, 51.6 per cent in 1938; Peru, 39.9 per cent in 1940, and Brazil, 34 per cent in 1940).

. . .

The Factory and Its Governing Elements

Venezuela, as has been repeated with monotonous insistence in this work, has suffered a dangerous distortion of its economy as a consequence of the growth of petroleum. The nation and the State have been depending for their survival more and more upon one single source of income: taxes, salaries and other contributions from petroleum to the Venezuelan economy.

The country has tied its destiny to an aleatory element—that is, what has brought such extraordinary natural wealth is not recoverable. And when one adds the fact that it is foreign capital that manipulates this mineral production, this is an unsteady base on which to raise the structure of the national economy and finances —a base as ostentatious as it is vulnerable.

Conscious of that dramatic reality, we patriotically bound ourselves to modify it. [The Democratic Action Party] started government action toward a rectification of the trends which the country was following. We proposed to halt its fall toward the condition of semi-colonial mining, of a "petroleum factory." The two correctives that began to be applied were those of increasing to reasonable limits the participation of the country in its subsoil wealth, and the reinvestment of a considerable part of the profits of petroleum in the development of a properly diversified economy, thus protecting and educating the Venezuelan people.

That [proposed] policy of defensive and creative nationalism brought about, even before it could be initiated in November, 1948, [the reaction of] a military dictatorship. The taxes imposed upon the concessionaires of the subsoil again became those typical of colonial possessions. And in an orgy of disarticulated and costly public works, and of private deals by the businessmen of the despotism, the major part of the public money was squandered. . . .

A certain self-serving propaganda, which is spread by the consortiums of petroleum and the present colonialist Government, tries to hide these realities. Venezuela appears—by means of that literature and the celluloid documentaries exhibited on the screens of all the movie houses of the continent—as a country in full development of an exceptional and privileged economic bonanza. Or as Senator Margaret Chase Smith, Republican representative, defined it in the Capitol of the United States on the 27th of April, 1954: ". . . a nation which has excellent reserves of gold and which seems to be making heaps of money with its petroleum."

The truth is quite otherwise. Venezuela is not receiving that which in justice belongs to it for its subsoil wealth. It is true that the high Budgets of the State are more than two-thirds covered by the income from petroleum, but this is at the price of an accelerated depletion of the mineral reserves so as to compensate for the other low taxes, which are less today than those received by countries with the tribal structure of the Middle East. The national income—without petroleum —diminishes year by year, to such an extent that we are approaching the moment at which the value of the mineral extracted will be greater than that income. Foreign trade is dominated, in a vassal-like form, by petroleum, and the real income *per capita* is progressively diminishing. Workers in the industry are not protected by strong unions of free choice: just as in the time of Juan Vicente Gómez, in the fields of "black gold" the will of the companies has returned to rule as the only law.

Venezuela, in spite of all the fanfares of the great columns of militarists and the spectacular annual celebrations of The Week of the Fatherland, is moving toward a situation similar to that which existed before 1810. It is going down an inclined slope toward the condition of a factory, a petroleum factory. The national sovereignty is a juridical concept, an abstraction of public law, which needs, for its full effect, to be placed on foundations of economic self-determination. These foundations are now cracked and unstable, precarious, so long as the country's economic destiny is left wholly in the hands of a dozen North American and British directors of great petroleum consortiums, which periodically deliberate in an office in Rockefeller Center, in New York City, or in another located in the business district of London.

8

Robert F. Smith

THE UNITED STATES AND CUBA

Our Cuban Colony was the title of a 1928 study by Professor Leland Jenks, which surveyed American relations with that unhappy island. Of all nations in which the United States has had large investments, none has been as thoroughly dominated, politically and economically, as Cuba. Made a legal protectorate in 1903, it remained under close official American direction until 1934, when that status was formally terminated as part of the Good Neighbor Policy, and unofficial guidance became the order of the day. As Dr. Smith, Professor of History at the University of Rhode Island, has demonstrated, the close ties between investments, trade and stability (i.e., a government acceptable to the United States) have dictated a continued policy of pressures just short of intervention—until the spring of 1961 and the Bay of Pigs. If foreign private capital ever had the chance, through its economic and political influence, to demonstrate

From *The United States and Cuba: Business and Diplomacy, 1917–1960*, by Robert F. Smith (New York: Bookman Associates, 1960), pp. 17–19, 22–24, 29, 32–33, 41, 175–178, 180–181, 183–184. Reprinted by permission of the publisher, Bookman Associates, Inc.

its ability to improve the lot of a people while still earning profits, American private capital did in Cuba. Castro is a chicken come home to roost.

The United States' declaration of war on Spain in April 1898 marked the beginning of a new period in Cuban-American relations. Some Americans had been concerned over the turbulence in Cuba which resulted from the revolutionary outburst in 1895, since this threatened to damage investments and disrupt trade. Although this concern may not have been the primary reason for the decision to fight Spain, the Spanish-American War nonetheless marked the beginning of active American intervention in the affairs of Cuba. As President William McKinley expressed it in his war message: "We have . . . become . . . the guarantors of a stable and orderly government protecting life and property in that island."

With the end of the war in 1899 the United States was faced with the problem of the status of Cuba. The Teller Amendment to the declaration of war had disclaimed any intent to annex the island, but the United States had no intention of handing Cuba over to the insurgents. A military government was set up in Cuba, and governed the island until the Cubans formed a native government in 1903. Before the occupation ended, however, a thorough protectorate was established by the Platt Amendment. This amendment to the Military Appropriations bill for 1901–02 was passed with little debate, then added to the Cuban Constitution, and finally embodied in a permanent treaty between the two countries in 1903. Thus, the United States became the "legal" guardian of the new republic.

With the end of the war the United States was also in a good position to work out the problems of Cuban-

American trade relations. As one author wrote in 1899: "To the United States, among the chief advantages of the liberation of Cuba will be a commercial one." These advantages were spelled out in terms of rich fields for investment and greatly expanded markets. American business interests began to discuss a reciprocity agreement as the best means of attaining both of these goals.

As early as June 1899, General James H. Wilson reported to Washington that establishment of proper trade relations between Cuba and the United States was of greater importance than the establishment of proper political institutions. This emphasis was repeated in General Leonard Wood's first annual report in 1900 in which he stressed the need for reciprocity in order to increase American exports. The issue was first brought up in Congress in February 1900 when a joint resolution was introduced in the House to admit sugar and molasses duty-free from Cuba and Puerto Rico. The Ways and Means Committee submitted an adverse report and the resolution was tabled.

. . .

The heated Congressional battle over Cuban reciprocity was prolonged for several months as the domestic sugar interests used various stratagems to defeat it. The reciprocity bill died in committee when Congress adjourned on July 1, 1902, but Roosevelt then proceeded to negotiate a treaty with Cuba, which he submitted to the Senate in December 1902. The treaty was approved several months later and became effective in December 1903. As a result, Cuban sugar received a 20 per cent preferential reduction in the American tariff, and various American products received from 20 to 40 per cent reductions in the Cuban tariff.

American trade with Cuba and the value of American investments in Cuba greatly increased after 1899. The

United States became Cuba's best sugar market as Cuban production increased—especially after 1903—and the Cuban share of the American market increased from 17.6 per cent in 1900 to 50.4 per cent in 1913. The value of American exports to Cuba increased from approximately $27,000,000 in 1897 to $200,188,222 in 1914. By 1914 Cuba was in sixth place among the customers of the United States. In 1896 American investments in Cuba were estimated at $50,000,000—chiefly concentrated in mining and sugar properties. This had increased to $265,000,000 by 1915, but European capital was still predominant in 1914. During World War I, however, the situation was reversed as American capital investments displaced European.

Enterprising adventurers swarmed to the island and formed the spearhead of American economic penetration. Some of these men set up their own companies, some became agents for American companies, and others went into the sugar business. This group formed an economic interest which was greatly in favor of "gunboat" diplomacy and its efforts helped to set the tone for American-Cuban relations for several years.

. . .

Between 1898 and 1919 a pattern of Cuban-American relations developed which involved a rather close connection between investments, trade, and Cuban stability. An official of the State Department's Latin American Division—Boaz Long—noted this development in a memorandum to Secretary of State Robert Lansing in February 1918. In a summary statement of the period since 1898, Long enthusiastically reported:

> The total trade of Cuba with the United States just prior to the end of the Spanish rule over that island (1897) amounted to about twenty-seven million dollars per annum. During the decade following the termina-

tion of our war with Spain the island of Cuba, guided
by American influence, increased her trade with us by
leaps and bounds and brought it to the startling total in
1917 of something over four hundred and thirty million
dollars. This unprecedented development of Cuba may
serve as an illustration of what probably would take
place in the Central American countries provided this
Government extended to them aid of a practical character as it did to Cuba.

The "aid" that Long discussed in more detail consisted
of the maintenance of stability, investments, loans, and
trade.

The protection of investments, the expansion of trade,
and the stability of Cuba were mutually dependent
parts of the pattern of relationships, and all in turn were
linked to the influence of the United States Government. Intervention by various means in the affairs of
Cuba, and the reciprocity treaty—which increasingly
tied the Cuban sugar economy to the United States—
were basic elements in this relationship. The nature of
this pattern of Cuban-American relations was clearly
illustrated by several events in 1917 and 1918.

Early in 1917 disturbances broke out in Cuba. The
United States issued instructions that it would not tol-
erate armed revolt, and small detachments of marines
were repeatedly landed from February to August in
response to numerous requests from American business
interests. Destruction of property increased during
April, however, and by May there was talk of sending a
large body of American soldiers. President Mario Menocal disapproved of such a step, but by the latter part of
May the State Department had definitely decided to go
ahead with this plan and had requested the War Department to begin preparations. In order to salve Cuban
feelings, and possibly the feelings of Americans who
might disagree with a policy of occupying a friendly

country, an artful plan was worked out. It was arranged for President Menocal to "offer" to the United States "sites for training camps . . . if it should be considered desirable to send troops to train in mild winter climate." This would make it possible to "impress eastern Cuba with [the] fact of [the] presence of United States troops" through the guise of "extensive practice marches." The American people were informed that the "friendly offer" had been accepted, and that it was proof of Cuba's desire to assist in the war with Germany. An Associated Press article had hinted at the real reason for intervention and this disturbed the State Department. For, as Minister William Gonzáles put it, "such publications . . . are embarrassing to diplomatic work."

Camp sites were rented in Oriente Province, and on August 16, 1917 it was decided to send a regiment of marines rather than a cavalry regiment. The marines arrived in force later that month, and the State Department received periodic "training" reports from the marine commander. Some historians have contended that this intervention was due to fear of German attempts to create trouble. There was one report of possible German activity, but it was received almost two months after the decision to send troops had been made. Frank Polk, the acting Secretary of State in July 1917, stated that troops were being sent "to aid in the protection of sugar properties and mining properties and in restoring complete order in the Oriente Province." The Military Attaché, in a report written in 1921, said that at the time he was not advised of the reason for intervention but that it was generally understood that it was to protect American property. In addition the marines acted as strikebreakers and strike preventers for the Cuba Railroad.

During the summer of 1917 Cuba began negotiations with the United States for a fifteen million dollar loan.

Secretary of State Robert Lansing informed Secretary of the Treasury William Gibbs McAdoo that Cuba's application for a loan offered a good opportunity to bring pressure on that government for a favorable settlement of the claims of the Ports Company of Cuba and the Cuba Railroad. Lansing noted that the loan should not be made until these issues were settled. The Ports Company claim stemmed from the revocation of the "Dragado Concession" in 1913. The company had obtained a concession to dredge the ports of Cuba in 1911, and had planned to make over 200 per cent profit on the operation. The Trust Company of Cuba—headed by Norman H. Davis—was deeply involved with the Ports Company. The Cuba Railroad claimed that the Cuban Government owed it $250,000,000 for damages suffered during the 1917 revolt. The Cuban Government stated that it was willing to loan money to the company, but that it did not owe damages.

Pressure was put on the Cuban Government to settle these claims. In October 1917 the Cuban Congress finally agreed to settle with the Ports Company, but the railroad claim was debated until the spring of 1918. The Cuban Government then agreed to pay the damage claims of the railroad out of the proceeds of the loan. On April 3, 1918 the Cuban President signed a decree which, in effect, returned to the Ports Company all of its assets while the Cuban Government assumed its debts. The first five million dollar advance to the Cuban Government was approved on March 27, 1918, and the two subsequent advances of like amounts were approved later that year.

. . .

The economy of Cuba was primarily dominated by sugar with tobacco, the second ranking Cuban export, playing a less important role. The story of Cuban economic development during these years was characterized by increased American penetration and control. As a result, the Cuban economy reflected some of the trends developing in the United States. The Cuban economy, however, was affected by the change in status of the United States and the legislative reaction to it. Here was the dilemma of American business interests during the period from 1919 through 1933. As American business became dominant in Cuba the value of Cuba's exports to the American market began to decrease, and the prosperity of Cuba depended on this market.

American investments in Cuba increased 536 per cent between 1913 and 1928. In 1913 the American stake was estimated at $220,000,000, which was 17.7 per cent of all American investments in Latin America. By 1929 this had grown to an estimated $1,525,900,000, or 27.31 per cent of the total Latin American investment. American-owned sugar mills produced approximately 15 per cent of the Cuban crop in 1906 and 48.4 per cent in 1920. By 1928 various estimates placed American control of the sugar crop between 70 and 75 per cent.

. . .

This was the economic setting of the period 1919 to 1930. Economic statistics revealed a growing American stake in Central and South America, the Caribbean area, and Cuba. Statistics in themselves do not reveal the entire picture, however. They must be interpreted and understood, at least in part, by men before actions and policies can be formulated. The views of businessmen and government officials which were presented, reveal several concepts: (1) that the American economy was characterized by a surplus production which could best be sold abroad; (2) that foreign investments and loans were vital to continued prosperity; (3) that Latin

American markets and investments, both actual and potential, were vital to the economy of the United States.

. . .

In spite of the generally improved condition of the national economy [after World War II], many of the basic problems of Cuba remained unsolved. Urban labor retained many of the reforms enacted in 1933, and the Constitution of 1940 embodied these—and subsequent—measures. Between 1952 and 1959, however, the Cuban Government modified some of these to meet business objections. The problem of illiteracy continued to plague Cuba, especially in the rural areas. No gain in literacy was made between 1931 and 1943. The 1953 census revealed a higher illiteracy rate among the 10- to 14-year age group than among the population as a whole. This indicates a possible increase in illiteracy.

The entire Cuban economy remained under the domination of "king sugar" and the United States market. In 1951 sugar accounted for 88.1 per cent of all Cuban exports. This declined to 79.8 per cent in 1955. In 1959 and 1960 Cuba exported about one half of its sugar to the United States. About 40 per cent of the profits from sugar exports went to American-owned companies, and this further complicated the economic problems of Cuba.

The most glaring problem of all was, and is, the extreme poverty of the masses. This has been especially true in the rural areas where the pattern of landholding has changed little since the early days of the Spanish Empire. In 1945, 7.9 per cent of the "farms" occupied 71.1 per cent of the land, while on the other end of the scale 69.6 per cent of the farms occupied only 11.2 per cent of the total farm land. There are more than 200,000 families with no land at all. These agricultural laborers rarely work more than three months out of a year. "The land is very rich, but the people are very poor," is an accurate summary of the situation in Cuba.

Thus, Cubans have lived in a country where most of the resources are controlled by a small minority, and part of this latter group are citizens of the United States. The power of the United States is an ever present element in Cuba. The naval base at Guantánamo Bay, and the frequent visits of naval vessels to Cuban ports give concrete evidence of this power. These factors have produced anti–United States feelings in Cuba, and many Cubans feel that their island is an "economic satellite" of the United States.

All of these factors worked together to produce the victory of the "26th of July" Revolutionary movement.

. . .

The policy of the United States, before and after the revolution, played into the hands of Cuban extremists. Support for Batista and the role of American capital in the Cuban economy—with its political implications— provided an initial residue of suspicion. The failure of the United States Government to give at least a measure of positive support to the Castro Government, at a time when moderate elements were still in control, gave the extremists another argument to cite as proof of American hostility to the revolution. The unfavorable reaction of the United States Government to the agrarian and business reforms—as in the demand for immediate cash compensation for property taken—provided additional fuel for the fires of anti–United States sentiment. Thus, the extremists in the movement skillfully utilized the actions—and lack of actions—of the United States to undermine the moderates and convince Fidel Castro of the need to draw closer to the Communist bloc in order to save the revolution.

． ． ．

In the long-range perspective of United States policy the emphasis has been placed on order, stability, and the protection of American interests. This has meant that the United States has generally opposed sweeping economic reforms, and Cuban nationalism—except that of the Machado and Batista variety. From the 1890's to the present the United States has supported the conservative upper classes and their American allies. The history of Cuban-American relations testifies to the consistency of this policy.

． ． ．

9

John F. Gallagher

THE SEARS, ROEBUCK AND COMPANY VENTURE IN LATIN AMERICA

While not as attractive a picture as the profits from auto financing, the work of Sears, Roebuck and Company in Latin America is a tribute to Yankee ingenuity and persistence in making money, and to the reciprocal advantages which may accrue from intelligent business leadership. Mr. John F. Gallagher, Vice President, Foreign Administration, Sears, Roebuck and Company, submitted the following account of his firm's operations to the Subcommittee on Inter-American Economic Relationships of the Joint Economic Committee of the United States Congress, when it was holding hearings on "Economic Development in Latin America."

Much has been said about private investment in South America. Some of what has been said has recognized

From 87th Congress, 2nd Session, *Hearings before the Subcommittee on Inter-American Economic Relationships of the Joint Economic Committee of the Congress of the United States,* May 10–11, 1962 (Washington, D.C.: Government Printing Office, 1962), pp. 78–82.

the value of and the need for more private investment—both national and foreign. More of what has been said has been critical of foreign investment—that it is a form of imperialism, and national investment—that it has not created a satisfactory society. In addition, misunderstandings and uncertainties have resulted from the fact that little has been said in Government circles about private investment and its role in the Alliance for Progress. In fact, it appears to some of us who have devoted much of our business lives to furthering our company's efforts and responsibilities overseas, that the role of private enterprise is conspicuously absent from any Government planning or discussions.

In your report, you made a statement about the role of private enterprise that I would like to give emphasis to by quoting:

> A major effort of U.S. policy toward Latin America should be to point up the merits of and assist these countries to develop a reliance on private enterprise and the processes of private investment decision-making. Every time we encourage reliance on centralized planning, we risk playing into Soviet hands, by showing a distrust of our own characteristic national method and encouraging the technique of our ideological competitors.

We, at Sears, agree with you and believe that the best argument in favor of this position is to review for you the story of Sears' operations in Latin America.

Sears' venture in Latin America began in 1942 with a store in Havana, Cuba. It continued postwar with expansion into Mexico in 1947. South America's first store opened in Brazil in 1949 followed by openings in Venezuela in 1950, Colombia in 1953, and Peru in 1955. The Sears' investment in capital stock in its subsidiaries in South America amounts to just over $22 million. In addition to the capital investment, the parent company had on loan to these units, at end of last fiscal year, a sum of $6,900,000. Over these years dividends in the amount of $12,062,000 have been paid the shareowners. The dollar value of reinvested profits at the end of fiscal year 1961 amounts to $9,352,000. The dollar value of the reinvested profits does not truly indicate the per cent of profits reinvested because it has been subject to the devaluation of the local currencies—94 per cent in Brazil since 1947, 72 per cent in Colombia since 1953, 29 per cent in Peru since 1955, and 26 per cent in Venezuela since 1950.

More important though than pure statistics like these is the human, technical, and economic interdependence which has developed between Sears and the consumer goods industries of South America. Originally our concept was to export goods as well as techniques, adjusting both to the relatively minor degree that might be necessary in order to conform to valid local requirements. This concept proved to be short lived, as immediately after World War II the major nations of Latin America, with populations that provided a relatively broad market potential, began to embark on vigorous programs of industrial development and national self-sufficiencies. Accordingly, we immediately began to develop local sources of supply. We did this on the basis of our time-tested stateside buying arrangements. Within Sears was the proven pattern of close working relationships with thousands of small manufacturers in the United States.

The relationship between Sears and its sources of supply, both in the United States and in Latin America, can best be described as a "partnership." One outcome of such a relationship is the considerable amount of technical assistance provided by Sears. Another is the financial assistance and equitable participation which Sears has provided, when necessary, for product development, product improvement, and for expanded production.

One such example is a story of a young, energetic, intelligent Venezuelan furniture manufacturer who was producing goods in a small shop with inadequate machinery and fewer than 20 employees. Sears went into partnership with him; technicians from the United States helped him lay out the factory for production; our accountants helped him set up an accounting system; our buyers gave him purchase contracts which permitted him to plan his buying of raw materials and schedule his production. Today, this factory employs 80 people making high-quality, excellently styled merchandise, to be sold by Sears stores and others, at attractive prices.

True, Sears in South America still imports merchandise, components for merchandise, parts, fixtures, and equipment. However, in 1961, the amount of goods purchased locally by each South American subsidiary was as follows:

	Per cent
Brazil	98.81
Colombia	98.82
Peru	70.96
Venezuela	51.22

These percentages, which accounted in 1961 for purchases totaling $25 million at cost prices, have been increasing annually.

Sears' purchases in South America are distributed among 4,600 suppliers, the majority of them very small in size. However, large or small, as a result of Sears' quality requirements, buyers and technical assistance, these manufacturers have raised their quality standards and have forced their competitors to do likewise. In addition, Sears' firm merchandise contracts have enabled the supplier to plan his production, and in many instances lower his costs. The beneficiary is the consumer, just as he has been in the United States for so many years through the application of these techniques which are inherent in the free enterprise system.

Throughout our South American development, Sears' stateside techniques of merchandise procurement have served us and our customers well. The same is true of selling.

We have installed all of the selling methods typical of our U.S. stores—fixed prices, outside selling, cash handling by sales personnel, and extension of consumer credit.

Every day that passes provides additional proof that we can and should apply the same criteria to our Latin American operations that we apply to our stores in the United States; high turnover at a reasonable markup; adequate sales per square foot of floor area; selling cost of sales personnel; commission rates; total payroll; advertising expenditures; return on advertising. These techniques, together with those involving sales promotion, are being passed on to our South American executives and, in turn, are being copied by our competitors. The result, the establishment of a new and respected profession, that of the retail salesman and retail executive.

No single aspect of Sears expansion into South America has been more satisfying—even dramatic— than the development of personnel to staff all aspects of our operation.

Initially, a nucleus of U.S. employees was sent to each South American country in which we started operations. It was their job to organize, supervise, and train people hired locally. While most Latin American countries permit corporations like Sears to employ stateside personnel up to a total of 10 to 25 per cent of the work force, Sears has progressively reduced the U.S. personnel assigned to South America, until today, only 45 of our 5,120 South American employees have been assigned by Sears from the United States. Each succeeding year shows a marked reduction in North American personnel—their positions being filled by properly trained nationals.

It is difficult to illustrate the diversification and responsibility of the executive and semiexecutive positions held by our South American employees without a detailed description of each Sears unit. However, 19 of the stores and all of the sales offices are managed and staffed totally by South American nationals. South Americans handle 90 per cent of Sears' total south-of-the-border buying, 95 per cent of the retail credit, 98 per cent of the retail merchandising, 98 per cent of the retail accounting.

Many of these men and women have visited comparable Sears operations in the United States of America for training. There is a constant interchange of ideas and information between parent company specialists and their South American counterparts. In each month and year, more of our South American employees advance in accordance with the long-established Sears policy of promotion from within. It is also Sears policy, both in the United States and in South America, that the pay of Sears employees in any unit of the company be equal to—or better than—the pay for comparable work in the community.

A wide range of employee benefits are, generally speaking, stipulated in Latin American countries by law which provide costly indirect benefits, considerably in excess of any found in the United States of America. Nonetheless, and in addition, two of our corporations have their own profit-sharing funds; a third will be added before the end of 1962, with the possibility of even a fourth being established this year if it is not in conflict with local legislation. Employee members of the funds (no U.S. personnel are permitted to join) contribute 5 per cent of their salaries up to a maximum amount. The company then makes a contribution annually of 5 per cent of its net profit before Federal income taxes. The major portion of the funds, thus made available, are used to purchase stock in the local company. At the present time, the Mexican employees of Sears de México own 20 per cent of the company—the Venezuelan employees own 13 per cent of Sears de Venezuela.

These principles and policies have established Sears as a good place to work and have enabled us to attract and maintain staffs of capable and loyal employees. In turn, they have been our best ambassadors of good will in the communities in which we are doing business.

Believing, as we do, that Sears must account for its stewardship, not only on the balance sheet but in matters of social responsibility, we have followed in Latin America our traditional policy of having Sears executives assume positions of responsibility in local civic and business organizations.

In addition to regular financial assistance to many charitable and social welfare organizations, we have a number of special activities, among them:

> Scholarship programs in national and regional universities—scholarships which are designed to assist both deserving students and the universities of their choice.
>
> Contributions to the growth and development of 4–H-type activities.

The complete support of a 50-pupil elementary school in one of the poorer sections of Caracas.

The establishment of manual training classrooms.

Aiding in equipping a vacation camp for under-privileged children.

Sponsoring, organizing, and financially supporting boys' baseball leagues and other youth programs.

Very active role in the organization and financial support of North American societies, whose purpose is the promotion of better understanding between the Americas.

I have used Sears as my framework of reference not because I think we are unique (although I am proud of our contribution to Latin America and the principles for which my company stands), but because I can speak from a broader knowledge of my own company than I can for American business generally. However, I know the thinking of other business leaders and can assure you that it differs in no way from ours at Sears—that the best kind of foreign aid this country can provide to countries in Latin America is the stimulus of American business in introducing modern, efficient, business methods which create jobs and raise standards of living.

It has been an honor for me to present this statement to you. I hope that it clearly indicates to you, as it does to me, the contribution which private investment can and does make to the societies of South America, not only in the area of providers of finance and technical knowhow, but also in the areas of total economic, personal, cultural, and community development, and will serve to emphasize that Government action, both in the United States and South America, should be directed toward stimulating rather than restricting the activities of private investors.

10

Henry Major Tomlinson

BUILDING A RAILROAD
IN THE AMAZON BASIN

H. M. Tomlinson dreamed of going to sea, but at the age of 39 he was still a Fleet Street clerk. One day in 1909, literally on the spur of the moment, he threw up his job and shipped as purser of the *Capella*, which was to take 5,000 tons of Welsh coal up the Amazon and Madeira Rivers to a point more than 2,000 miles from the sea. The coal was for the Madeira-Mamoré Railway, which was being built to link Bolivia to the Amazon River system and provide an outlet to the world for its rubber. The railway, crossing a terrifying jungle, is said by popular legend to have a corpse buried under each tie.[1] But the road was completed—in time for the spectacular collapse of the Amazon rubber boom. In *The Sea and the Jungle,* a minor gemlike classic,

Reprinted by permission of Gerald Duckworth & Co., Ltd., London from Henry M. Tomlinson, *The Sea and the Jungle* (New York: New American Library, 1961), pp. 121–125, 167, 174–181.

[1] According to his biographer, Percival Farquhar was led "to observe tartly that the [Madeira-Mamoré Railway] buried only 3,600 men to lay 615,000 crossties." (Charles A. Gauld, *The Last Titan: Percival Farquhar* [Stanford, California: Institute of Hispanic American and Luso-Brazilian Studies, Stanford University, 1964], p. 145.)

Tomlinson gives us, through the experience of an anonymous Englishman in charge of a supply depot, a picture of the driving force of capital in a hellish clime and the quiet, mad heroics of the men on the Job.

─────────

And now it seems time to explain why we are bound for the center of the American continent, where the unexplored jungle still persists, and disease or death, so the legends tell us, come to all white men who stay there for but a few months. If you will get your map of the Brazils, begin from Pará, and cruise along the Amazon to the Madeira River—you turn south just before Manáos—when you have reached San Antonio on the tributary you have traversed the ultimate wilderness of a continent, and stand on the threshold of Bolivia, almost under the shadow of the Andes. . . . As a reasonable being you would prefer to believe the map; and that clearly shows the only way there (when the chance comes for you to take it) must be by canoe, a long and arduous journey to a seclusion remote, and so the more deeply desired. It certainly hurts our faith in a favorite chart to find that its well-defined seaboard is no barrier to modern traffic, but that, journeying over those pink and yellow inland areas, which should have no traffic with great ships, a large cargo steamer, full of Welsh coal, can come to an anchorage, still with many fathoms under her, at a point where the cartographer, for lack of place-names and other humane symbols, has set the word Forest, with the letters spread widely to the full extent of his ignorance, and so promised us sanctuary in plenty. I suppose that in a few years those remote wilds, somehow cleared of Indians, jungle, and malaria—though I do not see how all this can be done—will have no further interest for us, because it will possess many of the common disadvantages of civilization's benefits: it will be a point on a regular route of commerce. . . . I had the fortune to go when the route was still much as it was in the first chapter of Genesis. "But after all," you question me, hopeful yet, "nothing can be done with five thousand tons of Welsh cargo in a jungle."

People with the nose for dollars can do wonders. It would be unwise to back such a doughty opponent as the pristine jungle with its malaria against people who smell money there. . . .

. . .

"Curious, this desperate haste, isn't it?" said the Englishman. "At every point of the compass from here there's at least a thousand miles of wilderness. Excepting at this place it wouldn't matter to anybody whether a thing were done tonight, or next week, or not at all. But look at those fellows—you'd think this was a London wharf, and a tide had to be caught. Here they are on piece-work and overtime, where there's nothing but trees, alligators, tigers, and savages. An unknown Somebody in Wall Street or Park Lane has an idea, and this is what it does. The potent impulse! It moves men who don't know the language of New York and London down to this desolation. It begins to ferment the place. The fructifying thought! Have you seen the graveyard here? We've got a fine cemetery, and it grows well. Still, this railway will get done. Yes, people who don't know what it's for, they'll make a little of it, and die, and more who don't know what it's for, and won't use it when it's made, they'll finish it. This line will get its freights of precious rubber moving down to replenish the motor tires of civilization, and the chap who had the bright idea, but never saw this place, and couldn't live here a week, or shovel dirt, or lay a track, and wouldn't know raw rubber if he saw it, he'll score again. Progress, progress! The wilderness blossoms as the rose. It's wonderful, isn't it?"

I was just a little annoyed. After all, I was part of the job. I'd made my sacrifices too. But I admitted what he said. Why not? It was something, that fancy that every rattle of the winch outside, bringing up another load, moved abruptly under the impulse of another thought from London Town—six thousand miles away; two months' travel. Great London Town! It was true. If London shut off its good will that winch would stop, and the locomotives would come to a stand to rot under the trees, and the lianas would lock their wheels; and in a month the forest would have foundered the track under a green flood. Where the American accent was dominant, the jaguars would moan at night. That long wound in the forest would be annealed and invisible in a year. While it persisted, the idea could conquer and maintain.

. . .

"In two hundred miles we reached a clearing [the Englishman continued]. Why it should have been at that particular place did not show. But there it was, the tangible link in an invisible, encompassing scheme. It was my place. I landed with my box. There was a white man on the river-bank, sitting on a sea-chest, his head in his hands. He looked up. 'You the victim?' he said. 'Well, there you are'—sweeping a lazy arm round the small enclosed ground—'that's your job. There's your store. There's your house. That's where the niggers live.'

" 'Pedro!' he called. A copper-colored native, in shorts

and a wide grass hat, loafed over to us. 'This is your servant,' he said. 'He's a bit mad, but he's not a fool. He's all right. Keep your eye on the niggers though. They are fools, and they're not mad. You'll find the inventory and the accounts in the desk in your hut. The quinine's there too. Take these keys. Oh, the mosquito curtain's got holes in it. See you mend it. I couldn't. Had the shakes too bad. Cheer up!'

"He went aboard. The steamer saluted me with its whistle, turned a corner, and the sound of its paddles diminished, died. I seemed to concentrate, as though I had never known myself till that instant when the sound of the steamer failed, when the last connection with busy outer life was gone. I could smell something like stephanotis. In that dead silence my hearing was so acute that I caught a faint rustling, which I thought might be the sound of things growing. I turned and went to my hut, sad Pedro following with my box. . . . I sat surveying things from a chair. Then leisurely took my envelope and read my instructions—how I was to receive and take charge of shovels, lanterns, machinery parts, railway metals, soap, cooking utensils, axes, pumps, and so on, which consignments I must divide and parcel according to directions to come, marking each consignment for its own destination. The names of a hundred destinations I should hear about in my future work were given. They were names meaning nothing to me. Then followed some brief rules for a novice in the governing of men. Through all the rules ran an incongruous note for such a place as that, a reminiscence of Leadenhall Street and its miserable whine. Yet it hardly disturbed me. . . . I was authority and providence, moulding and protecting as I thought right. This place should be kept reasonable, four-square, my plot of earth to be clean and unashamed, frankly open to the eye of the sky. I would see what I could do; and I would start now. I laughed at authority—all I could see of it—reflected in a fragment of mirror kept to a doortree by nailheads; the funny hat and the shirt which did not matter, bad as it was, for I was authority there by very reason of that white shirt; and the beard which was coming. Latitude, my boy, latitude! I strolled out to survey my little world.

"Of the weeks that followed, nothing comes back so strongly as some quite irrelevant incidents. A tiger I saw one morning, swimming the river. Pedro, insensible for two days with fever; and death, which came to overrule my viceroy authority. The first blow! There was a flock of parrots which visited us one day, and it surprised me that the men should regard them merely as food. But there was work to be done, and in a definite way; but why we did it—and I know we did it well—and how it joined up with the Job, I could not see. That was not my affair. There was the inventory to be checked, for one thing, and before I was through with it the work had fairly imprisoned me, and the new romantic circumstances became blurred and overwritten. That inventory was so extravagantly wrong that in a week I was going about heated and swearing at the least provocation. It was fraudulent. There was a sporadic disorder of goods irreconcilable with their neat records, though each record bore the signs and countersigns of Heaven knows how many departments of the Company. All an inextricable welter of calm errors, neatly initialled by unknown fools.

"Every few days a steamer of the Company would call, loaded with more goods, or would come down river to me to take goods away. The confusion grew and interpenetrated, till I felt that nothing but dumping all that was there into the river, and beginning again with a virgin station, would ever clear the muddle. The place grew maddening through ridiculous blundering from outside. I had six men to attend to, all with temperatures and all useless. The arrears of accounts, my work on sweltering nights while the very niggers slept, the arrears grew. A steam-shovel came, without its shovel, and not all my written protests to headquarters could complete that irrational creature lying in sections rotting in sun and rain, minus the very reason for its existence, an impediment to us and an irritation. Constant urgent orders came to me from up country to ship there this abortion. I declined, in the name of sanity. There followed peremptory demands for a complete steam-shovel, violent with animosity for me, the unknown idiot who obstinately refused to let a steam-shovel go, just as though I was in love with the damned thing, and could not part with it. But I understood those letters. They were from chaps irritated, like myself, by all this awful tomfoolery. And from headquarters came other letters, shot with a curt note of innocent insolence, asking whether I was asleep there, or dead, and adding, once, that if I could not keep up communications better I had better make way for one who could. There were plenty who could do it. Pleasant, wasn't it? They complained querulously of my accounts, almost insinuating that I debited more wages to the Company than I credited to the men. I had too many sick men, they said. Did I pamper them? And again, I had too many who died; I must take care; they did not want the local government to get alarmed.

"The time came when I got amusement out of those letters from headquarters; for their faults were so plain that I conceived the headquarters staff having much time to spend, and a sort of instruction at large to administer ginger to men, like myself, on the spot, on general principles, so to keep us not only alive, but brisk and anxious; and doing it with the inconsequential abandon of little children playing with sharp knives. I got comfort from that view; and when I looked round my placid domain where my men, with whom I was on good terms, labored easily and rightly under the still woods, I told myself I was still fretting because the business was new, that things would come easier soon. But at night I felt I was anxious exactly because it was all so old and familiar to me. . . .

"Next morning I woke late, feeling I had gone wrong. My hands were yellow and my finger-nails blue, and I was shaking with cold. But the tootling of an up-coming steamer forced me to business. The steamer was towing six lighters, filled with laborers. They were Poles, I think. Afterwards, I learned, some hundreds of these men had been collected for us somewhere by a clever, business-like recruiting agent, who promised each poor wretch a profitable time in the Garden of Eden. My responsibility, thirty of them, was landed. They stood by the river, gaping about them, wondering, some alarmed, more of them angry, most clad in stuffy woolens, poor souls. Having the fever, I was not very interested. I told my Negro foreman to find them shelter and to put them to work. We were making our clearing larger, and were building more storehouses.

"Something like the pale morning light which wakens you, weary from a fitful sleep, to the clear apprehension again of an urgent trouble which has filled the night with dreams, I came through each bout of fever to know there was really trouble outside with the new men. Daily I had to crawl about, shivering, my head dizzy with quinine, till the fever came near its height, when I got into my hammock, and would lie there, waiting, burning and dry, tremulous with an anxiety I could not shape. Sometimes then I saw my big Negro foreman come to the door, look at me, as though wishing to say something, but leave, reluctantly, when I motioned him away.

"One morning I was better, but hardly able to walk, when shouts and a running fight, which I could see through the door, showed me the Poles had mutinied. There was a hustling gang of them outside my door, filling it with haggard, furious faces. I could not understand them, but one presently began to shout in French. They refused to work. The food was bad. They wanted meat. They wanted their contracts fulfilled. They wanted bread, clothes, money, passages out of the country. They had been fooled and swindled. They were dying. I argued plaintively with that man, but it made him shout and gesticulate. At that the voices of all rose in a passionate tumult, knives and axes flourishing in the sunlight. In a sudden cold ferocity, not knowing what I was doing, I picked up my empty gun—I had no ammunition—and moved down on them. They held for a moment, then broke ground, and walked away quickly, looking back with fear and malice. Next day they had gone. Yes, actually. The poor devils. They had gone, with the exception of a few with the fever. They had taken to that darkness around us, to find a way to the coast. Talk of the babes in the wood! The men had no food, no guide, and had they known the right direction they could not have followed it. If the Company did not take you out of that land, you stayed there; and if the Company did not feed you there, you died. No creature could leave that clearing, and survive, unless I willed it. The forest and the river kept my men together as effectively as though they were marooned without a boat on a deep-sea island. Those men were never heard of again. Nobody was to blame. Whom could you blame? The Company did not desire their death. Simply, not knowing what they were doing, those poor fellows walked into the invisibly moving machinery of the Job, not knowing it was there, and were mutilated.

"We had news of the same trouble with the Poles up river. Some of the mutineers tried to get to the sea on rafts. Such amazing courage was but desperation and a complete ignorance of the place they were in. One such raft did pass our place. Some of them were prone on it, others squatting; one man got on his feet as the raft swung by our clearing, and emptied his revolver into us. A few days later another raft floated by, close in, with six men lying upon it. They were headless. Somewhere, the savages had caught them asleep.

"No. I was not affected as much as you might think. I began to look upon it all with insensitive serenity. I was getting like the men I met on the island, months before. I saw us all caught by something huge and hungry, a viewless, impartial appetite which swallowed us all without examination, which was slowly eating me. I began to feel I should never leave that place, and did not care. Why should others want to leave it, then? Often, through weakness, the trees around us seemed to me to sway, to be veiled in a thin mist. The heat did not weigh on my skin, but on my dry bones. I was parched body and mind, and when the men came with their grievances I felt I could shoot any of them, for very weariness, to escape argument. The insolence from headquarters I filed for reference no longer, but lit my pipe with it. But the correspondence ceased at length, and because now I was callous to it, I failed to notice it had stopped.

"Some vessels passed down river, coming suddenly to view, a rush of paddles, and were gone, tootling their whistles. The work went on, mechanically. The clearing grew. The sheds spread one by one. The inventory was kept, the accounts were dealt with. There came a time when I was forced to remember that the steamer had not called for ten days. We were running short of food. I had a number of sick, but no quinine. The men, those quick faithful fellows with the doglike, patient eyes, they looked to me, and I was going to fail them. I made pills of flour to look like quinine, for the fever patients, trying to cure them by faith. I wrote a report to headquarters, which I knew would get me my discharge; I was not polite. There was no meat. We tried dough fried in lard. When I think of the dumb patience of those black fellows in their endurance for an idea of which they knew nothing, I am amazed at the docility and kindness inherent in common men. They will give their lives for nothing, if you don't tell them to do it, but only let them trust you to take them to the sacrifice they know nothing about.

"That went on for a month. We were in rags. We were starved. We were scarecrows. No steamer had been by the place, from either direction, for a month. Then a vessel came. I did not know the chap in charge. He seemed surprised to see us there. He opened his eyes at our gaunt crew of survivors, shocked. Then he spoke.

" 'Don't you know?' he asked.

"Even that ridiculous question had no effect on me. I merely eyed him. I was reduced to an impotent, dumb query. I suppose I was like Jack the foreman, a gaping, silent, pathetic interrogation. At last I spoke, and my voice sounded miles away. 'Well, what do you want here?'

" 'I've come for that steam-shovel. I've bought it.'

"The man was mad. My sick men wanted physic. We all wanted food. But this stranger had come to us just to take away our useless steam-shovel. 'I thought you knew,' he said, 'The Company's bought out. Some syndicate's bought 'em out. A month ago. Thought the Company would be too successful. Spoil some other place. There's no Company now. They're selling off. What about that steam shovel?' "

III

ATTITUDES

In human societies truth and necessity are more often determined by the ideas in men's heads—usually preconceived ideas—than by subjective analysis. Men's notions of themselves as altruistic profit seekers or merely victimized expropriators of foreign-owned property fixes their view of the world and its human relations. What one swears is meat another condemns as most surely poisonous. While one regards his actions as part of his God-given role as his brother's keeper and helper, the other regards himself as the virtual or incipient prisoner of a rapacious and self-righteous intruder. In the complexities of world society and world history there are enough incidents and viewpoints to prove anything.

The following selection of readings is designed to contrast the views of American with Latin American analysts and with several impartial observers. The American Secretary of State, Dean Rusk, sets the stage for Americans by informing them that they have a duty to invest abroad because their activities are vital to strengthening Latin American economies and hence are saving them from the Communist menace. But a curious counterpoint is supplied by a United States Senate discussion of an agrarian reform law in Honduras, which is seen as threatening the interests of the United Fruit Company and therefore putting that nation in the position of losing United States government aid—so vital to its economic betterment. As for the American businessman himself, H. W. Balgooyen, Vice-President of American & Foreign Power Company, sketches his contributions to the Latin American economy in detail and looks with a jaundiced eye on various schemes to curtail or even supplement the activities of business-men. A rather important note is struck by an analysis made by the Corporation for Economic and Industrial Research, which brings out the fact that private invest-ment in seeking profitable ventures neglects many areas needing development. These gaps, the Corporation con-cludes, necessitate United States government invest-ment. A more critical view is that of the Marxist-oriented economist, González Casanova who finds that the purported necessity of United States business to invest abroad can lead Latin America into becoming either subservient to American economic direction or, since the American *must* invest, the investments can be directed into channels deemed appropriate by the host country. Still, he believes that the more domestic and the less foreign investment, the better. Alfonso Bauer Paíz also denounces the activities of foreign investors in his native Guatemala where concessions and political skulduggery went hand in hand, finally culminating in a United States–inspired invasion to oust a leftist-nationalist government. The actual laws enacted to control foreign investment are the subject of the next two documents, and they indicate that the viewpoints of sundry Latin American governments are far from being in agreement concerning the role of foreign capital and its relations with domestic capital. Finally, two economists, Baer and Simonsen, attempt to elucidate and explain the misunderstandings on both sides which make for problems in maintaining good relations between hosts and investors.

11

Dean Rusk

TRADE, INVESTMENT, AND UNITED STATES FOREIGN POLICY

While American businessmen feel themselves pushed by economic commandments to expand operations abroad, the United States State Department sees the necessity of encouraging them as part of its cold war offensive against Communism. Dean Rusk, the Secretary of State, in the following excerpt apprises American businessmen of the anticommunist base of our foreign policy and the role of business leadership abroad in combatting Communism by helping underdeveloped nations develop strong, viable economies. Insisting that the "socialist-minded leaders" of these nations are beginning to appreciate the value of American private enterprise, he urges businessmen to get into these lucrative markets, with assurances that their government will do all in its power to back them

From Dean Rusk, "Trade, Investment, and United States Foreign Policy," *Department of State Bulletin* (November 5, 1962), pp. 683–688. Originally presented as an address to the National Business Advisory Council, Hot Springs, Virginia, October 19, 1962.

up with investment guarantee programs and embassy representation. An outside observer cannot help but sympathize with the Latin American who strongly suspects a new "dollar diplomacy": the United States government using a red scare to foist United States investments upon Latin America and thus extend United States power by reducing the economies of the Latin American countries to colonial status.

what a commie

I welcome this opportunity to talk with this distinguished group of American business leaders. I shall talk about the contribution of American business to furthering the key foreign policy objectives of the United States. I should like to see the business community focus its unique skills and resources on this great task.

I am not suggesting that businesses should make uneconomic investments or sacrifice the interests of stockholders, employees, or old customers. Quite the contrary. It is precisely those skills of management and organization, the imagination and the flexibility which a firm must have to operate at a profit, that make the contribution of business so essential to our foreign policy.

What is the basic goal of our foreign policy? In President Kennedy's words, it is: ". . . a peaceful world community of free and independent states, free to choose their own future and their own system so long as it does not threaten the freedom of others."

This is the kind of world community envisioned by the Charter of the United Nations and, we believe, desired by the great majority of mankind. . . .

In carrying out our foreign policy American business has two fundamental roles. First, business is the key factor in maintaining a dynamic domestic economy.

Secondly, business must expand its present important role in the world economy. The dynamism that has been central in the development of the United States must now be employed on a global scale.

. . .

The Role of Foreign Investment

I turn to the role of American investment abroad. Its relationship to our foreign policy is complex. It cannot be judged merely in terms of dollars. In the long run the flows of managerial skills and attitudes, and the ties developed between American businessmen and their counterparts in other lands, may prove far more important than the flow of capital alone.

Especially in less developed areas foreign private enterprise can be of critical importance. It can demonstrate how man, by his own ingenuity, can improve his lot. It can prove the necessity for managerial as well as technical skills. It can reveal to often socialist-minded leaders that modern private enterprise can spearhead economic growth. It can refute Communist claims that foreign business feeds off, rather than builds up, the local economy.

Most of American private investment abroad is in the advanced nations. Of a total of $34.7 billion in direct investments, as of last year, $11.8 billion was in Canada and $7.7 billion in Europe—of which $3.5 billion was in the United Kingdom and $3 billion within the European Common Market. During the past decade American businessmen have seen the great investment potential in Europe. In the short run the outflow of capital has placed a strain on our balance of payments. In the longer term, however, the return flow of earnings, foreign subsidiaries' procurement from the United States, and more generally the global scope, vitality, and profitability of American firms all strengthen both the international position of the dollar and our domestic economy.

As against $19.5 billion in direct private investment in Canada and Europe, we have only $2.5 billion in Asia and $1.1 billion in Africa. And these latter investments, like the $8.2 billion we have in Latin America, are largely in the production of oil and ores.

I should like to see American business expand substantially its role in modernizing the economies of the less developed countries. Admittedly, in many instances, the returns may be slower and less certain. In some countries the risks, both political and economic, may be prohibitive. Yet American firms who participate in development in its early stages have the prospect of securing ground-floor positions in great markets of the future.

In considering risks I shall address myself particularly to the political risks. If we can find ways to minimize political risks, I am confident that American business ingenuity will overcome the economic obstacles.

The most immediate political risk for foreign investment is, of course, expropriation. This can take either the direct form of a quick government takeover or a variety of indirect or partial forms by which the host government discriminates against foreign business or makes it impossible to operate at a fair profit.

Any sovereign nation has the right to expropriate property, whether owned by foreigners or nationals. In the United States we refer to this as the power of eminent domain. However, the owner should receive adequate and prompt compensation for his property. Moreover, a legal right is not the same thing as a wise policy. Economic growth requires the expansion of capital resources. If an underdeveloped nation is to achieve self-sustaining growth in a reasonable period of time, it must, as a rule, obtain external capital. The amount of outside public funds available for investment is limited. And over the long run these public funds will tend to go to those countries which are pursuing policies that hold the prospect of achieving self-sustaining growth. We consider it extremely unwise for developing nations to alienate foreign investors, thereby stunting economic growth.

The United States Government is prepared to intercede on behalf of American firms and make strong representations to host governments in cases of economically unjustified expropriation or harassment. Various forms of investment guaranties are also available as insurance against certain political risks. I am happy to announce that we are making substantial headway in as difficult an area as Latin America in putting our investment guaranty program into effect. We have recently reached an interim agreement with the Colombian Government under which we are to extend our investment guaranty program to cover inconvertibility; expropriation; and war, revolution, and insurrection risks. And we have high hopes of getting similar bilateral guaranty agreements signed in the near future in Argentina and several other Latin American and African countries. We currently have one, two, or all three guaranties effective in 46 less developed countries. I hope you will make use of these insurance devices and suggest ways in which they can be tailored more closely to your requirements.

Despite the importance we attach to dissuading governments from expropriating foreign investments, merely to forestall expropriation is not enough. . . . We cannot assume that operating procedures, community relations, and governmental relations will be identical in advanced and developing nations. A primary responsibility for avoidance of political risk, therefore, rests with the firm.

I am confident that American firms can, through their own efforts, avoid a large part of the political risk inherent in operations in developing nations. They can, if they retain maximum flexibility of operations, if they focus skills and imagination on satisfying both their own imperative requirements and the imperative requirements and sensitivities of the developing country. As many of you know from experience, it is often helpful to provide for substantial participation by local partners and to employ and train as many local citizens as possible. In some cases it may be possible to work out management contracts or other arrangements which keep the essential American skills and attitudes in the plant while leaving our flag off the roof.

No matter what ingenious formulas we work out, however, difficulties do and will continue to arise between American business and foreign governments. We are seeking to make our embassy staffs from the ambassador down alertly aware of their responsibility to handle such matters expeditiously and to make necessary representations to the host governments concerned.

Also, we have just established in the Department of State a Special Assistant for International Business to handle the not infrequent cases when American business firms find they are discriminated against in one form or another in their investment or trade relations with a given country. It is the duty of this Special Assistant for International Business to see that U.S. business does get prompt representation in such matters. It is hoped that the business community will take advantage of this facility, which should not be viewed as competitive with existing facilities for the business community but rather as a focal point for them within the Department of State.

In assessing the risks and opportunities of investment in less developed areas we should try to keep a proper perspective. We must remain fully aware of the deep nationalistic, anticolonialist, often socialistic sentiment in most developing nations. Private enterprise, and particularly foreign enterprise, is often highly suspect. And yet as these new nations and their leaders realize the factors necessary for development, as they see the private sector in many instances pacing their nations' growth, their hostility is softening. In part this results from the performance of the private sector. It also results from the poor performance of the Communists. The Communist bloc economy is, of course, pallid in comparison to the West. The abysmal failure of Chinese development is evident for all the world to see. Soviet incompetence in both the aid and trade fields has led to disillusion and the search for closer ties with the West on the part of several African and Asian nations which earlier seemed to have been taken in by the grandiose Soviet economic line.

Unhappily a few countries which previously were receptive to private foreign investment are now alienating it by expropriation and harassment. However, in many developing nations the climate for private enterprise is improving.

There are strong incentives for American firms to stake their claim now in these great potential markets. As nations develop, business opportunities are being created. Future profits will go to the firms which are enterprising and foresighted today. An American firm whose managerial skill, political sophistication, and contribution to development win the confidence of a developing nation should be in an enviable position. The risks are there; the long-term opportunities are there. The developing nations represent a classic challenge to American private enterprise.

12

"WE HAVE THE SOVEREIGN RIGHT TO PROTECT OUR INVESTORS ABROAD": A CASE AND A COMMENTARY

The United States State Department has had to struggle manfully, tactfully, and with sympathy to balance foreign and domestic pressures. The Latin American nations' desire to treat foreign capital as they wish, while receiving United States aid, conflicts with domestic pressures to push and protect American capital seeking outlets abroad. Reflecting a popular feeling of frustration at the Latin Americans' "ingratitude," the United States Senate finally balked at State Department policy by passing the Hickenlooper Amendment, Section 620(e), to the Foreign Assistance Act of 1962. This amendment provided that unless a nation which has expropriated or nationalized American capital takes definite steps toward settlement within six months, the President of the United States is to suspend assistance to that government. The Senate believed that too many governments were regarding United States aid as a right rather than a privilege; a right which would

From 87th Congress, 2nd Session, *Congressional Record* (Washington, D.C.: Government Printing Office, October 2, 1962), pp. 20,455–20,462. (This selection was suggested by N. Gordon Levin, Jr.'s article, "Our Men in Honduras," *Dissent,* Vol. X, No. 4 [Autumn, 1963], pp. 375–380.) Mr. Vernon's letter of November 21, 1963 is reprinted by permission of the author and the publisher. © 1963 by the New York Times Company.

have to be honored no matter how they treated United States businessmen. The Senate wanted to make clear that, while it did not question a nation's right to nationalize or expropriate property, it expected that the owners would be given a fair deal—"the one compensation that means anything, and that is hard, cold American dollars," in the words of Senator Wayne Morse. If American businessmen were not given "payment in an established currency which can be traded and utilized on the world markets," in the words of Senator Allott, such governments had no right to expect American taxpayers to devote part of their tax moneys to aid them. To the Latin American governments, depending upon United States aid for development while struggling with desperate internal political and economic problems, the Hickenlooper Amendment smacked of intervention: either treat American businessmen as we say you ought, or we will cripple your domestic economic growth. Arthur Krock, doyen of *The New York Times* columnists, in discussing American aid in general, noted the existence of "the belief that this Government can persuasively maintain the pretense of exerting no pressure in the internal affairs of other nations of the hemisphere in the presence of the plain fact that millions of United States dollars spent of the Alliance [for Progress] will otherwise be fruitlessly squandered." (November 21, 1963.) Commenting on the Hickenlooper Amendment specifically, N. Gordon Levin wrote: "This conflict between the needs for structural change in Latin America and the needs of American business as a system of power may be irreconcilable. . . . Since corporation ideology is entrenched in the heart of the Alliance for Progress by Section 620(e), the chances are that these business values will exert a final veto on the social change this country will be willing to underwrite in Latin America."

A series of letters by officers of the United Fruit Company was triggered by the passage of a Honduran law which the United Fruit Company believed threatened its holdings. They in turn resulted in the following speeches which illustrate the almost reflex response of a group of Senators. Speaking their fears of a growing wave of expropriations, they demand that the Administration and the State Department make known to the Latin American governments, in no uncertain terms, the legislative requirement linking continued aid and fair nationalization policies. A year later, Raymond Vernon, Professor of International Trade and Investment at Harvard University, wrote a letter to the editor of *The New York Times* after the Argentine and Peruvian governments began moves to nationalize the property of United States oil companies operating in their countries. He pleaded for an understanding of the Latin American position and warned that, do as we may, the ultimate *political* reality is that "Latin America shares a continent with us and it will not go away."

Two short addenda are appended to provide food for thought. As Sinbad the Sailor found out when he took the Old Man of the Sea on his shoulders to help him, the Government of the United States has learned that aid to the less fortunate builds ties of dependence and obligation which cannot be easily severed.

The Correspondence

BOSTON, *September 7, 1962.*

The Honorable EDWIN M. MARTIN,
Assistant Secretary of State,
Department of State,
Washington, D.C.:

. . . Events today indicate the situation in Honduras is getting more serious with the passage of time. Despite assurances by the President in the presence of the American Ambassador that copy of the proposed law would be shown us today, Government officials have now declined to show us the proposed law. Apparently American Ambassador does not have copy of this proposed law although we understand that he has requested a copy. We urgently need action by State Department through American Ambassador to get copy of this proposed law before it is too late to take action to protect American interests. Responsible officials of ours now in Honduras continue to have the impression that Honduran officials believe this so-called agrarian reform law either has the tacit approval of the United States or that in any event the United States does not object strenuously to its passage. Imperative that you correct this misimpression on the part of officials of Honduras, otherwise American property apparently will be subject to expropriation without normal judicial and constitutional protection and without any prompt adequate and effective compensation. We have attempted to point out provisions of the Hickenlooper amendment but our representatives in Honduras have been unable to find that the Honduran Government has been advised as to the seriousness of this portion of our law. Appreciate the difficulties under which you are working and know of your desire to protect American investment abroad. We hope that this telegram and previous letters from Victor Folsom supplementing what you are getting from your Ambassador will help you to take the necessary action which I am sure the Department desires under circumstances of this kind.

THOMAS E. SUNDERLAND,
President, United Fruit Co.

Boston, September 18, 1962.

The Honorable EDWIN M. MARTIN,
Assistant Secretary of State,
Department of State, Washington, D.C.:

Supplementing my telegrams of yesterday and today, our representatives have been informed by the Embassy in Honduras that the U.S. Embassy there has not even called to the attention of the Government of Honduras the existence of the Hickenlooper amendment to the 1962 Aid Act and the fact that the proposed agrarian law would be inconsistent with said amendment. Our representatives also were told that the U.S. Embassy had received instructions not to make representations to the Government of Honduras based upon the Hickenlooper amendment, because it would be premature. As you know, matter is most urgent as bill may become law unless the misimpression that the U.S. Government approves the proposed law is corrected.

THOMAS E. SUNDERLAND,
President, United Fruit Co.

OCTOBER 1, 1962.

Hon. BOURKE B. HICKENLOOPER,
Senate Building,
Washington, D.C.:

Yesterday the President of Honduras signed so-called agrarian reform law but did not repeat nor issue statement regarding modifications of law but on the contrary made speech praising the law. We had understood from State Department that President was to issue statement pointing out that it would be necessary to amend the law to make it consistent with Alliance for Progress program and international law. Now that law adopted and held up as being praiseworthy and in accordance with the Alliance for Progress program it will be very difficult to secure its modification. Therefore State Department solutions appear highly improbable.

VICTOR C. FOLSOM,
Vice President, United Fruit Co.

OCTOBER 1, 1962.

Hon. BOURKE B. HICKENLOOPER,
Senate Building,
Washington, D.C.:

I have sent following message to Assistant Secretary of State Martin:

"Thank you for your message of September 30, and your promise to send us a copy of the so-called agrarian reform law signed by the President of Honduras yesterday. Reference your point 1 you must recognize how difficult it is for us to comment on laws the exact text of which we have not yet seen. The clear implication given Members of Congress from the memorandum delivered to them was that the State Department had the law and had carefully examined it at the time the memorandum was written. Reference point 2 new law by its terms gives agrarian reform institute overriding powers not subject to normal constitutional guarantees and access to the courts and we know of no legal opinion in Honduras which disagrees with this point of view. Reference point 3 we are advised by the American Ambassador that no representations were made by him regarding the Hickenlooper amendment prior to September 11 or 12 after passage of law but that he could not say what the State Department might have done. We have checked with Honduran Ambassador and he did not receive any representations regarding Hickenlooper amendment prior to September 12. Reference point 5 confiscatory taxation provided for in articles

63–65 makes 'voluntary expropriation' anything but voluntary. Provisions obviously call for forced transfer without the payment of prompt, adequate and effective compensation and this is confiscation. Reference point 7 cannot understand your statement that no defensible analogy can be made between this program and Communist agrarian reform particularly since you state that you have not read the 'exposición de motivos' or statement of purposes attached to the law. The President of Honduras signed the law yesterday without making any statement whatsoever regarding its future amendment to eliminate the conflict of its provisions with the Constitution of Honduras and international law. We had understood that the President would make such a statement at the time the law was signed."

> VICTOR C. FOLSOM,
> *Vice President, United Fruit Co.*

The Senators' Response

MR. HICKENLOOPER: Mr. President, I wish to discuss for a few minutes a subject which I think is of vital importance to the United States, to our foreign policy, and to our relations with other countries. As I view it, it is the attitude of our Government toward the expropriation or seizure of American property in foreign countries. Repeated instances of expropriation have arisen, specifically, instances which occurred early this year; namely, a couple of expropriations in Brazil, some expropriations in Ceylon, some threatened expropriations in other places, and a general beginning of a wave of seizure of American property by foreign governments without adequate purpose or sufficient payment of the property. This action has aroused the indignation of many Members of Congress.

It has always been my concept that one of the duties

of the U.S. Government is to protect the reasonable, fair, equitable rights of American citizens abroad. I submit that that is not being done, that it has been neglected, and that American citizens and their property are being discriminated against. Not only is their property being seized in certain countries without adequate, fair compensation, but the State Department and the administration are not exercising vigorous care or attention to see to it that the traditional protection given to their rights—not the unusual or extraordinary territorial rights, but merely the basic rights of American citizens abroad—is being afforded American citizens.

Early this year, when the Foreign Assistance Authorization Act of 1961 was before the Senate for consideration, I filed with the Committee on Foreign Relations, for the reference of the Senate, an amendment which sought to reach this situation. There had been two expropriations in Brazil. No real provision had been made to pay for the seizure of that property. Other expropriations were threatened. Bills were introduced in the legislatures of a number of countries throughout the world providing for the expropriation and seizure of foreign property under various types and kinds of alleged payment, most of which were long-term bonds of questionable value and having no certainty of convertibility. In effect, this action merely amounted to expropriation and seizure of the property.

There are other countries where unfair and inequitable tax exactions or other business requirements were placed upon American nationals doing business in those countries, requirements which were not applied to the nationals of the countries.

In many nations throughout the world the U.S. citizens were being put upon. They were being treated without equity as compared with the nationals of those countries. Americans were being discouraged in their business operations.

Meanwhile, there was lip service from the U.S. Government. It was said that we were encouraging American investment abroad and were exporting American knowhow. At the same time the basic interests of Americans abroad were not being protected.

The amendment to which I refer, which was considered by the Committee on Foreign Relations, provided that the United States would not attempt to control the sovereignty of any nation in the expropriation of property for public convenience as that nation saw it, or for the exercise of eminent domain, which we recognize as a sovereign power of a sovereign government. The amendment provided, in effect, that when any nation seized the property of an American citizen or imposed exactions by way of regulations or taxes upon Americans doing business abroad that were not equitably applied to all people in that country, the United States would withhold foreign aid from that country; and the President was directed to withhold foreign aid. We did not seek to dictate the sovereign rights of any country; but we reserved the right, under the amendment, to say what we would do with our money if foreign countries abused American citizens by denying them their rights.

The State Department raised all kinds of objections. They wrote memoranda; they appeared before the committee; they said, in effect, "We will protect American rights. Please do not write any such laws. Some of the countries will take offense at us and will not take our money."

The committee held a hearing, and considerable influence was brought to bear by administration sources to soften the amendment. The amendment provided that the Foreign Claims Settlement Commission of the

United States, which has had a long history of surveying foreign values, has the legal machinery to determine the reasonable value of American property seized abroad. If a foreign country did not wish to accept the findings of the Foreign Claims Settlement Commission as to the facts and pay the claim in convertible currency—not in so-called bonds of questionable value or in long-deferred payments that could be subject to deception in one way or another, according to strange manipulations of foreign governments—then we would withdraw our aid. It was our view that if a foreign country wished to take American property, they should pay for it; but that if they did not want to pay for it, we would withdraw our aid.

. . .

Mr. President, the amendment was not adopted. It was modified. It went to the House. The House further modified it. Eventually, after the conference report was adopted, we ended with a provision in the Foreign Assistance Act of 1962, section 620(e).

Mr. President, I think perhaps I had better read this provision into the Record, so that Senators can understand just what this provision is. It is an addition to the Foreign Assistance Act of 1962. Section 620(e) of the Foreign Assistance Act of 1962 reads as follows:

> (e) The President shall suspend assistance to the government of any country to which assistance is provided under this Act when the government of such country or any governmental agency or subdivision within such country on or after January 1, 1962—
>
> (1) has nationalized or expropriated or seized ownership or control of property owned by any United States citizen or by any corporation, partnership, or association not less than 50 per centum beneficially owned by United States citizens, or

(2) has imposed or enforced discriminatory taxes or other exactions, or restrictive maintenance or operational conditions, which have the effect of nationalizing, expropriating, or otherwise seizing ownership or control of property so owned,

and such country, government agency, or government subdivision fails within a reasonable time (not more than six months after such action or after the date of enactment of this subsection, whichever is later) to take appropriate steps, which may include arbitration, to discharge its obligations under international law toward such citizen or entity, including equitable and speedy compensation for such property in convertible foreign exchange, as required by international law, or fails to take steps designed to provide relief from such taxes, exactions, or conditions, as the case may be, and such suspension shall continue until he is satisfied that appropriate steps are being taken and no other provision of this Act shall be construed to authorize the President to waive the provisions of this subsection.

That is what was written into the law by Congress. . . . As I stated a while ago, the ink on that act is scarcely dry; but today I am persuaded that this provision of law, which was written in by Congress, and the declaration of Congress which was made as a result of this provision, are being disregarded by the State Department, and the spirit of the law is not being put into effect. For some reason, which I do not know, this provision is being soft pedaled.

The point is that we were forced—as often is required by legislative procedure—to compromise somewhat from my original amendment, which I thought was airtight and would not permit any escape. We were forced to compromise somewhat; and apparently the difficulty arises from the last paragraph of the law which was enacted—section 620(e) of the Foreign Assistance Act of

1962—at the point where it reads: "and such country, government agency or government subdivision fails within a reasonable time (not more than six months after such action or after the date of enactment of this subsection, whichever is later) to take appropriate steps."

At the time when we adopted that language, I pointed out that those were weasel words, and that they left the gate wide open for the Executive or the State Department to say that the steps were reasonable or were appropriate, or to say that the time was reasonable—in other words, that there could be endless delay without making these countries come up to the till and lay the money on the line, if they were going to seize American property.

Mr. President, I think that is what has happened, and I shall state why I think so. I am not talking now about expropriation proceedings already going on, those which have not yet been settled in Brazil, or those which have not necessarily been settled in Ceylon, nor am I talking about other countries in which there is still the threat of the seizure of American property. Sometime ago I learned that a bill before the Honduras Legislature provided for the establishment of an agency or commission which would have the right to seize and take over foreign property in Honduras, but with no specified method of payment, except as the commission might determine, and that there would be no appeal to the courts from the action taken by the commission, or no appeal from the commission's decision. In short, the commission could do as it pleased, and could fix such payment, or even a specious payment, as it might wish to fix; and it has openly announced that its purpose is to seize American property in Honduras. The officials have stated that sometime it will get around to issuing some sort of bonds, payable at some distant time in the future, but that in the meantime Americans or American companies will lose their property.

The reason why I say I wonder how much attention is being paid by the responsible U.S. officials whose duty it is to see to it that U.S. citizens property is given equitable treatment, is that 2 weeks ago or so I called the State Department and asked about this matter. I received a vague reply to the effect that something was being considered, but nothing was being done in Honduras.

A few days later I called and said, "I understand that the law has been passed in Honduras."

The reply was, "If it has been, we don't know anything about it."

Later I called again; and then the reply was, "We assume the law was passed, but we understand they will not be as hard on foreign property as the law might permit them to be."

On September 20, I asked the acting chairman of the Senate Foreign Relations Committee to send a letter to the State Department, because I had also heard indirectly—and I believe it to be a fact, although I cannot allege it, because I was not present when the conversations took place; but I heard it from sources which I believe to be accurate—that specific instructions had gone from our State Department, to our representatives abroad, to soft pedal this amendment, and not to emphasize it to foreign governments, because it might disturb our relationships; and our people abroad were told to be careful about what they said to foreign governments about their responsibility under this amendment.

MR. SALTONSTALL: Mr. President, will the Senator from Iowa yield to me?

MR. HICKENLOOPER: I yield.

MR. SALTONSTALL: I point out that the property in

Honduras belongs to one of the best companies in Massachusetts, the United Fruit Co. Not only does the institute or commission have the right, as I understand, to make such a decision, without the right of appeal, and to establish the amount to be paid, but I also understand that it is stated that this matter would be handled under the principles of the OAS, in order to help carry out the intention in connection with the OAS—although in my opinion it would be directly contrary to the purpose of the OAS, as I understand it.

MR. HICKENLOOPER: I agree with the Senator from Massachusetts. Furthermore, in addition to the United Fruit Co., a number of other companies are involved.

At this point I shall refer to the United Fruit Co. I know every Senator wishes to have equitable and proper treatment accorded his constituents. Furthermore, in this connection it is important to note that the United Fruit Co. has done in Honduras many things which no other company has done.

It has established schools. It has established hospitals. It has brought about the highest wage scales in the country. It has brought about better living conditions. United States companies have done more for the countries where they operate than the local governments have even approached doing for their own countries, but the property of the various countries is proposed to be seized under laws which we knew about, but apparently which we did nothing to attempt to stop. When I say "stop," I mean that we still recognize the right of sovereignty, but we did nothing to attempt to see that fair payment was made for the property seized. That is the point involved. . . . On last Sunday, day before yesterday, with a great deal of ceremony in Honduras, the bill was signed——

MR. MORSE: By the President?

MR. HICKENLOOPER: Signed by the President, and there was a great deal of speechmaking to the effect that they are going to take this property now and it will belong to the Hondurans. Apparently one of the major speechmakers at that time had just recently returned from Castro's Cuba and he spoke of the great day on which the land of Honduras is being returned to the Hondurans.

. . . On yesterday I called the State Department again and I said, "I understand the bill has been signed down there." The person to whom I spoke said, "Well, we did not know it, if it had been." I received a call at 2 o'clock in which I was told, "Well, we called the Ambassador down there and we learn it was signed yesterday."

I knew it before that. Apparently the State Department did not know about it. There is something rather mysterious about the whole thing.

MR. MORSE: Does the Senator know of any official protest on the part of the State Department to the Honduras Government in opposition to the passage of that bill?

MR. HICKENLOOPER: I know of no vigorous protest. Furthermore, I know of no vigorous calling to the attention of the Honduran Government prior to the contemplated action as far as concerns the possible results which might flow under the law which passed here.

. . . I think the facts show that a perfunctory report was made to the Honduran Government of the action in the foreign aid bill. I am now talking about going in and saying, "This is the policy which has been written, and I want you to know we must stand behind the legislative policy written by the Congress of the United States." I do not think it went that far. I think perfunctory information was given on it.

I also have information, as I stated, that our people were told to soft pedal it, not to emphasize it. . . .

Mr. Morse: I call to the attention of the Senator from Iowa that we have been privileged for the last several days to have the galleries loaded with representatives of the State Department and the Pentagon Building as we have debated the foreign aid bill, but the galleries have been emptied of the legislative representative sections of the State Department and the Pentagon Building. I think they have one or two representing each department now, instead of the 15 or 20 who have been present during the last several days. They had due notice that we were going to discuss the Honduras matter. I can understand why they cannot "take it." They have had such an unfortunate attitude with regard to this matter that they just cannot take the criticism. But they are going to have to take the criticism and to answer for their course of conduct in the hearings the committee has officially approved, and which the subcommittee will start this fall regarding what I consider to be the bad record the State Department has been making with regard to the whole Alliance for Progress program, of which this is, as I shall show, an integral part.

Mr. Hickenlooper: These communications set forth the activity and the vital concern of these people in the seizure of their property, and indicate their concern with the inaction or failure to get something done.

I shall conclude my statement, and then yield to Senators.

I conclude by saying that, as I tried to point out, and as other Senators tried to point out when the bill was considered earlier in the year, the success of expropriation in one country will stimulate expropriation in other countries by dissident groups. The success of expropriation in Ceylon and in Brazil will stimulate expropriation in other countries. Now it is coming in Honduras, and Panama is also threatening expropriation. There are bills in the legislatures of Chile and Peru—to do what? To seize American property.

MR. LAUSCHE: It began in Cuba.

MR. HICKENLOOPER: People in those countries are pointing to the success Castro had in Cuba in seizing American property.

I sat in Bogotá at a conference with a Cuban representative, still in the OAS organization at that time, a year ago, who said to the Latin American countries, "If you need help, do what we did. You have $10 billion worth of American property investments in Latin America. Take it. That is the way to get your money. Take American property in those countries."

The Cuban representative advised them to do that, and I wonder if some of those countries are not taking the advice of the Cuban representative.

If our State Department and the administration supinely do not protest, if they do not protect the equitable and fair right of American citizens, all this property may be lost. We are not talking about unfair claims of rights, or rights which some owners might wish to claim which are unjust. We are talking about fair and equitable rights of American people abroad. That is the issue.

The law is sufficient. The law which is already on the books is sufficient, if there is an intention on the part of the administration to implement the law in good faith. That is the whole burden of my discussion.

MR. LAUSCHE: Mr. President, will the Senator yield?

MR. HICKENLOOPER: I yield to the Senator from Ohio.

MR. LAUSCHE: I should like to relate a bit of the background leading up to this discussion of foreign nations confiscating without due compensation property of U.S. citizens.

In the Committee on Foreign Relations the subject of Cuba came up for discussion. It was then pointed out that the confiscation which was tolerated in Cuba in all probability would lead to confiscation of property in Brazil. It was further pointed out in the Committee on Foreign Relations, and especially by the Senator from Iowa, that the sufferance of what happened in Cuba brought on what happened in Brazil and, following what happened in Brazil, what happened in Ceylon. Bolivia was then discussing confiscation. Now Honduras is doing so.

Mr. President, it cannot be escaped that the supine acceptance of one grave offense gives encouragement to all other nations around the world that they can proceed in the fashion of Cuba and Brazil to confiscate American property without fear.

What disturbs me is that in the Committee on Foreign Relations, when minds were in agreement about the need to forbid the granting of foreign aid to countries which confiscated American property without compensation, we had difficulty in procuring the approval of the State Department to the ultimate language which was to be used.

MR. HICKENLOOPER: The Senator is correct.

MR. LAUSCHE: With that difficulty in mind, we now have difficulty in procuring a compliance with the language which was finally agreed upon as a compromise.

MR. HICKENLOOPER: It is inconceivable to me that we cannot get compliance by the administrative branch of this Government with the law and the intent of the law which the Congress passed, but I am sorry to say there is foot dragging some place which prevents the operation of the law in its full vigor.

MR. LAUSCHE: We have been pushed around in Laos and in Vietnam, and by the building of the wall in

Berlin. We have been pushed around in the Congo. We are now being pushed around by international law being violated. Our sovereignty and our honor are being insulted by this confiscation of property throughout the world.

If it were at an end now, I would say we probably could suffer through it, but it is foolish to think it is ending now. What has happened will give added encouragement to other nations to confiscate our property.

We have been pushed and pushed. We have retreated and retreated. Our honor has been assaulted. I do not know where it will stop. I know the problem gets worse each day.

The law prohibiting aid to countries guilty of expropriating property of U.S. citizens without compensation has been written. The State Department officials must abide by it, and for compliance, the Congress should voice its vigorous demand. . . .

MR. MORSE: . . . The State Department knew that that was a part of the law. As chairman of the Subcommittee on Latin American Affairs, I am keenly disappointed that the State Department has not taken a more adamant and persistent attitude in regard to what they knew was the plan of Honduras to enact the kind of law that was referred to by both the Senator from Iowa and the Senator from Massachusetts. The law enacted by the Honduras Parliament and signed by the President in recent days becomes meaningless so far as concerns giving any assurance to American property owners in Honduras that they will receive just compensation for property seized.

There is no question that the Government of Honduras has a sovereign power to expropriate the property of the United Fruit Co. or any other American investor in Honduras. I am not at all concerned with any controversy that may exist between the United Fruit Co. and the Honduras Government in regard to past differences.

But I am concerned with the question of U.S. sovereignty. We have the sovereign duty to protect our investors abroad. When we cooperate with our investors and when we urge them to invest in Latin American countries, as we have done time and time again, and when we have urged foreign governments to offer them such terms and conditions as will encourage them to invest in a foreign country, I say that a relationship is developed between the U.S. Government and the foreign government that imposes upon each the duty and the obligation to see to it that foreign investors, be they U.S. investors, British, Dutch, Canadian, or any other, receive fair compensation for their property when a foreign sovereign decides to seize and expropriate all property.

It is not happening in Honduras. It is as simple as that. The Senator from Iowa pointed out that it is contemplated that some script or bond or paper may be offered in payment for this property. Mr. President, there is only one compensation that means anything, and that is hard, cold American dollars.

There is nothing in the Honduras law that gives the United Fruit Co. or any other investor in Honduras any assurance that it will get payment in convertible foreign exchange.

In fact, it is perfectly clear from a reading of the law that they are not going to give any, and the American investors are not going to get any.

Therefore, I believe that our Government has an obligation to make clear to Honduras that there is something they are not going to get, and that is foreign aid, until they pay in convertible foreign exchange for American property. . . .

I hope the Government of Honduras will take note,

and that other Latin American countries will take note.
I serve notice today that, although I opposed the more
drastic form of the Hickenlooper amendment in committee on expropriation, next year I will support even
stronger language, if we are to be faced with this kind
of evasion of the purpose which, in my judgment, Honduras is on the road to committing.

We must make clear to American investors that if
there is a seizure of their property they will get fair
compensation. If they do not get fair compensation, we
do not propose to take American tax dollars and pour
them into any country by way of foreign aid, so that
they will in effect get a double take—the property of
American investors and the taxpayers' money.

What kind of prestige and respect does that build up
for the United States in Latin American countries, or
anywhere else in the world?

MR. ALLOTT: . . . I agree that a part of the sovereign
right of any nation is to effect expropriation, if that is
the nation's will. But it is also a part of our doctrine and
understanding that no nation will effect expropriation
without payment in an established currency which can
be traded and utilized on the world market.

Although I have steadily supported foreign aid, and
intend to vote for the bill this afternoon, I have been
concerned for a long time that the State Department as
a whole, not only under this administration, but also
under the previous administration, has taken a very
immature, unknowledgeable attitude toward countries
we are trying to assist. I am concerned because the
people in those countries have come to believe that the
money we are sending to them in the form of foreign
assistance is no longer something we are providing them
of our own will, but rather something in which they
have a right to share, namely, the prosperity of the

United States. During my attendance at interparliamentary meetings and other similar meetings, I have heard this view expressed.

I do not believe that any foreign nation has a right to share in our prosperity or in our goods. If we wish to share our prosperity with them—and I have felt that I wish to do so—that is another thing. But no nation has a right to the wealth, the money, or the goods which the people of the United States have developed through hard work, imagination, initiative, courage, and brains, when other nations themselves are unwilling to exert the same qualities to raise the standards of their own countries.

At Punta del Este, the United States agreed to provide $14 billion to Latin America during the next 10 years. We contributed the first portion of that sum last year, and more will go into the *Alianza para el Progreso* this year.

I do not know how we can impress the State Department with the fact that in our constant help throughout the world, when other countries repeatedly and constantly kick us in the teeth, the rest of the world can only regard us as weaklings, as vacillators, as a people who have lost their national purpose, when we have rewarded other nations after they have kicked us in the teeth by continuing to supply them with huge sums for their own advancement, to provide the basic, decent things that I believe all men are entitled to. As a Christian, I believe that I am my brother's keeper. Therefore, I am willing to devote a part of my taxes to the help of other countries; to bring to the poverty stricken countries, whose living conditions are beyond imagination, the basic rudiments of health, living standards, and education.

I endorse what other Senators have said in this respect. I think we must take a hard look at the situation. From this time forward, let no one make the mistake that we will dispense our aid and spend our money, to use a common expression, "like a drunken sailor on a Saturday night"; but that we will dispense aid to countries which at least recognize the principles of basic law which we recognize. I feel certain that Congress is of the mind that there will be no further aid to countries which practice expropriation against the United States.

. . .

A Letter to *The New York Times*

To THE EDITOR OF THE NEW YORK TIMES:

The recent measures of the Argentine and Peruvian Governments against foreign oil companies operating in their countries are having their predictable aftermath in this country—a sense of frustration, of impatience, even of outrage at governments which feel the need to hamper the productive work of foreign investors in order to satisfy internal political pressures.

The sense of outrage is all the stronger because so many here in the United States feel that these governments are biting our right hand while being fed from our left.

Outrage and frustration, however, are not very creative reactions. What is needed for our future policy toward Latin America is to gauge the power of the forces we are up against; to try to change what we do not like; and to accommodate ourselves to what we cannot change.

Old Order Under Attack

On any reading of Latin-American history it seems overwhelmingly clear to me that we are in for a long period of tension or hostility toward foreign companies producing inside that area. The hostility may vary from year to year and from country to country, according to the tactical concepts and personalities of their leaders. But the pressures in that direction are deep-seated, based on long-term historical and psychological forces.

Make no mistake about the direction from which these forces come. Only a tiny part of the pressure to curb the foreigners comes from Marxists. Only a little more comes from the national socialists. Much more probably comes from those who in a fine rage are indiscriminately against all the symbols of the old order—symbols that, as they see it, include the landlords, the generals and the foreign investors.

But finally, importantly, there are the pressures from the new business class, the new technicians, the new administrators. These are men who feel fully as competent as the foreigner to run their national industries and who are impatient to prove that fact to themselves and the world. Few Latin American governments can stand up against such forces for very long.

Uneasy Decade

So the foreign investor is in for an uneasy decade or more in Latin America. This does not necessarily mean that it will be an unprofitable decade. Despite all the excursions and alarums, Latin America continues to be one of the faster growing areas of the world and it continues to offer splendid opportunities from time to time to carefully selected projects.

The threat of nationalization and expropriation is far larger than the actual performance. If the investor manages to withstand the sporadic measures of restraint and hostility that Latin American governments are bound to decree from time to time, he may come out all right in the end. At best, however, he can only hope for prosperity without peace.

But there is no use baying for the moon. Latin America shares a continent with us, and it will not go away. If our own long-term interests require that Latin America should grow, we shall have to frame our plans and expectations to accommodate to those forces in its growing patterns that we cannot change.

RAYMOND VERNON.

Cambridge, Mass., Nov. 18, 1963.

Following the anti-American riots in Panama and the Canal Zone in January 1964, Panama severed diplomatic relations with the United States, demanded a revision of the canal treaty immediately, complained to the Organization of American States, and threatened to take its charges before the United Nations. Under the circumstances, the United States suspended aid under the Alliance for Progress for several projects involving schools, roads and housing construction, "not as a political matter but for purely practical reasons because United States personnel have left Panama." The Panamanian Government, citing its fear that the suspension would "result in large scale unemployment and heighten the country's already simmering political and economic ferment," was then reported as having considered pressing charges of "economic aggression" against the United States if it persisted in its suspension of aid programs. (*The New York Times,* January 22, 1964, pp. 1–2.)

Having annulled its contracts with six American oil companies, the Argentine Government entered into negotiations to settle upon a proper sum for reimbursement for their properties. In February 1965, the Argentine Government "became convinced" that aid money for the construction of new silos to store surplus wheat that was to be advanced by the Agency for International Development (AID) was being held up because "the oil companies have used political pressure on AID and the [State] department." An AID spokesman stated, "The matter is still under study." President Arturo U. Illia was reported as being "dismayed" at the oil companies' attempts to take advantage of his government's difficult position. Significantly, the report noted the "apprehension and confusion" the AID inaction had caused among many American "officials . . . interested in developing better political and economic relationships," and "raised again" the question of whether pressures of private business should be permitted to endanger United States policy to rally support for defense efforts in Vietnam and to consolidate a political alliance against Cuba. (*The New York Times,* February 10, 1965, pp. 55 ff.)

13

H. W. Balgooyen

PROBLEMS
OF UNITED STATES
INVESTMENTS
IN LATIN AMERICA

Mr. H. W. Balgooyen, Vice President of the American & Foreign Power Company, has spent some 25
years in businesses dealing with Latin America. An
intelligent, perceptive, and well-spoken advocate and
defender of the role of American private investments
in the Latin American economy, he presents here a
telling exposition of the role and position of the
private investor vis-à-vis government and international agencies, the aspirations and policies of the
Latin American nations, and the changing economic
conditions. He is a firm believer in the thesis that an
increased flow of private capital to Latin America is
in both parties' mutual self-interest. And he recognizes the need for flexible policies of cooperation to
meet new situations over the years.

I believe a good point of departure in any discussion of
Latin American investment problems is to try to de-

From Clement G. Motten, *et al.*, *Latin America: Development
Programming and United States Investments* (Philadelphia: University of Pennsylvania Press, 1956), pp. 49–70. Reprinted by
permission of the publisher.

velop a clear understanding of the reasons for our interest in Latin American investment from a national as well as from an individual viewpoint. As a spokesman for private investment interests, much of what I shall have to say will be from the private investor's viewpoint—a viewpoint which must be understood both here and in Latin America if any real progress is to be made; but behind the problems of the individual investor there is a broad public interest which all Americans, both North and South, cannot afford to ignore.

Let us examine, first, the reasons that we, as United States citizens, should feel an interest in the industrial and general economic development of Latin America and in the related investment problems. . . . With a per capita income which averages only one eighth of ours, they still consume one fifth of all our exports, and these exports are heavily weighted with capital goods to supply industries established by United States investors. The nations of Latin America represent one of the world's greatest storehouses of natural resources and one of the most accessible. Roughly one third of our imports come from Latin America and thirty per cent of all the exports of these countries result from the investments of United States citizens. . . . Here is a three and one-half billion dollar market for our goods—a market at the very beginning of its growth and development and expanding in terms of purchasing power at a rate much faster than our own. . . .

Our private investments in Latin America are playing an important role in facilitating this progress. Latin America abounds with practical examples of the increased productivity, the enhanced earning power, the higher living standards and, in some areas, the improvements in health, sanitation, and education that have resulted where a fair opportunity has been provided for the productive investment of private United States capital with the experienced management and advanced techniques that accompany it.

The nations of Latin America must be able to count on this type of assistance on an increasing scale if they are to maintain their recent rate of progress. Even now, there are indications that the pace of economic growth is beginning to slacken. The remarkable expansion in economic activity since the war has outrun the capacities of the Latin American countries to finance their capital requirements. Efforts of government to maintain the rapid pace of industrialization, to determine its direction, and to finance more and more of the cost have contributed to an unbalanced economic development in some countries, to a serious inflationary situation, and to the persistence of foreign exchange problems long after the original reasons for their existence ceased to be important factors. Regardless of the reasons for their difficulties, these countries need our help, both in capital investment and in the technical assistance to assure its most productive application . . .

Our country has had much recent experience in helping other nations and other peoples. . . . I believe we have learned some valuable lessons. One is that friends are not bought with gifts or money; another is that the most valued assistance is that which enables the recipients to help themselves; but perhaps the most important is that there is no substitute for the drive and creative force which the system of free, private, competitive enterprise, with its incentives for effort and its rewards for accomplishment, can impart to the productive process.

It can be said to their credit that our Latin American friends are not looking for charity. They are eager to help themselves and, despite some unfortunate socialistic experimentation, their chief reliance still is placed on private enterprise. It is in their own self-interest as well as ours that our help should be extended in the most practical way—by increasing the flow of private investment capital, with the technical assistance that comes with it—to those nations that seek it intelligently and are willing to give it encouragement and protection. I am sure that United States private investors have done more in the field of technical training and assistance in both industrial and agricultural pursuits than have all the official technical assistance agencies together. And they have done this not out of charity but because they believed it was in their own interest.

This is not intended as a criticism of the very fine work that governmental and intergovernmental agencies have accomplished in fields where they have demonstrated their competence. The Joint Technical Assistance Programs of our government, working in cooperation with the governments of Latin America, have many constructive accomplishments to their credit in such fields as health, sanitation, education, public administration, and improved agricultural methods. Although some errors have been made, the balance is sufficiently favorable to justify the continuance of these efforts.

I believe that the case is equally strong for continuance of the fine work which our government is doing, directly through the Export-Import Bank, and indirectly through its contribution to the capital of the International Bank, in assisting to finance the construction of basic services in Latin America. I am sure that officials of these banks are sincere when they say that their aim is to assist private investors rather than to increase their problems. Both institutions, however, are under constant pressure to lower their lending standards, and to enter questionable fields of activity. It isn't right for private

enterprise to look to government or to government-sup-
ported agencies for protection against the consequences
of its own poor business judgment, ill-considered investments, or overzealous sales efforts. It is our responsibility, as citizens and taxpayers, to keep ourselves
informed and vigilant so that we may help the conscien-
tious officials of these institutions to resist the pressures
of politically influential groups who would break down
the standards that have been set and divert these agencies from their proper functions. . . . It must be made
clear that neither the United States government nor the
financial institutions it supports will provide funds, now
or at any other time, to finance exports to countries
whose shortage of capital is due to their unwillingness
to provide an economic environment conducive to domestic capital formation and the attraction of foreign
investment.

Since it is generally conceded by practical people that
the major financial burden of the economic development of Latin America must be borne by private investors—domestic and foreign—let us consider, for a
moment, some of the motives which might induce a
private investor to take all or part of his capital out of
the relatively safe and profitable environment of the
United States, to undergo the foreign exchange risks
and other economic and political hazards incident to
Latin American investment. In special cases, the motive
may be a desire to protect an existing investment, to
maintain a market position by getting behind tariff
walls, or to assure a source of essential raw materials.
But the overriding motive, and the only one which will
bring about a broad flow of new capital into the main-
streams of Latin American industry and commerce, is
the profit motive. Private enterprise in the United States
has always been known for its initiative and its willing-

ness to venture. The urge to pioneer, to accomplish, and to build is part of our American heritage; but the driving force behind it all is the desire to produce something of recognized value for which adequate compensation will be received in the way of earnings or profits, and the greater the risks, the greater should be the opportunities for profit.

There really is nothing complicated or obscure about the reasoning of an investor when he lists the plus and minus factors of a contemplated venture in a foreign country. It must all add up to a reasonable opportunity to operate his business with a minimum of government interference and, with good management, earn a profit commensurate with the risk and with the value of the service rendered. The infinitely complicating and confusing element too often is the irrational and unpredictable behavior of the governments with which investors must deal: governments of capital-hungry nations who profess their eagerness to receive private investments, while promoting state-owned enterprises which encroach upon and narrow the field for private endeavor, and while making no effort to remove obstacles which make it impossible for existing enterprises to flourish; and governments of capital-exporting countries, who sometimes urge their citizens to invest abroad while their policies, in the fields of taxation, foreign trade, and diplomacy have the effect of inducing investors to keep their money at home.

As a private investor, I would not be moved to action by any talk about our collective responsibility to invest abroad. Nor would I concede that American investors are, in any way, derelict in their duty or unduly timid in failing to measure up to the expectations of theorists who calculate how many billions should be invested each year, in this industry or in that country, to raise productivity or living standards to a level they consider appropriate, or to rectify an imbalance in our international payments. Individual investors will not be stampeded into unwise ventures, into uninviting places, by arguments that a disproportionate amount of total private investment is going into this industry or that country; or that, in certain areas, the inflow of new investment funds is failing to keep up with earnings remittances on existing investments.

As to the first of these arguments, I would say that there are excellent reasons, from the viewpoint of both the investor and the recipient, for the large petroleum and iron ore investments that have been going into Venezuela, for the expansion that is taking place in North American utility properties in Cuba and Brazil, and for the great increase in our investment stake in the friendly environments of Peru and our immediate neighbors, Canada and Mexico. (This is by no means a complete list of Latin American countries which are providing, or making an effort to provide, a favorable environment for foreign investments.)

I would like to consider the second argument, that the inflow of investment funds should exceed the outflow of earnings, in some detail, since it is cited, in some Latin American countries, as a reason for restricting earnings remittances of present foreign investors, and because it had been given new life and a certain pseudo-respectability by two recent studies originating in United Nations agencies.

To appreciate the full impact on the Latin American investment picture of these two United Nations studies—*International Cooperation in a Latin American Development Policy,* prepared by the Economic Commission for Latin America, known as ECLA, for the use of delegates to the recent Rio de Janeiro Economic Conference, and *Foreign Capital in Latin America,* prepared for ECLA by the United Nations Department of Economic and Social Affairs—it is necessary to understand the enormous prestige enjoyed in Latin America by ECLA and by its Director, Raúl Prebisch. The studies, reports, and pronouncements of ECLA are accepted, without question, as the final word in matters of economic theory and policy.

The ECLA study, which gave the United States delegation so many headaches in Rio, made these interesting suggestions: that an investment target of a billion dollars a year should be set up for Latin America, of which about one third should be supplied by private foreign investment, and two thirds by the International Bank and the Export-Import Bank; that there should be created an Inter-American Fund for Economic Development, with half the capital furnished by the United States out of taxes levied against the income of United States investors in Latin America; that a larger proportion of the new investment in Latin America should come from "public sources" rather than "costly" private investment, and that, in developing countries, new investment should exceed earnings remittances on existing investments.

The study on *Foreign Capital in Latin America* followed up the last-mentioned suggestion by pointing out that, over a period of some twenty-five years, our private investors had taken out more than they had put into Latin America. This was hailed by a large segment of the press as a startling discovery—and a "little-known situation." As I pointed out in an article in the *New York Journal of Commerce:* "If this is truly a 'little-known situation' and, of itself, is considered to be cause for alarm, it is only too evident that we have not progressed very far in our understanding of foreign investment fundamentals." If investments are made for profit, and if profits, to be useful to a company's shareholders must, eventually, be translated into cash income in a currency investors can use, why should a private United States company be expected to put into foreign investment over a period of years more than it takes out? And, if not one private company, why should [this reasoning not apply to] the sum total of all private companies?

The real question, of course, is not whether, during a specific year, or over a period of years, the inflow of private United States capital to Latin America has exceeded the outflow of profit remittances. Neither is it merely a question of balancing foreign exchange income and outgo, although it can easily be demonstrated . . . that United States private investments in Latin American countries, by earning them a billion dollars a year on export accounts, by saving them a billion and a half dollars annually on import account, and by paying them taxes estimated at one billion dollars annually do produce an annual net gain in dollar exchange of very sizable proportions. The significant question is whether, all things considered, these investments have been beneficial to the countries which have received them.

It is only fair to say that the U.N. study on *Foreign Capital in Latin America* did concede that "comparison of particular items in the balance of payments are of limited significance. . . . The basic questions are how a given amount and composition of foreign investments affect the country's output and international payments position." But this was almost completely ignored in the sensational press reports which heralded the study. . . .

I would now like to turn from consideration of the general background and problems of Latin American investment to the more specific problems of an actual, long-term investor in a key industry in that area and tell you, from personal knowledge, some of the problems my own company, the American & Foreign Power Company, has had to face during more than thirty years in the Latin American investment field. And I want to talk not only of problems but also of opportunities and accomplishments.

The Foreign Power System has investments of over a billion dollars in the public-utility industry in eleven Latin American countries. Over the years, we have met with more than our share of obstacles and frustrations; and our earnings have been considerably less than they would have been on the same amount of capital invested in the United States. This has been partly due to economic conditions beyond the control of the countries where we have invested, but, too often, it has been due to the failure of responsible government authorities to come to grips with some of their most serious economic problems—to their tendency to do that which is politically expedient, rather than financially sound.

The Foreign Power System was faced, early in its history, with a variety of economic problems that could scarcely have been anticipated by its founders. Our Latin American investments were made in the 1920's when currencies were stable, exchange was convertible, governments paid their bills and tried to keep out of debt, and individuals, rather than governments, complained of a dollar shortage. We had just completed the acquisition of our properties when the 1930 collapse of commodity prices hit Latin America and ourselves with the full impact of the world depression. As commodity prices fell and demand for foreign currencies exceeded the supply, the foreign exchange reserves of the countries we served diminished rapidly and the international values of their currencies dropped precipitously. . . .

Not only did the decline in exchange rates drastically reduce the dollar value of our earnings, but country after country imposed strict exchange controls which severely restricted their remittance to the United States. In some cases, dollars were not available even to pay for essential materials and equipment. Although the first shock of these developments was the hardest, this was only the beginning of a long and difficult period of declining currency values and exchange restrictions which still are a factor to be reckoned with in some of the countries where we operate.

Next to these currency difficulties, our most serious economic problem has been the inflationary trend which got under way in earnest during the early years of World War II, rapidly picked up momentum, and today, in some countries, seems to be out of control. . . . Yet, the problems of the utilities in Latin America are not insoluble, provided that the regulatory authorities have the courage to face up to their responsibilities.

Electric power and transportation are the keys to an expanding economy and a rising standard of living and there is no logical reason for the rate of return on investments in these industries to be among the lowest in Latin America, and lower than they are in the United States. Interest rates in Latin America are extremely high. In some countries, they run up to twelve per cent or more, while returns on equity investments outside the public utility field may reach thirty, forty, or fifty per cent annually on invested capital. In such an economic environment, the nominal yields on investments in electric power and transportation are a curious anomaly, and one which must be remedied if the economic development of Latin America is to go forward.

Since the governments concerned fully realize the

urgent need for additional investment in electric power, the reluctance of some of them to authorize remunerative service rates would make no sense at all if they did not believe they have an easy alternative, and one that possesses much political appeal. It is the entry of government into the electric power business, financed with money raised through the taxing power or by long-term borrowings at low interest rates. Several Latin American countries have created government power agencies to construct costly power plants, financing their cost with funds obtained through taxes, government borrowings, and outright inflation of the currency; but still the power shortage continues and the countries which have gone farthest down the public power road—even in one instance to the point of confiscating foreign-owned utilities—are among the chief sufferers.

Despite the recent emphasis on public power programs, the provision of electric power in Latin America is still largely in private hands, and most of the governments continue to emphasize their desire for additional private foreign investment in the industry. Naturally, those countries that have been realistic and fair in their treatment of the foreign-owned utilities are the ones that are receiving the bulk of the new investment.

The Foreign Power System, alone, has spent $400 million since the war on new construction in Latin America and, if present trends continue, this amount should double in the next ten years.

We are sometimes asked why we continue to spend so much money on new construction in Latin America. The first reason is the obvious one: we are in the power business, and the first responsibility of any electric power company is to make all reasonable efforts to meet demand. However, we do not consider that this responsibility extends to countries where we have had a history of unfair treatment or where there is no reliable promise of fair treatment for the future. Sometimes a commitment to expand our facilities does result in more favorable consideration by government of our essential requirements in the way of service rates, foreign exchange authorizations, and local financing, and there are, of course, important savings in operating expenses to be gained by replacing obsolete and inefficient equipment with facilities of modern design and efficient operation. While we must be realistic about our problems, we cannot allow them so to preoccupy us that we lose sight of our opportunities; and however difficult the financing problem it creates, we must look upon the dynamic growth of local industry and the soaring demand for power as an opportunity and a challenge, rather than as an obligation.

It is quite an understatement to say that it has not been easy to find the money to carry out our post-war construction program. The disastrous collapse of currency values during the depression left us with an unwieldy capital structure and an overpowering burden of fixed charges and dividend obligations on senior securities. A complete and thoroughgoing corporate reorganization was necessary, and it required some seven years of continuous negotiations and hearings before our reorganization became effective in 1952.

Here was a company in the throes of a long and costly corporate reorganization, under the necessity of coping with a serious power shortage, requiring substantial new investment in countries with long records of currency problems and foreign exchange difficulties —countries with undeveloped capital markets and unsolved inflationary problems which exerted a continuous upward pressure on operating expenses and construction costs. Yet, there was no alternative, as we saw it, but to go ahead.

Foreign Power's own resources were exhausted before the program was well under way and the development of new financing mechanisms soon became a matter of urgent necessity. . . . Well, we did something quickly —several things, in fact. We pioneered and met with some success in developing local capital markets in the interior of Brazil, in Cuba, in Costa Rica, Panama, and other countries. We raised some twenty million dollars by means of common stock sales in Brazil alone, not on the basis of the yield, which was relatively low, but by emphasis on the safety factor and on the absolute necessity of local participation in the financing of badly needed additions to power supply. We also sought the assistance of the Export-Import Bank, which responded by extending credits totalling over seventy million dollars. We secured a loan of ten million dollars from a group of private banks in the United States. We sought, and obtained, the assistance of government sponsored development banks and financing institutions, both in Cuba and Brazil. We sold securities of our Cuban subsidiary to the union representing its employees and to the Cuban public and, when necessary, we borrowed from local banks at high rates of interest. Still, it was necessary to finance more than fifty per cent of our postwar construction program from retained earnings.

This percentage, of course, is much higher than it should be, and we are making every effort to cut it down by raising a larger portion of our construction requirements in the areas which directly benefit. Within the past two years, we have been successful in obtaining loans totalling eighteen million pesos for our Cuban subsidiary from *Financiera Nacional,* a subsidiary of the Cuban Central Bank, and our Brazilian subsidiaries have obtained a quarter of a billion cruzeiros from the National Development Bank in that country. Additional loans are under negotiation from financing institutions in Mexico and Brazil. In this way, we are developing an effective partnership between private investors and government institutions in Latin America and the United States to share the task of building and expanding modern, efficient electric power facilities, under private management and control. The gradual development of local capital markets, and the growing acceptance by government of the proposition that the private companies should be given every encouragement to expand their facilities—despite the noise of the nationalistic element and the clamor of the advocates of public power —is providing Foreign Power and other foreign-owned utilities in Latin America with one of their greatest opportunities, and we are determined to make the most of it.

I am citing some of our experiences in Foreign Power because I believe that the very fact that a privately owned utility company, operating entirely in Latin America, and faced since its inception with the hazards of currency depreciation, exchange controls, inflation, economic and political instability, and the rising tide of nationalism, can somehow manage to survive and grow and render real service to its customers is indicative of the results that can be achieved by investors in basic industries as these hazards are mitigated and the obstacles are overcome. . . .

It is obvious that the solution of the problem of rising costs of operation, which derive largely from inflation, must be found in more efficient operations, in higher service rates, or in a combination of both. If foreign exchange restrictions threaten to block the remittance of dollars, the authorities must be shown that the requirements of such key industries as electric power, upon which the industrial life of the country depends, should be a first charge against their foreign exchange resources. The solution to the problem posed by the drying up of the traditional sources of capital investment in Latin American utilities must be found in the development of new sources of both debt and equity capital, and if conditions in the industry are such as to render a direct appeal to the profit motive ineffective, another type of appeal must be devised to interest the equity investor until conditions improve. . . .

None of these results can be achieved without a great deal of educational work and constant attention by utility management to its public and government relations, and wherever a good job is being done, management is spending a major part of its time and effort on this type of activity. It is not easy to operate a price-fixed industry profitably in an inflationary economy. Problems related to the necessary revision of rates require constant attention. Their solution requires the understanding cooperation of the highest authorities in government and a high degree of economic statesmanship and courage on their part. And this is equally true whether electric service is provided by private utilities or government agencies. No one likes to pay higher rates for electricity. Yet, the provision of remunerative rates is the only answer to the problem of assuring adequate power supplies to the power-hungry economies of Latin America while maintaining the solvency and financial responsibility of their governments. . . .

I have tried to give you a broad picture of the need, the desire, and the reasons for private foreign investment in Latin America. I have made no attempt to gloss over any of the problems and uncertainties that continue to face the private investor in this largely undeveloped area, with its enormous potential for growth and progress, and, finally, I have told you something of what is being done by one of the largest North American investors, despite obstacles, to preserve and expand the opportunities for private enterprise in Latin America. Given the opportunities which these nations hold for foreign capital, and given their recognition of their need for foreign capital, it is unthinkable that mutual self-interest will not result in removal of the obstacles which impede its flow. Foreign Power is only one of many United States investors who have the courage to face the problems, the determination to work for their resolution, and the faith to believe in the opportunities. We, in Foreign Power, look upon our system of electric properties as an integral and essential part of Latin America's vigorously expanding economy and despite the problems, we continue to have faith in Latin America's future, for, in a very real sense, it is also our future.

14

The Corporation for Economic and Industrial Research, Inc.

PRIVATE INVESTMENT AND UNITED STATES FOREIGN POLICY

In 1959 the United States Senate Committee on Foreign Relations contracted for a series of reports by various organizations to survey all facets of United States foreign policy. The Corporation for Economic and Industrial Research, Inc., in its study of private foreign investments, brought out the fact that investors were quite selective as to nations and industries into which they put their money. Hence, private investment has had to be supplemented by politically directed government loans and protective policies. This point is generally not emphasized outside of academic or inner government circles.

It is official U.S. policy to encourage private investment abroad, portfolio and equity, and official state-

From 86th Congress, 1st Session, U.S. Senate Committee on Foreign Relations, *United States Foreign Relations: Worldwide and Domestic Economic Problems and Their Impact on the Foreign Policy of the United States* (Washington, D.C.: Government Printing Office, 1959), pp. 60–62. This study was prepared by The Corporation for Economic and Industrial Research, Inc., August, 1959.

ments increasingly indicate that private U.S. investment should play the major role in international economic development. This view arises in part from a desire to reduce the burden of Government aid and in part from a nostalgic belief that the U.S private enterprise system offers the most effective way to achieve economic growth regardless of the environment or the availability of human and national resources.

This position as it presently stands has its limitations. In terms of U.S. aid policy, private U.S. investment abroad is highly selective. It tends to favor the more developed and to ignore the more backward areas, unless nature by chance provided them with petroleum or mineral resources. Adverse government policy in many areas also leads to their avoidance by U.S. investors.

Selectivity is even more pronounced with portfolio than with direct investment, due largely to the painful past experiences of U.S. investors. In the postwar years, only the Western European countries, Israel, and those of the British Commonwealth have been successful in floating sizable bond issues in the United States. There may be some slow relaxation in the attitudes of the U.S. capital market as policy and economic conditions elsewhere improve, but the likelihood is small that there will be more than a trickle of sales of public issues for the more underdeveloped areas in the next decade.

As of the end of 1957, the book value of U.S. direct private investments abroad came to $25.3 billion. Of this total, about half, or $12.3 billion, was in Canada and Western Europe. In the countries of Latin America and the Middle East, to take two major underdeveloped areas, total private direct investment amounted, at the end of 1957, to $8.8 billion but, of this total, $5.6 billion, or 63 per cent, was in the extractive industries

—petroleum, mining and smelting. These extractive industries, with their associated industrial processing, contributed to economic growth and development in the countries concerned. But again, within the geography of Latin America and the Middle East, such investments were concentrated in four or five countries. This is typical of the selective pattern of international private investment, caused by differences in economic opportunity and the investment climate in the underdeveloped areas.

In the years from 1955 to 1957, about half of the increase in U.S. direct foreign investment went to Canada and Western Europe. With the steady expansion of the economies of Western Europe, and the continued growth of Canada, it appears probable that an increasing share of such investments will go to the developed rather than to the underdeveloped areas of the world. However, the latter areas will undoubtedly gain in absolute amount on a selective basis, depending on economic opportunity and the policies of the foreign governments. Selectivity is wholly understandable; business executives are obliged to exercise discretion. In the absence of special inducements and guarantees, the more backward areas will be avoided.

Much tribute has been paid by the Government to the need for increasing the volume of foreign investments, and the agencies of the U.S. Government which do foreign financing have, of course, been continuing and even expanding the U.S. role in world economic development.

The countries of Western Europe, long associated with colonial development, have been important sources of private capital for most areas of the world for many generations. Their long experience and tradition in this field will make of them major and often competitive sources of private financing in both the developed and the underdeveloped areas of the world. On the other hand, their own capital needs for continued economic growth and expansion will be great, so that there will be balancing forces at work. Their private investments overseas are likely to be influenced by political as well as economic considerations, and hence will tend to go, as they have done in the postwar years, to their own colonies or areas of influence. Hence, large portions of the world will have access to only relatively small private investments from the European countries.

Of the total of $3.8 billion included in the international flow of private capital in 1956, of which reinvested profits constitute a part, over 33 per cent was invested in Canada so that this 1 country of 17 million persons received about as much private external capital as the 20 countries of Latin America combined, with about 10 times the population.

Conclusions: Patterns of Capital Flow

1. Non-U.S. foreign government loans and grants concentrate in areas of political influence, such as the Commonwealth or the French Community. This flow can and undoubtedly will increase.

2. Non-U.S. foreign private investment to underdeveloped countries tends to follow the direction taken by Government financing, and within these bounds, concentrates in the most promising places—for example, private British investors favor India. Undoubtedly these investments will grow.

3. Most U.S. private foreign investment goes to developed countries, and the balance goes selectively to (a) a few rapidly developing countries, mainly in Latin America, and (b) the oil-and-mineral-rich regions. These

investments will probably increase in line with present patterns.

4. The U.S. Government is, in a sense, left with the rest—the least promising places from the investment point of view. At the same time it contributes substantially to other, more promising countries, such as India.

5. The private patterns of investment are understandable; important as their efforts are, private investors are not in the business of economic development per se. Development is a byproduct. If private investment is to go to areas, and for purposes, important to U.S. foreign policy, specific incentives will need to be devised for specific purposes.

6. Both the needs for capital in general and the present patterns of supply to the least developed countries make many of them vulnerable to Soviet advances—and some acutely so.

7. The Soviet pattern of economic assistance is highly selective at present, concentrating on areas having difficulties of one sort or another with the West and on those in which neutralist tendencies are strong or where the U.S.S.R. wants to promote such tendencies.

15

Pablo González Casanova

THE IDEOLOGY OF THE UNITED STATES CONCERNING FOREIGN INVESTMENTS

Pablo González Casanova of the Instituto de Investigaciones Económicas of the National University of Mexico, is an ardent nationalist who fervently believes his country to be threatened with economic subjugation and political and cultural servitude by United States investments in the Mexican economy.

González Casanova's nationalist-Marxist analysis emphasizes "conceptual unities," "the idea of necessity," and "the concept of contradictions." He first dwells on the American businessman's purported point of view that it is a *necessity* for him to invest abroad—necessary for his business and the American economy—but he ends with the twist that if Americans are driven by the idea of necessity to export

From Pablo González Casanova, *La ideología norteamericana sobre inversiones extranjeras* (Mexico: Dirección General de Publicaciones, Universidad Nacional Autónoma de México, 1955), pp. 66–69, 172–182. Translated and printed by permission of the publisher.

capital, they will and must do it no matter what may be the policies of the underdeveloped, capital-importing nations. He concludes that Americans are not free since they are the prisoners of their system's necessities, while the capital-importing nations are free to set the terms on which they will accept foreign investments.

He reaches the same conclusion by another tack: Mexico, as a sovereign nation and cultural entity, cannot afford to permit foreign capital to enter, except under tight controls, without sacrificing her freedom. To the extent that foreign capital enters, Mexican capital is discouraged and the internal dynamics of Mexican growth is hindered. Starting with the improvement of the terms of trade as the basic panacea for Mexico's troubles, he also urges that the American exporters' interest be cultivated by Mexican policy in lieu of that of American foreign investors. He suggests appealing to the exporters' interest in a strong Mexican economy. Exporters know that Mexico can buy their products only as it develops its own domestically-owned productive capacity. He also suggests that Mexico appeal for support (e.g., pressure on United States government policy to favor exports of goods over exports of capital) from small businessmen in the United States who would be hurt by the various competitive advantages already held by the businesses large enough to invest abroad.

For González Casanova, a thorough understanding and appreciation of this reality by all classes of Mexicans is the *sine qua non* for the nation's future development.

The idea of the necessity for making foreign investments, particularly in underdeveloped areas, establishes, among other things, a correlation [a mutual relation] which is in keeping with the commercial practice of United States producers. This correlation is limited to the idea: contraction of internal demand—national unemployment—losses; foreign investments—foreign demand—national employment—profits. The frequency with which this idea appears in industry, in commerce and, in part, in the capital market is beyond question. More than a simple opinion, it is the result of commercial practice. A very precise example of the formation of this idea is found in the words of W. Gifford, of the Detroit Board of Commerce: "The Detroit area," he says, "is the major producer in the world of industrial goods destined for foreign markets. The wellbeing of the city and of the State of Michigan depends on a high level of international commerce and a relative freedom and possibility of competing in world markets. Around 800 firms in Michigan are occupied with or busy in some type of foreign commerce, and hundreds of other firms in Detroit and Michigan, which are not directly engaged in export or import, use foreign raw materials or manufacture products needed by firms which will export them. It has been estimated that, of every seven workers employed in the Detroit area, one is employed as a direct result of foreign trade. . . . the present situation of the dollar will become more and more critical if the nations of the world cannot produce the wealth necessary to trade merchandise among themselves. . . ." He set forth this line of reasoning before the Senate [Banking and Currency] Committee in order to explain the necessity for making investments in underdeveloped areas and of increasing their productivity, and thus of augmenting the necessary profits. Afterwards, as a personal opinion based on his experience, he made this even more daring observation concerning the degree of necessity to which American capital finds itself subject in the matter of being sent abroad: ". . . I believe that it was Senator Tobey who suggested the idea that people go abroad because they hope to obtain greater profits. . . . That is one reason, but it is by far the lesser reason. In my opinion, in business the reason frequently is: either you go abroad or you lose your business." Leaving for later analysis the idea of profits and the rate of return, we see here in a common form the mutual relation between the supersaturation of the internal capital markets and the necessity to export capital, a correlation which frequently comes into conflict, as we will see, with the correlation between the saturation of the market for goods and the export of capital. . . .

With this in mind, it is advantageous to analyze four principal propositions: First, the necessity to export capital is affirmed. Second, it is affirmed that the export of capital is the solution to the problems of the internal economy, which in turn break down into: (a) the scarcity of demand for goods, (b) national unemployment, and (c) the cost of capital. Hence the solution to the problem of the scarcity of dollars abroad is what in turn solves the problem of the scarcity of foreign demand. Third, the unity of this thought excludes all internal contradiction [i.e., inconsistency] while [at the same time] it closely approaches the practical thought of each firm. The solution without internal contradictions appears obvious: "Only to the extent that there may be dollars abroad can American exports be bought abroad. I believe that this is a perfectly simple and obvious proposition." ([Nelson] Aldrich, [Senate] *Hearings*, p. 29.) But this coherency, which is as free of internal contradiction as is any practical unity, finds itself making for a logical incompatibility abroad which forms another conceptual unity which is an obstacle to the solution. This latter conceptual unity [the fourth principle]

denies the idea of this *necessity* itself by way of a
perception that forms a concept of *self-liberty* and includes *altruism*. (We shall return later to this conceptual
unity for detailed analysis, but at present it is useful to
see how we find its genesis in the analysis of *necessity*
itself.) After having heard the remarks of the representative of the Department of State on the *necessity* for
the export of capital, and being already convinced of
this, Senator Flanders says: "I would be a little inclined
to do whatever might be necessary to fortify the idea
that these investments are so necessary to us that the
unstable countries can count upon receiving what they
may wish without promising anything." In this way the
idea of *necessity* is negated by (a) the exclusion of all
internal contradiction, and (b) political rationalization.
Thus the very idea of the necessity to export capital,
given the practical and political categories, incorpo-
rates the bases of the concept of one [nation's] *liberty*
[to accept or reject foreign capital] side by side with
that of another's *necessity* [to export capital].

. . .

Conclusions

. . . To continue, we will show, in summary, the
principal facts and relationships and how these appear
in the United States' ideology on the matter. To that let
us add the following derived conclusions:

I. The object of foreign investments is to solve the
economic problems of the United States, which are
related to overproduction and the accumulation of capital: i.e., overinvestment, underconsumption, competition for markets, unemployment, etc.

II. The necessity for foreign investments comes from
the dangers of overproduction, overinvestment, over-
fiscalization, unemployment, and the contraction of the

internal and external market; it appears, or we recognize it as such, not only in periods of contraction but during relative expansion, in the forecasting of the cyclical phenomenon and as an anti-cyclical policy.

III. The policy of investments abroad is designed to stabilize the rate of profit of domestic investments, given overinvestment, and to obtain a higher rate of profit, given the favorable difference of costs in the underdeveloped nations.

IV. Obtaining profits, stabilizing those already existing, and achieving the maximum profit rate, are the essence of the practice of investors.

V. The obstacles to investments which the government of the investor presents are eliminated (or tend to be eliminated, other factors being equal) principally by finance capital and the great monopolies. The particular solutions of stronger effect (and those which imply greater intensification of the incompatible relation between finance capital and productive capital, between the foreign market and the internal market, between the sources of domestic and foreign labor) are those which now prevail. The theoretical and pseudotheoretical struggle against the intervention of the State has this meaning: it is a struggle for the freedom (the absence of obstacles) of United States finance capital and the monopolies to operate unhampered at home and abroad.

VI. The obstacles that the host countries place in the way of foreign investments have to do with the protection that these countries give to their own industries (such as the intervention of the State in productive matters, tariffs and protectionist tribute, exchange control, etc.), and to their workers, so as to create or conserve an internal market, or for other reasons of national social or economic policy (such as the right to strike, legislation concerning salaries, maximum hours, etc.).

The breaking or weakening of these obstacles, by means of intervention by the Government of the United States and by the media, or social agencies of publicity, is an objective directly related to the size of the enterprise and investments placed abroad. The achievement of that object affects all facets of the life of the host country: political, economic, and cultural. It tends to change the political, cultural, social, and productive forces as much as it does the political, cultural, social, and productive relationships.

VII. Even though there does exist a pressure or compulsion from finance capital and the monopolies which shows itself in the fact that the Government of the United States applies pressure on the economic and political life of the under-developed colonial and semicolonial countries, this pressure is not coherent and unequivocal, nor does it have only one course. In the United States itself, there is a maladjustment, a friction, a difference and opposition of interest, between finance capital on one side and productive capital on the other, between domestic competition and the foreign competition which is encouraged by investments abroad. Or, to put it another way: [a conflict] between the export of capital and the export of goods and services, between the protection of American industry and the necessity that export industries have of breaking the protective tariffs of other countries (a necessity which is bringing them [in reciprocity] to break their own protective tariffs, to the detriment of the smaller American industries). The present fight for "freedom" of commerce and for the reduction of the tariffs and protective measures of the United States, thus appears as a form in which to demand reciprocity in the extension of freedom of trade by other countries. Faced by the obstacles which foreign markets present (from the tariff point of

view), and the obstacles which domestic, non-monopo-
listic production presents (from the point of view of
[small enterprises] who find it necessary to protect
themselves against foreign competition), [export indus-
tries] have decided to break the first [obstacles, i.e.,
tariffs] even if it means doing away with the second [set
of obstacles, i.e., small enterprises]. As a result—other
factors being equal—the monopolies of the different
countries of the world, and not only those of the United
States, will find themselves in a more advantageous condition, to the detriment of the small enterprises of the
United States as well as those of the rest of the world.
The disequilibrium which such a step would provoke in
the world economy, if other factors are not efficiently
interjected, is almost unthinkable.

VIII. In the ideological terrain, the underlying theory
of investments is formulated in terms of ethical ideas,
for the purpose of having it accepted unconditionally
and, by way of this psychological control, eliminating
obstacles to it. The American cultural structure, with its
functional character, generally succeeds in creating this
acceptance. And the persuasion may be genuinely effective, above all in the country of origin. The use of those
emotional means which the researches of social psy-
chology have proven to be effective in the persuading,
propagandizing, and reinforcing prejudices . . . are
among their most general characteristics; they partially
affect all levels of internal and external perception, both
in the United States and in the countries to which they
are directed.

IX. From all of the foregoing it can be seen, in summary, that foreign investments are not a purely economic
phenomenon, but an integrated social phenomenon,
whose origins and repercussions cover the entire social
life of the investing nation and of the nation in which

the investment is made. They also tend to alter the to-
tality of the economic, social, and cultural structures of
the underdeveloped countries. As is obvious, implicit in
these trends are found the contrary trends [of thought
and action] of the underdeveloped countries and of the
United States itself. This makes it impossible, from a
scientific point of view, to think in [terms of] "historical
inevitability" so much as of an "historical immutability,"
in which one can foresee concretely how things will
develop in the future. The scope of human action and
the possibility of intervening in the development of
the process in which men find themselves are immense,
given the diverse currents which exist within, as well as
outside of, the United States. This scope of human
action in each actual case, in each country, in each
economic and social relation, domestic and foreign,
ought to be studied objectively in order to determine
concretely up to what point it is possible to control
foreign investments. The possibility of a policy counter-
ing foreign investments does not appear to be a purely
economic one; on the contrary, it is political, social,
cultural and ideological, like the investments themselves. Their concrete study requires finding that possible policy and its limits in relation to: (a) the internal
contradictions of investments, (b) the external contradictions of investments, (c) the internal and external
conflicts of the countries in which the investment is
made. This must be done with the object of determining
(a) up to what point in a given situation it is possible to
utilize the internal and external contradictions of the
investments in order to prevent them, control them, or
channel them, and (b) up to what point in a given
situation it is possible to lessen the internal conflicts of
an underdeveloped country in order to strengthen its
position against outside influences—that is, to succeed

in preventing, controlling, or channeling foreign investment.

The only guarantee of a truly national policy for
controlling foreign investments is to be found in a
coherent internal policy, which tends to diminish conflicting internal relations. In order to gain recognition
for its international position, Mexico has to look for all
those economic and political means that will tend to
strengthen it internally and against outside [pressures].
There are various ways to reach this stronger position.
One of the most important, which merits the deepest
study and application, consists in the betterment of the
terms of trade. This will, at the same time, permit the
capital of Mexico to increase and a greater gain to
emerge in economic and social justice—which is to say
it will permit an increase at the same time of Mexican
capital, salaries, and jobs. The betterment of the terms
of trade is a measure which will keep the increase of the
income of capital from being incompatible with the
simultaneous increase of the income of labor; it will also
resolve economic problems of development and political
problems of social justice, by making for an increase in
the internal market that in its turn will rebound in
capital growth.

Up to what point is it possible to better contemporary
Mexico? Is Mexico doing, in this respect, all that it can
do? Does the magnitude of the volume of our exports
match our maximum productive capacity? Is it possible,
and under what concrete conditions, to better our selling and buying prices in the international market? Is it
possible, and under what circumstances, for our producers to obtain the exact and adequate information
concerning market conditions that will permit them to
carry on transactions from a more advantageous position? Or are they already in that situation, given the

facilities which they now have for becoming acquainted with market conditions? Many of these questions have received an answer in economic studies; but it is appropriate to formulate them as part of a specific social, cultural, and political objective, and not solely an economic one. This objective relates the increase of income by betterment of the terms of trade to the less inequitable distribution of the augmented income and the political and social effects that change will have; it relates the increment of productivity to the expansion of the market and its possibilities, and not, as at present, in an isolated form which necessarily diminishes our sources of work.

On the other hand, the intervention of the State in the key parts of our economic life will promote the growth of the capital of Mexico. The protectionist policy of national industry (falsely called "discriminatory"); the policy of high wages; the policy of giving preference to foreign industries which do not compete with national industry (and which by the [small] amount of their capital invested in Mexico would not lead to interventionist acts)—these depend, at this moment, on the social forces of Mexico. These forces must see that the lack of an integrated democratic policy, along with the absence of a policy for the control of foreign investments (while still permitting certain sectors to continue provisionally to maintain and even increase their profits) will subject Mexico in a short time to the most "disloyal" competition of capital, goods, and services, such as will limit our capacity for independent as well as dependent development.

What idea do Mexican businessmen have of economic time [the business cycle]? What idea do these businessmen have of the key importance of the increase of profits, and its repercussions on contraction and a more distant depression? What are the possibilities of these problems being consciously recognized, and what of the methods to be employed in dealing with the different sectors? All these are questions which, so long as they are unanswered, delay the process of putting into execution the economic development of Mexico down to its social foundations, its social, political, and cultural conditions, and which indicate the necessity for studying not only the economic foundations of national policy, but also those social foundations that will make possible the use of the proper economic measures. This explanation and [the spread of] ideological information has a very important function which cannot be disregarded, in so far as it is in a certain way the foundation for the social factors. How will you be able to make palpable the fact that nationalist principles are part of our economic, social and cultural reality? That is, how do you reinforce the ideas of protection of industry and the national economy, ideas which have been defended as much by the conservatives of the 19th century as by the ideologues of the Mexican Revolution? And up to what point is it possible in a country like our own—which represents a considerable market for American products —to dwell upon the need that foreign investments have for economic and political security in the country in which they are made?

How is it possible to demonstrate in an objective and constant form that if the investors and the most aggressive ideas of the monopolies and/or American policy operate freely, there will inexorably occur (in a direct relation to the impoverishment of the country and to the "aggressivity" of the investors), an economic disequilibrium and domestic political insecurity, which will threaten to reduce the Mexican capacity to buy in the American market? It is evident that the problem is not a simple one and it would probably be a puerile illusion to try to convince the investors that they ought to

operate in another manner. But in our relations with the
American people, it is possible to persuade certain
sectors and to manipulate certain problems by pointing
up the meaning of their own arguments. Persuasion has
a most important function in our country; the objective
elucidation and the knowledge of the absolute truth of
our problem can have the function of organizing the
forces and creating the social foundations for economic
development, thus permitting to be set forth an alternative to the United States [investor] in the terms most
favorable for national independence.

Generally speaking, when one studies foreign investments scientifically, purely economic correlations are
established and [even] then only one part of them—that
which pertains to the *technique* of investment. Do not
think that the idea assumes and covers social correlations which far surpass its narrow meaning. Nevertheless, as we have seen, the idea of "foreign investments"
appears under the most diverse categories and assumes
profound changes in the economy, the politics, and the
culture of the underdeveloped countries. The possibility
or impossibility of the development of a national economy, the development of a national policy, and the
conservation and development of a national culture,
depend in good part on the [people's] consciousness of
the idea and on whether the theoretical and practical
problems we have sketched out above are examined by
all social groups in our countries.

These problems are generally treated emotionally—
which at times may be necessary in the political terrain,
but in the scientific terrain is always sterile. Thinking of
the actualities of contemporary Mexico, we believe that
our country does not have any topic more important, as
much for the determination of its national policy as for
economic and social investigation.

16

Alfonso Bauer Paíz

HOW YANQUI CAPITAL WORKS IN CENTRAL AMERICA
(The Case of Guatemala)

For years Guatemala had been one of the "Banana Republics" facetiously immortalized by O. Henry in *Cabbages and Kings*. But beneath the surface of these nations' daily life lay the hard realities of power and wealth, poverty and ignorance. And in time there arose a generation of young men who wished to lead their Fatherland out of thralldom to foreign economic interests and build a viable nation.

Alfonso Bauer Paíz was a member of the university generation that led the Revolution of 1944 in Guatemala; it overthrew the dictator, General Jorge Ubico, and brought a breath of the modern world to their

From Alfonso Bauer Paíz, *Cómo opera el capital yanqui en Centroamérica (El caso de Guatemala)* (Mexico, D. F.: Editora Ibero–Mexicana, S. de R. L., 1956), pp. 52–56, 59, 365–366, 375–376, 379, 382. Translated and printed by permission of the publisher.

nation. As a lawyer and government functionary in the liberal, anti-foreign administrations that followed Ubico's downfall, Bauer Paíz was a deputy in Congress, and head of several state-owned enterprises and agencies, as well as an "interventor" in the affairs of foreign-owned corporations. Driven into exile by the successful *coup* of Castillo Armas in 1954 (now known to have been organized by the United States Central Intelligence Agency), Bauer Paíz, with many fellow exiles, has written of the traditional plight of his nation, the attempts to find remedies, and the forces of reaction (anti-Communist movements, driven by their monomania, often use unsavory characters and groups to accomplish their purpose) who seized power with American help in 1954. Here we have a romantic description of domestically financed public works under the Liberal president Justo Rufino Barrios and a polemic directed against the economic influence and political intervention of American corporations—particularly United Fruit and Electric Bond and Share—during the succeeding regimes.

In the last quarter of the last century the government of General Justo Rufino Barrios was re-established in Guatemala. He was a distinguished personality of the progressive currents of the time, rivaling the worthy Benito Juárez. Barrios led the liberal revolution in Guatemala with unusual energy and unyielding decision. He had to face the reactionary forces of clerical conservatism, whose powerful economic machine was based on a system of large landed estates and the concentration in its "dead hands" of the main agricultural and manufacturing activities of the country. . . . The Liberal Revolution started the Era of the Railroads in Guatemala.

. . .

Barrios, being convinced that, in order to hasten the economic progress of Guatemala, it was necessary to construct harbors and railroads, set up the legal and financial measures that were needed. He was careful not to compromise the State, as was then the fashion, with the British moneylenders, or to acquire obligations with the still inexperienced promoters of the United States. Being confident of the capacity of his people, he decreed the subscription of an internal loan to finance the railroad and the construction of a harbor in the Bay of Amatique. Understandably, it now carries his name: Puerto Barrios.

The funds were provided by Guatemalan investors of average income, and even people of low income contributed to this patriotic work. Among the people who helped were public employees, from whom a reasonable percentage of their pay was deducted. The generous effort of the people of Guatemala, despite their limited economic means, made an appreciable success possible and put at the service of the export and import traffic the wharf of Puerto Barrios and two thirds of the route from the Atlantic port to the interior of the Republic. The other part would have united the town of El Rancho with the Capital.

Perhaps if we were now to judge the value of the task carried out by the Guatemalans in the construction of their first interoceanic railroad—guiding ourselves by the advance of technology and keeping in mind the relatively small distance that the railroad runs—it might seem to us to be an easy job of engineering; however, our judgment ought not to be based on these points of view, but rather on those [points of view] that make the obstacles that had to be overcome clearly visible. In the first place, [there were] the difficulties presented by the mountainous character of the region, which had to be overcome at a time when knowledge and technical skill had not yet been diffused through the country. In the second place, [there was] the nation's precarious economic situation, whose characteristics, typically feudal, made for a self-sufficiency completely outside the workings of a money economy.

If we do not underestimate our abilities to make judgments, we would not be exaggerating if we were to characterize the work done at that time by the Guatemalans as heroic. They developed to the maximum their constructive power, toward the end of creating their own destiny with their own national resources and manpower, and without having to ask for foreign aid—which, then more than today, was granted only at a very high price and under the condition that the borrower should give up to the lender part of his sovereignty, if not all of it.

The feat directed by Barrios more than half a century ago has a symbolic meaning for the present. His saga is a living example for all those underdeveloped nations in which the United States' cultural and economic penetration has tended to create feelings of inferiority, which proclaims *yanqui* superiority and Latin America's insurmountably inferior condition. The depraved imperialist propaganda wishes to make them believe—and has succeeded in great part in doing so—that, for large sectors of the economic activity of nonindustrialized nations to overcome their backwardness, and to establish and operate enterprises for the exploitation of their natural resources and wealth, they must inevitably accept the subjection of their developmental plans to the interests of the great monopolies, since the men and countries of the South have demonstrated a continuing incapacity [to do these things themselves].

The fallacy of that preaching has been demonstrated by other people, as well as by our own. The Guatemalan example irrefutably reveals that if, in those days long past, a small and unprepared country could undertake to build and successfully build a railroad estimated to cost nearly eight million dollars, [one has the right to ask] why it should be impossible to imitate such an example now? And why should we renounce that right which belongs to us, as sovereign countries, to use for our own benefit the exploitation of public services and industrial activities of general utility?

They can achieve these goals today, when the influence of imperialism each time manifests itself as more threatening, provided they march down the only road to achieve it—that of cooperative self-help among similar peoples. It is not possible if our efforts are separated by the desiderata of anti-national oligarchies—most times —so that we urge each other to compete even more strongly in order to appear in the eyes of the yanqui bosses as their most tested and loyal servants.

The preceding affirmation represents nothing more than the "Americanistic" wish of the author for a patriotic solution of the common problems of the republics of the Continent.

. . .

The governments following Barrios—those of Barrillas, Reina Barrios, Estrada Cabrera, Carlos Herrera, Orellana, Chacón, Ubico and Ponce—for one reason or another abandoned the task of economic emancipation in order to serve those regressive interests of Guatemalan society that were dependent upon the United States.

The first two Presidents cited above exercised their office still under the mandate of the liberal revolution. They respected certain forms, and Reina Barrios at least planned to finish the construction of the railroad to the North by concessions to United States companies.

At the beginning of this century, Manuel Estrada Cabrera, ex-Secretary of Government, took over the presidency of the Republic, and from then on the enslavement (*via crucis*) of the people of Guatemala started. This government usurped power for twenty-two years; since that time, the identification of the governing regimes with the interests of the White House and Wall Street has been accentuated.

The transitory government of Carlos Herrera, brought into power by the majority vote of the Guatemalans, does not count in the chain of dictatorships, but neither does it contradict the aforemade assertion.

It may be noted how the contracts and concessions signed between the governments of that era and the United States monopolies coincide with critical situations in local politics. For example, the 1904 contract that gave to the railroad monopoly power over all railroad communications—under shameful conditions, as we shall explain further on—was the price paid by the dictator of the two decades in order to continue in power with yanqui help. The contract of 1923, signed with the same railroad company to build, under similar conditions, a track that would join Guatemala with its neighboring Republic of El Salvador, along with the contract signed between the Bond & Share Company and the same government, secured the full recognition by the United States of the government of General José María Orellana. The contract of 1930 signed between the Government of General Lázaro Chacón and the United Fruit Company had as its goal obtaining the help of the fruit monopoly for the plans for presidential succession of the "chaconistas" of that time. Finally, the 1936 contract signed between the latter company and the government of Jorge Ubico guaranteed the re–election of that President, who secured himself in power for fourteen years.

The people of Guatemala did not give the Government of Frederico Ponce enough time to repeat that feat. The democratic revolution of 1944 prevented it.

The contracts of December 1954 between the Government of Castillo Armas and the United Fruit Company, and the concessions granted in the year 1955 to Pan American Airways, Bond & Share and other yanqui enterprises, are the result of the policy of "Liberation" of the present regime.

These examples are enough to prove the close relationship that has existed—and this in only one of the Central American countries—between the prostitution of democracy and American private enterprise, backed by the political interests of the United States.

Colonization Against Sovereignty

This is how an almost insurmountable difficulty comes into the lives of the American peoples—the opposition of American economic interests to the institutional development of our nations. If a country, by democratic elections, has created a government ready to respect the wishes of the majority and respond to the dictates of national interest, those American interests will immediately block its administrative action. The dilemma is placed before the government: either respond effectively to the popular desires and the necessity of organizing the institutions required for economic and social development—in which case it knows beforehand that it will suffer a defamatory assault and economic (if not military), pressure instigated by the American financial corporations in alliance with the unpatriotic elements of the Nation—or else, in order to avoid such injuries, fall into a greater evil: to draw back from its position, betray the interests of the people, and transform itself into a servant of imperialistic capital.

. . .

The propaganda of the monopolistic circles, as distributed by the national sectors tied to them, asserts to the whole world that the flow of private American capital has been the decisive factor in the successful functioning of public utility or industrial enterprises in the underdeveloped countries. It is said that the scarcity of capital and of technical resources, as much human as material, would have made it impossible to exploit the sources of production and to take advantage of these natural resources, if it had not been for the capital and administrative direction of foreign monopolies. This statement is false; the experience of Guatemala proves so.

Antipatria

Guatemala enjoyed its democratic glory from October 1944 to June 1954. The juridical and work chains that had enslaved the country's workers since the colonial period were broken; the law of the dictator Ubico, which established forced labor for peasants, was overthrown, and never again would the peasants of Guatemala give free forced labor in the public or private works of the government bosses. The Agrarian Reform had destroyed the feudal power, and would consummate the definitive freedom of the peasant. The workers of the city, also free for the first time, organized the workers' movement—backbone of the social Revolution —and contributed to the consolidation of democracy. Industrialists and businessmen saw the perspective of wider internal markets and prepared to widen their workings, which would start the capitalist era. Students, teachers, priests, professionals, and artists learned, taught, preached, served and created—without limitations. Guatemala, the Fatherland, obtained international prestige. Man was free, and the Fatherland was worthy. That was the spectacle that Guatemala offered to the face of the world: a nation ruled by the democratic, humanizing and anti-imperialistic October Revolution.

On June 27, 1954, the Constitutional President of Guatemala, Jacobo Arbenz Guzmán, broadcast his resignation from his position, without giving any reasons. The country had been invaded, on the 17th of that same month, by mercenary hosts in the service of powerful yanqui interests coming from the sister Republic of Honduras. A popular regime, which had been the exponent of the democratic aspirations of the people for ten years, had fallen in ten days, because of the brutal yanqui conspiracy.

We will not go into details. Recent books written by Guatemalan authors (J. J. Arévalo, G. Toriello, R. Osegueda, L. Cardoza y Aragón, and M. Galich), explain sufficiently how these events came about, and describe with all trustworthiness the gangsterlike methods [used by] the foreign aggressors and the national traitors in order to consummate their felony. We will, nevertheless, show the principal protagonists of this infamous action: Peurifoy, United States Ambassador; Castillo Armas, henchman (*jerifalte*) of the United Fruit Company and of the State Department; Elfego Monzón, ex-Minister of the Interior for President Arévalo, ex-Minister Without Portfolio for Presidents Jacobo Arbenz and Arévalo, and archetype of military disloyalty and the most heinous treason. We cannot keep to ourselves the name of Mariano Rossel Arellano, Archbishop of Guatemala, and spiritual spokesman for the

eternal exploiters of our people: feudal landholders and
aristocratic families; fierce preacher of violence, hate
and fanaticism. And finally, the Apostolic Nuncio, Gen-
aro Verollino, inspirer of the Falangist movement in
Guatemala.

Four important forces came together to destroy
Guatemalan democracy: Yanqui Imperialism, the military cliques, the Archbishopric and latifundism. The
three last constitute the *Antipatria*. In its service are
mercenary journalists and intellectuals, pseudo-univer-
sity oligarchs, servile politicians of the Dictatorship,
agricultural barons, and stateless traffickers. This crew
maintains the usurper in power. Guatemala is subju-
gated today by Washington gold, the bayonets of treason, the clerical Inquisition, and the revived masters of
forced labor (*la encomienda rediviva*). Its task? The
most execrable in history!

. . .

It is also logical that Central America should observe
the North American watchword of "peace and order."
. . . The abjectness of the Government of the Antipatria
with regard to expressions of international policy is such
that it has gone to the extreme of designating the
representative of another country as the representative
of Guatemala. One of the representatives of Castillo
Armas to the Ninth Meeting of the General Assembly of
the United Nations was the protagonist in the following
anecdote. Before he left on his mission, a friend asked
him about the statements or points of view that the
Guatemalan delegation was going to present in the
conference. He answered: "This time there will be no
problem to afflict us. According to what my traveling
companion, Licenciado Luis Beltranena (a prominent
member of the delegation), has said, President Castillo

Armas has decided that the representative of the Dominican Republic should be the Guatemalan spokesman in the General Assembly of the ONU. Therefore (he sighed deeply as he said it), the Guatemalan vote will always agree with the vote of the United States. . . ."

. . .

The realistic and practical plan of rural credit set up by the Revolution will be replaced by a deceitful project called "Supervised Rural Credit." Those who understand these matters know that such a system requires a larger staff, more money, and more [bureaucratic] machinery than would be necessary to buy all the land of Guatemala and donate it to the landless peasant. It is an attempt to fool the people, to make them believe that the "Americans" know what they are doing and that the Guatemalan technicians are incompetents. These are projects that will never be accomplished because they cannot be accomplished—and also because the peasant himself resists the repulsive demagogy of his oppressors.

In order to throw the servants of the State out of their jobs, it was necessary to receive technical help. The journal of the reaction says that the "bureaucracy" of Arbenz is going to be finished, and to accomplish this objective they called in the best experts of the FBI, who were empowered to draw up interminable lists of "reds" that have been ousted from their work without regard to their competency or technical efficiency. The imperial persecution is called today in Guatemala "improvement of the public administration."

. . .

Pharisees! scribes and centurions of the Empire! do not forget that in Asia and in Africa (soon it will be in America), the slave countries have set out for the crusade of their liberation! The Colonial subjugation, regardless of its actual power, will collapse like a colossus of clay before the rebellion of the people. The solidarity of the despoiled victims will smash the pride of the exploiters. The cupidity of the powerful will carry them to their own destruction. Asian, African and American *natives*—as you call them contemptuously—will demolish your imperial idols. And the people of Guatemala, who for ten years lived in an anarchistic communion, are standing up and are on the eve of going into liberating battle.

17

*Consultant Group Jointly
Appointed by the Economic
Commission for Latin America
and the Organization of
American States*

LATIN AMERICAN VIEWS
AND OPINIONS ON
FOREIGN INVESTMENT

The Latin American Free Trade Association
(LAFTA) was organized by the signing of the Treaty
of Montevideo on February 18, 1960, among seven
nations: Argentina, Brazil, Chile, Mexico, Paraguay,
Peru, and Uruguay. Designed to promote economic

From report of the Consultant Group Jointly Appointed by
the Economic Commission for Latin America and the Organization of American States, *Foreign Private Investment in the Latin
American Free Trade Area* (New York: United Nations, Department of Economic and Social Affairs, 1961), pp. 18–19. (Sales
No. 60. II. G. 5.) Reprinted by permission of the United Nations
Publications Board.

development by reducing tariffs and stimulating intra-regional exchange of commodities, LAFTA also made for a number of problems, including policies toward foreign investment with its effects upon economic growth and trade. A joint committee was set up by ECLA and the OAS in December 1959 to study the problem of foreign investment in the LAFTA area. In its report the Committee summarized and compared the laws and attitudes affecting foreign investment in the seven countries. If there was a "Latin American Viewpoint" it seems to have escaped the Committee, which found that each nation had a distinct set of laws and views.

Only a few generalizations can be safely made with respect to the opinions and views on foreign private investment in the seven signatories of the Montevideo Treaty. Among these might be mentioned *official policies* recognizing the need for a foreign capital and assigning to it an important role in the economic development process; *business opinion,* which favors foreign capital in joint ventures and in non-competing activities; and *public opinion,* which is usually uninformed and uninterested.

It must be noted, however, that while the above generalizations are more or less relevant to all seven member States, opinion varies in each country and in each economic sector from deeply rooted anti-foreign sentiment to outright approval of unlimited foreign enterprises, the majority opinion being rather against than in favor of foreign capital.

Underlying these reactions are various historical, political, and economic factors. The first two are of long standing and are compounded of many elements, including the effects of the social radicalism of recent decades, the alleged colonial policy of more developed areas and the universal popular fear of size and influence. Economic factors, however, have also become major determinants of long-term governmental policy, and it is in this area that is centered the conditional support of foreign investment, influenced by the theory that profits and remittances form an uncompensated drain on exchange resources, by demands that foreign capital should complement and not compete with domestic industry, and by pressure on Governments to channel foreign investment into basic or new sectors, limit profit and dividend remittances and progressively nationalize foreign enterprise.

It is natural that the official policies, deriving from each country's needs as well as from the pressures and influences briefly noted above, should differ considerably from country to country. Peru, which has the most simplified official regulations for the entry of foreign capital, is among the industrially less developed countries, while Chile, which has one of the most elaborate systems for determining the advisability of each foreign investment, is—in relation to its market—very highly industrialized. Argentina and Brazil occupy intermediate positions, both having approval systems which take into account the interests of established industrialists, although this characteristic is much more pronounced in the case of Argentina than of Brazil. The systems in effect in Uruguay and Paraguay are more promotive than restrictive or selective in character.

Mexico occupies a somewhat unique position; while legally making no distinction between foreign and domestic enterprise, it quite frankly assigns a complementary role to new foreign capital and holds that "it should not compete favorably with existing Mexican enterprises nor displace national capital nor frustrate its future development." Further, "such capital should not utilize national savings" in such a manner as to reduce resources "which naturally correspond to national enterprises." Within the Government itself there are powerful sectors which hold that private foreign capital should only be encouraged to enter basic industries if willing to accept a minority participation in joint enterprises.

As regards regulations governing the remittance of dividends and profits, governmental attitudes have become more liberal in the last decade. In no LAFTA country is there any control exercised over such remittances at the present time, although policies and existing regulations with respect to capital imports vary considerably. In the case of Peru, the legal prerequisites for establishment are precisely the same as for domestic investors, while in Chile an application has to be made to the Foreign Investment Committee (*Comité de Inversiones Extranjeras*) prior to registration of a foreign enterprise for the purpose of securing certain remittance guarantees. In Mexico, the legal requirements are much the same as in Peru, although in practice new industries, if they wish to have the good will of the Government—an essential element for successful operation—must keep within the policy boundaries previously described. In Argentina and Brazil, existing regulations provide for an application to the Advisory Committee on Foreign Investments (*Comisión Asesora de Inversiones Extranjeras*) in the former, and to the Foreign Trade Department (*Carteira de Comércio Exterior*) of the *Banco do Brasil* in the latter. In the case of Brazil, the regulations fall within the category of import control rather than that of foreign investment control, while the reverse is true in Argentina.

It should be stressed that, legally speaking, firms do

not have to take advantage of foreign investment incentive laws and, except where special restrictive legislation rules otherwise, are free to establish themselves and to make their remittances through free-exchange markets. In practice, the additional guarantee of future free access to such markets is usually sought by the foreign investor through registration.

In general, special tax and other incentives, when provided, are extended equally to foreign and domestic investors. In Brazil and Chile, the only advantage not extended to domestic enterprise is the right to import equipment without the payment of exchange surcharges (prior deposits in the case of Chile), although in Brazil, in cases considered of special interest to economic development, both foreign and local investors may be granted a rate of exchange (the so-called "cost of exchange rate") more favorable than the free-market rate.

Domestic business attitudes towards private foreign investment may be summed up as favoring such investment in basic or new fields, opposing it in competing fields and favoring joint domestic foreign ventures over outright foreign enterprise.

These generalizations must be refined, however, to portray correctly the varying degrees to which they are valid in business and particularly in industrial circles in the LAFTA countries.

Top officials of the leading industrial associations in Argentina and Chile, as well as many of the larger industrialists, tend to stress equality of opportunity for domestic industries rather than protection from competition from enterprises established by foreign capital. However, the rank and file of the membership of those associations was found to be far less reticent in demanding that fields developed by domestic capital be reserved to it. In Brazil, both views are held, the latter predominating over the former. In Mexico, feeling reflects government attitudes far more than is the case in the other three most industrialized countries of the Free-Trade Area, the opinion being very strong indeed that foreign capital, especially in the case of basic industries, should associate itself with domestic interests.

The preference for joint ventures is nowhere so strong as in Mexico, although sentiment in this regard is growing in Brazil. Reactions in both Argentina and Chile tend to be more theoretical than in Brazil and Mexico, where experience with joint ventures is much more extensive.

Support for foreign private capital is stronger in those countries where industrialization is less advanced. Thus, in Peru the domestic business community appears to be quite favorable to foreign investment although some reserve was encountered, particularly in the case of the textile industry, where opposition to further new investments from abroad was voiced.

18

Mario Ramón Beteta

MEXICAN GOVERNMENT POLICY TOWARDS FOREIGN INVESTORS

The following selection spells out in detail the conditions placed upon foreign investment in Mexico, one of the LAFTA countries surveyed in the preceding document. In contrast to the strong anti-foreign stands of González Casanova and Bauer Paíz, Mario Ramón Beteta, manager of the Banco de México, recognizes the utility of foreign investments in fomenting economic development. However, he notes, foreign capital must accept the limitations imposed by Mexican nationalist policies and legislation. These government actions mark out large areas of the economy for state and private national ownership, control and development. They also place burdens on foreign-controlled businesses. But the rewards offered by the dynamic Mexican economy, he contends, provide sufficient balm.

The economic and social prosperity of Mexico must depend basically on the efforts of the Mexican people, and on an intensified and constant endeavor to in-

From Mario Ramón Beteta, "Government Policy Towards Foreign Investors," *The Statist* (London, January 8, 1965; Mexico: "A *Statist* Survey"), pages 21–23. Reprinted by permission of the publisher.

crease domestic savings. We are aware, however, that the achievement of economic progress in the shortest possible time demands our very scrupulous attention to the complementary part that foreign resources and investments from abroad can play concurrently with Mexican resources. An accelerated rate of investment is needed to reach higher levels of employment and production, and since Mexico adheres to a non-inflationary policy, resources from abroad constitute a very important contribution and augment attainable goals in domestic savings. Thus, the first thing to be said is that Mexico does want foreign investment.

In our view, the encouragement of investment in general, and foreign investment in particular, does not depend on artificial incentives but on a healthy, stable and dynamic economy. An unstable, weak or stagnating economic system will be viewed with distrust, even when artificial measures are taken to attract and protect foreign investments. Moreover, Mexico enjoys a social order and political stability that we include among our most valuable assets. And then, again, in the words of the just retired President López Mateos: "Foreign investors obtain reasonable profits and are free, if they so desire, to export both profits and the amortization of their capital. . . ." Indeed, Mexico has a very deep-rooted tradition of free convertibility and transferability of its currency which the country has lived up to even in times of crisis. We are one of the very few members of the International Monetary Fund that has not, at one time or another, imposed exchange restrictions, and we have the firm intention not to do so in the foreseeable future.

Type of Foreign Investment Desired

A second point to be clarified is what kind of foreign investment Mexico wants. This follows directly from our concept of foreign investment as an integral part of the general plan to promote the economic advancement of our people. We have no Foreign Investment Code but Government policy, as expressed in several laws, administrative regulations and public pronouncements, consistently underlines three basic ideas: that foreign investment must promote our economic development, must be adjusted to our social environment and must be carried out in accordance with our legal structure.

To take the last point first. Inasmuch as foreign investors are going to operate and obtain their profits in Mexico, they must submit to the laws, the courts, and the institutions of this country. If this places some limitations upon them, it also grants them the protection and security of an established legal order. We believe that it is extremely difficult for any sovereign state to give greater protection and security to foreign capital than to its own. But let me emphasize that foreign capital is treated with the same respect and has the same effective legal safeguards as does domestic capital. Several constitutional and legal dispositions guarantee the legitimate interests of all private investors in Mexico.

Outside certain specified fields of activity, foreigners are free from any legal restrictions on investing up to 100 per cent in an enterprise as long as they consider themselves as Mexican with respect to their investments and do not invoke the protection of their respective governments. There have been several attempts to promote an International Investment Code that would guarantee a special status to foreign investments. Our country has always refused to participate in any such agreement.

In general, Mexico feels that foreign investment can be particularly beneficial when it stirs the mobilization of internal savings for investment purposes, when it brings about technological and productive advance, and when it puts special emphasis on the utilization of our natural and human resources. We look for foreign enterprise taking roots, understanding our ways of life and adapting to our own idiosyncrasies. In other words, foreign investors should not be inspired exclusively by the desire to obtain profits, but should rather determine to become a permanent part of the nation's productive process.

There is also a tendency to grant special facilities to those mixed-capital corporations in which the majority of the stockholders are Mexican. This is the case, for instance, with the Mining Law which provides that new mining concessions can only be granted to Mexican companies or to mixed corporations with a maximum foreign participation of 49 per cent. Impressed by the fact that ownership of the large corporations in other countries is widely distributed and that often there are more stockholders than employees, we would like to see something similar in Mexico. We would be glad to have the ownership of enterprises operating here divided among numerous shareholders and for foreign or mixed-capital corporations to be no exception to this principle.

Joint Ventures

We have deliberately stimulated joint ventures through various measures and incentives. Experience has shown that the combination of capital is useful from many points of view. Public opinion is much more favorable towards companies that follow this policy than towards those exclusively foreign-owned. Domestic investors and workers, in particular, react favorably and perfectly aware that foreign participation means not only additional capital but also administrative experience and technological know-how. A healthy mobilization of domestic capital is frequently stimulated. But the advantages of partnership are not all on the Mexican side. Apart from creating a favorable public opinion, Mexican associates can contribute greatly to the joint investment through their knowledge and experience concerning local environment, labor relations, commercial channels, distribution services, official paperwork and so on. And it should be remembered that the foreign investor who acquires 49 per cent, or even less, of a company's stock, can still have decisive influence on the direction of the company, since it is most likely that the remaining stock will be distributed among several domestic investors.

Specific Fields for Foreign Investment

In strong contrast to the situation at the beginning of the present century, or even 30 years ago, the tendency now is for foreign investment to go into secondary and tertiary activities. One of the causes has been the Mexican Government's policy of nationalising basic resources and directly operating basic utilities; but another has been the growth of the economy and our domestic market, with the result that these activities have come to be regarded as dynamic investments with a promising future.

Mexicans are not particularly happy about foreign investment being attracted to commerce as such, i.e., to mere distribution activities. On the other hand, we believe that investment in industry, and particularly manufacturing, contributes in a real and effective way to our industrialization process. Moreover, we are trying to diversify industrial production not only to substitute imported products but also to increase our capacity to export manufactured products.

We also believe that Mexico's economic development

has reached a stage when reasonable possibilities exist for investment in capital goods industries. We realize that difficulties are involved, but consider it worth investigating specific projects where the size of our domestic market along with export possibilities offer real prospects for the production of capital goods under internationally competitive and attractive conditions.

Among specific expanding industries, one might mention electronics, the chemical industry—especially petrochemicals and pharmaceuticals—and the manufacture of electrical and mechanical goods. One need only refer to the 500 new industrial activities listed by the Government just over three years ago as fields of insufficient investment, to realize the wide investment opportunities that Mexico has to offer; moreover, about half of the new industries listed have already been taken up and are in varying stages of planning or completion. Another useful guide to Mexico's industrial needs can be found in circulars of the Ministry of Finance, indicating what new and necessary industries are eligible for diverse incentives, mainly tax reductions, that can be authorized by the Federal Government. Similar incentives are available in most of the individual States of the Mexican Republic.

. . .

A Few Misunderstandings

One question that gives rise to frequent discussion—even among our Mexican entrepreneurs—is the position of private enterprise *vis-à-vis* State participation in the economy. We believe that private initiative has a principal part to play. President Díaz Ordaz reiterated during his election campaign that "Mexico needs more and better private enterprise and better State enterprise . . . these two factors can and should work har-

moniously for the achievement of faster economic development. . . . As a general rule . . . the State should
confine itself in this respect within the limits clearly
marked by the Constitution, as, for instance, the general
fields of petroleum, coal, power and communications.
However, this should not be construed as meaning that
the Government will abstain from participating whenever the negligence and/or omission of private entrepreneurs should make it advisable to do so."

There is some investment that cannot be left undone,
whether it be undertaken by private enterprise or by
public agencies, without holding back economic progress and falling into a retrogressive state, with consequences difficult to imagine. And, as the Punta del Este
Charter points out, foreign capital must be combined
with public funds as well as private domestic capital.

This position is perfectly consistent with an attitude
of respect and stimulus to private business. As long as
businessmen are active and dynamic in their authorized
activities, they should not be fearful of unfair competition from the Government. There is no danger that the
State will invade their general territory, nor is there a
threat to a legally established business of ever finding
itself under pressure by the Government to sell out to
the State.

The Mexican Constitution guarantees the right to
hold private property and prohibits confiscation. It also
regulates the procedures of expropriation, demanding
that it must be for reasons of public welfare and
through indemnification. There have, after all, been
only two important cases of expropriation in the recent
history of Mexico, those of the oil companies in 1938
and those of rural properties divided up in our Agrarian
Reform Program. It should be stressed that the more
recent purchases of certain companies and their stock

by the Government were normal business transactions. Actually, the shares of the Mexican Light and Power Company, for instance, were acquired by the State in 1960 above the normal market price and the foreign stockholders stated publicly that they were satisfied with the transaction.

Although Mexican nationalism is traditionally strong, we are convinced that the present stage of history demands an interdependence of nations and mutual co-operation. We thus regard direct foreign investment favorably when it serves to complement our economic development efforts, and we accept as justified the foreign investor's preoccupation with security and reasonable profits. Isolationist ideas on national economies as autocratic entities, maintaining only the most indispensable relations with the outside world, are outdated. At the same time, present thinking assumes a spirit of mutual benefit and respect and equity in commercial relations. Mexico wholeheartedly welcomes anyone who wishes, within our social environment and legal framework, to participate in our task of promoting economic progress.

19

Werner Baer and
Mario Henrique Simonsen

AMERICAN CAPITAL AND
BRAZILIAN NATIONALISM

Werner Baer, of the Economic Growth Center of Yale University, and the Brazilian economist Mario Henrique Simonsen have examined the role of American capital in Brazil and the Brazilian reaction to it. With a deft touch they bare a number of fallacies believed by both sides, indicate areas of misunderstanding, and explain the work and function of foreign capital and why it often rubs Brazilians the wrong way. In a succinct article they have successfully summed up many of the pros and cons of foreign investment, answered questions, rebutted arguments and pointed out problems which resist solution.

That this article is based on Brazilian experiences is fortuitous. Much the same could be written about any Latin American nation receiving large foreign investments.

Many North Americans can hardly believe how much Latin American nationalists dislike and distrust foreign

From Werner Baer and Mario Henrique Simonsen, "American Capital and Brazilian Nationalism," *The Yale Review*, Vol. LIII, No. 2 (Winter 1964, December 1963), pp. 192–198. Copyright Yale University. Reprinted by permission of the publisher.

capital. North Americans know that wherever industrialization has taken place in Latin America, foreign capital has played a major role. In Brazil, for instance, it was foreign capital that built the first railroads, the communication and light systems, the automobile industry, the new consumer durable industry, and the capital goods industry. The North American sees all this as an occasion for gratitude, but the Brazilian nationalist sees it as exploitation. He argues that, far from really adding to the national well-being, foreign capital (by which he usually means United States capital, though in fact investors from many other countries have participated in financing Brazil's new industries) has been bleeding the country, that it has taken more money out than it has brought in. He claims that, far from helping the country to industrialize, it has distorted investment to such an extent as to postpone "real" industrialization.

The arguments against foreign capital all center on the subject of exploitation. Nationalists claim that foreign capital has come to Brazil only because it has seen there the possibility of earning exorbitant profits, profits many times greater than it could earn at home. This attitude was unforgettably presented to the Brazilian people in the late President Vargas's widely publicized suicide letter, where the despairing president dramatically accused foreign firms of making profits as high as five hundred per cent a year. The figure, needless to say, was based on erroneous calculations, but it has been firmly imprinted in the minds of countless Brazilians. Another claim is that direct foreign investment often consists of obsolete machinery, already fully depreciated for tax purposes in the country of origin, which enters at an overvalued price. (This charge has been most often made against the automobile industry.) Nationalists further maintain that the outflow of profits to investors is many times as great as the inflow of new capital, with the result that the country is bled of its resources. They argue that foreign concerns actually bring in relatively small amounts of capital and, whenever possible, use local sources of credit, that is, the savings of Brazilians. Resentment against foreign banks operating in Brazil is particularly strong. Nationalists see the chief function of such banks as capturing the deposits of Brazilians in order to lend them to foreign enterprises, and thus direct domestic savings away from Brazilian investors. Finally, nationalists maintain that foreign capital has concentrated on industries producing "superfluous" goods—television, Coca-cola, automobiles, and so on. This argument goes beyond the purely economic by suggesting that there has been a conspiracy to create tastes for the frivolous products of light industry so that the development of heavy industry, which would make Brazil more economically independent, will actually be delayed.

With some exceptions, these arguments do not find much support in the facts. Foreign banks do not siphon off Brazilian savings into enterprises controlled from abroad; the largest proportion of their deposits comes from those very enterprises. The majority of foreign enterprises do not produce "superfluous" goods; for example, only one American company produces passenger cars, while the other two produce only utility vehicles and tractors. The outflow of profit is not greater than the inflow of capital. In the years 1955 to 1961, a period when there were no restrictions on the movements of capital or its earnings, the inflow was much greater than the remittance of earnings. When nationalists reply that a large part of the profit remittances do not appear in the balance of payments because they are hidden in such items as payments for royalties and technical assistance or in the form of overvaluation of imports and undervaluation of exports, the figures still do not support them.

The one economic argument that finds support in the facts is that foreign capital will not go to Brazil (or to other underdeveloped countries) unless it can expect a larger profit than it makes at home. The expectation of higher profits is necessary not only because of the greater trouble of setting up an enterprise abroad, but also because of the greater risks, real or alleged, of carrying on business in uncertain political conditions such as most investors believe prevail in Brazil and elsewhere in the underdeveloped world. The investor thinks that he has to earn his money back fast, because nobody knows what will happen in a few years. To an American businessman all this makes perfect sense, but many Brazilians cannot understand why Americans expect to earn higher profits in a poor country like Brazil than in a rich country like the one they come from; they cannot understand why foreign investors have to earn their money back with such speed when it means that the foreign resources introduced into Brazil will be quickly offset by the fast withdrawal of resources when earnings and the original investment are repatriated.

These objections are probably unanswerable, until and unless Brazilians achieve a far greater sophistication in economic understanding than they now have. Objections to the high profits made by North American investors may be in some measure met by the steps currently being taken by the United States to offer better insurance against the hazards of investing in underdeveloped countries. A good deal of the responsibility for Brazilian misconceptions of the actual operation of foreign capital in their country lies with the foreign firms themselves. They simply do not make any effort to get

their side of the story before the Brazilian people. The
advertising of United States firms in Brazil is limited to
the direct selling of products; the kind of institutional
advertising that has been so successful in selling business, in getting its aims and problems before the public,
is unknown. One never sees in Brazil advertisements
showing what a company does for its workers, what
community programs it has developed, etc. This lack
could be easily remedied.

There are other changes that could be made with no
great trouble or expense to create a friendlier atmosphere. For example, a great many foreign enterprises
use the untranslated name of the parent company, a
daily reminder to a sensitive people of foreign economic
domination. Everywhere the consumer turns he is faced
by foreign, especially North American names—Palm-
olive, Willys, Esso, Shell, Gillette, Crush, Spray, General Electric, and on and on. The foreign name is often
localized by adding "do Brazil" to the name of the
parent company, but that does little good, especially
when *Brasil* is spelled with a foreign *z*, which is galling
to many people. Sometimes, of course, the foreign name
should be retained; when it designates a famous brand,
the name increases sales and thus creates jobs for
Brazilians. But some of the companies can make no
such claim for the names they use. Light for the city of
Rio de Janeiro, for instance, is furnished by a company
that calls itself "Rio Light." Brazilians who object may
be oversensitive, but many New Yorkers would dislike it
if in 1963 they paid their light bills to the Allgemeine
Lichtgesellschaft von Neu Jork.

Another thing that could be done with some ease
would be a planned effort to improve the integration of
North American businessmen in Brazilian society. Brazilians, like the residents of other underdeveloped coun-

tries, resent the fact that outsiders come to their country to make money but otherwise isolate themselves from it. United States executives and their families do not expect to settle there permanently; often the man sees his period of work in Latin America as simply one rung in a ladder of success most of which is to be climbed elsewhere, and his family are not necessarily the most willing camp followers. They do not learn Portuguese, the children do not attend local schools, the parents keep to their own clubs and social activities. Back in the United States these same families might keep to their own clubs and social activities, and the Brazilian businessman may sometimes be just as exclusive socially, but the fact remains that the isolationism practiced by the American business community gives a most unfavorable impression of colonialism. The government of the United States, working discreetly through the trade associations, could have considerable influence in persuading companies with substantial interests overseas to establish training programs for their personnel going abroad similar to the training programs for foreign service officers.

Some changes need to be made that are more significant economically. North American firms should not have Brazilian technicians working side by side with colleagues from the United States at a third the salary, yet one often hears of such situations. The subsidiaries of North American firms in Brazil should open their capital to Brazilians. Many are now closed companies, or offer only nonvoting stock to Brazilian investors. If they were to open up and spread their shares among the rising middle classes, they would automatically receive widespread support by an influential section of society. Wherever the shares of a company are commonly traded on the Brazilian Stock Exchanges, such as Belgo-

Mineira (Benelux), Souza Cruz (British), Mannesmann (German), and Willys (United States), that company is never singled out for criticism by nationalist groups. The usual argument against opening the companies to Brazilian investment is that, in an inflationary atmosphere like Brazil's, the reinvestment of profits necessary for expansion would be impossible if a large portion of the profits had to be distributed to shareholders. It is well known, however, that most Brazilian corporations distribute a very small proportion of their earnings and that the growth-conscious Brazilian investor is quite happy with a very low dividend to stock value ratio in companies with a high growth potential.

Foreign firms also need to be more respectable in their use of money to secure economic advantage. Bribery is frequently charged against outside enterprises by Brazilian nationalists, and in some instances the charge is accurate. Newspapers receive financial rewards for favoring policies friendly to foreign enterprises; a few years ago a prominent United States–dominated public utilities company was reported to have bribed a substantial number of representatives in a local legislature to get a favorable vote on a rate increase. Other companies, especially mining, cold storage production, and the pharmaceutical industry, have been accused of bribing officials. The fact that bribery cannot exist unless there are bribable officials, or that Brazilian firms use bribery too, does not refute the charge; it only increases the odiousness of foreign capitalists who exploit weaknesses in the local society to their own advantage.

A more general problem is sometimes involved here. In the United States businesses think it is only natural and right to attempt to influence legislation, and in a pluralistic society they are right, so long as they recognize and observe proper limits for such activities. But when American businessmen abroad try to put pressure on influential politicians or buy up or finance newspapers favorable to their interests, quite a different interpretation will be put on their efforts—they will be seen as illegitimate interference by foreigners in domestic affairs.

The record, then, of foreign capital in Brazil is not all favorable. Its economic effects have been undoubtedly beneficial, but its social side-effects have been sometimes unfortunate. Yet even these social side-effects are hardly sufficient to account for the bitterness of nationalist resentments and their great popular acceptance, so apparent to anyone who has lived in Brazil. There are increasing numbers of "nationalists" in the Brazilian Congress, recently severe profit remittance laws have been passed, currently there is a wave of sentiment for nationalizing public utilities.

The North American is likely to look for Communism behind all this, and in fact the anti-foreign capital arguments of the nationalists agree perfectly with the Communist line, and there is a distinct possibility that Communists have played an active part in formulating, elaborating, and propagating those arguments. But Communism fails to explain their popularity. There are very few Brazilian Communists and very many Brazilians who believe in the villainy of foreign capital. Other explanations must be sought.

One explanation lies in the need for a scapegoat, so marked in many underdeveloped countries. Poor people with no training in economics need an emotionally satisfying explanation of their plight, and opportunistic politicians throw them the foreign capitalist for the purpose. Soon perfectly sincere politicians echo the explanation, and soon it has countless believers.

Brazilian industrialists concerned about foreign competition contribute to the support of nationalist, antiforeign groups. They are much given to the argument that foreign capital is monopolistic, that it uses its resources to eliminate competition from local producers and thus control the domestic market. This argument, which was recently successful in keeping out foreign competition in aluminum, textiles, and metallurgy, has some basis: there are some prominent instances of monopolistic practices by foreign firms. But the Brazilian industrialists are really trying to maintain or regain the monopolistic positions they enjoyed before the arrival of foreign competition.

The fact that Brazilian nationalism so often finds its target in North American business may seem puzzling, since Germans, Japanese, and Italians have substantial investments in Brazil. But there is more capital from the United States in Brazil than from any other nation, and besides the United States today happens to be the major power in the world, with all the conspicuousness that comes with size. Furthermore, there are many Brazilian immigrants from Germany, Japan, and Italy, so that capital and its accompanying management are less suspect when they come from those countries. The American businessman is nearly always a temporary resident; he sees Brazil as a place to make money but rarely as a place worth settling in.

The United States government seems to be confronted by a dilemma. On the one hand, it seeks to encourage private capital to go to underdeveloped countries and help them develop; one of the objectives of the Alliance for Progress is to encourage private investment in Latin America. On the other hand, private capital will inevitably create some, if not all, of the kinds of problems that have been described here. But the facts are the facts. If private capital had not flowed into Brazil in the last fifteen years, the economy of the country might have grown at a much slower rate, and the resulting social tensions might have been a good deal more severe than the tensions created by the presence of private capital from the United States.

Suggestions for Additional Reading

While there is no single bibliographical guide to the topic of foreign investments in Latin America, several of the general guides to Latin American studies and general economics provide listings of pertinent sources. For historical coverage of this topic, see the two volumes compiled by the Staff of the Bureau for Economic Research in Latin America of Harvard University entitled *The Economic Literature of Latin America; A Tentative Bibliography* (Cambridge, Mass., 1935). Recent coverage is provided by the indispensable *Handbook of Latin American Studies* (Gainesville, Fla., 1935–   ), the social scientist's excellent guides: *Bulletin of The Public Affairs Information Service [PAIS]* (New York, 1915–   ), the UNESCO-sponsored publication by the International Committee for Social Science Documentation, *International Bibliography of the Social Sciences: International Bibliography of Economics* (Paris and Chicago, 1955–   ) which lists numerous European and foreign-language publications, and the lately deceased monthly, *Hispanic American Report* (Stanford, Calif., 1948–1964) with a most complete annual index, which gave a fine detailed account of political developments in Latin America, many of which affected and were affected by foreign investments. S. A. Baytich's *Latin America, A Bibliographic Guide* (Coral Gables, Fla., 1961) and Robin Humphreys' *Latin America; A Guide to the Literature in English* (Oxford, 1958) are also helpful. A fine guide has also been compiled by the Bank of Mexico, as number four in its *Serie de estudios especiales* entitled *Inversiones extranjeras* (Mexico, 1962). A wealth of information can be gleaned from United States Government documents which are listed monthly and indexed annually in the *Monthly Catalogue of United States Government Publications*. Equally valuable are the documents prepared by the United Nations, particularly the Economic Commission for Latin America, which are indexed in the *United Nations Documents Index*. The two guides to the scholarly *Hispanic American Historical Review*, edited by Ruth Latham Butler, *Guide to the Hispanic American Historical Review, 1918–1945* (Durham, N.C., 1950), and Charles Gibson, editor, assisted by E. V. Niemeyer, *Guide to the Hispanic American Historical Review, 1946–1955* (Durham, N.C., 1958) provide some material, while Simon Hanson's journal, *Inter-American Economic Affairs* (hereinafter cited as IAEA) (1947–   ), indexed by the *PAIS*, presents some of the best writing on Latin American economic problems in general. Excellent articles are also to be found in the *Journal of Latin American Studies* (1959–   ). The journals *Revista de economía* and *Investigación economica* of Mexico often feature articles concerning foreign investment, usually sharply nationalistic or even Marxist.

Problems of methodology and definition are treated in detail in Samuel Pizer and Frederick Cutler's study for the Office of Business Economics of the U.S. Department of Commerce, *U.S. Business Investments in Foreign Countries* (supplement to the *Survey of Current Business*) (Washington, D.C., 1960), pp. 76–85. Not all nations offer clear-cut figures or estimates. The difficulties of working with British figures are explained in the Royal Institute of International Affairs survey, *The Problem of International Investment* (London, 1937), Appendix I, pp. 333–346.

FACTS AND FIGURES

It will probably be impossible to ever total the entire amount of capital which has been invested in Latin American government bonds and direct investments. The best running accounts of the status of Latin American government bonds are found in two series of reports to disappointed bondholders: the *Annual Report of the Council of the Corporation of Foreign Bondholders* has been issued in London since 1873, and its American counterpart, the *Annual Report of the Foreign Bondholders Protective Council, Inc.*, has been issued in New York since 1935. Both reports contain much data on government issues from the mid-nineteenth century to the present. A list of British loans during the first decade of independence is given in Charles K. Webster's *Britain and the Independence of Latin America, 1812–1830*, Vol. I (Oxford, 1938), p. 560. For a full discussion, see J. Fred Rippy, *British Investments in Latin America, 1822–1949* (Minneapolis, Minn., 1949). The United States had an unfortunate experience with Latin American government bonds in the 1920's—the object of much of the Foreign Bondholders Protective Council's work —which is covered in the hearings before the U.S. Senate Finance Committee, 72nd Congress, 1st session, *Sale of Foreign Bonds or Securities in the United States* (Washington, D.C., 1931–1932), and Ilse Mintz, *Deterioration in the Quality of Foreign Bonds Issued in the United States* (New York, 1951). For further information on this matter, see Ralph A. Young, *Handbook of American Underwriting of Foreign Securities*, Washington, D.C., 1930 (U.S. Department of Commerce, Trade Promotion Series, No. 104), and Paul Dickens, *American Underwriting of Foreign Securities in 1931*, Washington, D.C., 1932 (U.S. Department of Commerce, Trade Information Bulletin No. 802).

Over-all summaries of investments in Latin America are hard to come by; many nations do not keep track of their nationals' activities and even the host countries keep only sparse records. (One exception is Mexico, where the annual report of the Bank of Mexico, *Asamblea general ordinaria de accionistas*, has, since 1940, included detailed estimates of investment in that country.) Almost unique is the compilation made by the Department of Economic and Social Affairs of the United Nations, *Foreign Capital in Latin America* (New York, 1955), which not only attempts to total all investments in Latin America, but summarizes national policies toward investments and the experience and position of the individual countries. This report is supplemented by the one prepared by the Consultant Group Jointly Appointed by the Economic Commission for Latin America and the Organization of American States, *Foreign Private Investment in the Latin American Free Trade Area* (New York, 1961), UN sales number 60.II.E.5. A short concise survey of foreign investments in Latin America in 1930 by totals of the major investing countries and by individual Latin American nations is to be found in M. Poblete Troncoso, "L'influence du capital étranger dans le développement économique de l'Amérique Latine," *Revue de L'Amérique Latine*, XXIII (Paris, July–September, 1932), pp. 245–260. The general trend of investment flow in the period 1919–1939 is covered in the United Nations study, *International Capital Movements During the Inter-War Period* (New York, 1949), sales number 1949.II.D.2., while a second monograph, *The International Flow of Private Capital, 1946–1952* (New York, 1954), sales number 1954.II.D.1., carries the coverage down to the decade of the 1950's. These studies show that Latin America has been a relatively minor field for investment by European nations in the twentieth century and that there is a lack of precise data on investments made by nations outside the United States. The flow of capital into Latin America during the decade of the 1950's is covered by the report of the United Nations Economic Committee for Latin America, *External Financing in the Economic Development of Latin America* (Mar del Plata, Argentina [?], May, 1963), document number E/CN.12/649, which also includes a long section on the activities of United States and international lending institutions in Latin America. The Office of Economic Affairs of the General Secretariat of the Pan American Union has prepared a factual monograph, *The Flow of Capital from the European Economic Community to Latin America* (Washington, D.C., 1963). A continuing series of reports prepared for the General Assembly of the United Nations, *International Flow of Long-term Capital and Official Donations*, is issued periodically and covers the entire globe as well as Latin America. The latest report, for 1960–1962, was issued on October 24, 1963 as document number A/5546. The Economic Commission for Latin America's annual, *Economic Survey of Latin America* (New York, 1949–   ) usually has some material on foreign capital in the region as does its periodical, *Economic Bulletin for Latin America* (New York, 1956–   ).

By far the most extensive coverage of foreign investments by a single nation has been carried out in the United States by government agencies and private investigators. Cleona

Lewis' *America's Stake in International Investments* (Washington, D.C., 1938) is probably the classic study, which is supplemented by her book, *The United States and Foreign Investment Problems* (Washington, D.C., 1948). Professor J. Fred Rippy succinctly summarizes most of the national summaries turned up in individual estimates and government reports, tempered with his own extensive researches and that of other investigators, in *Globe and Hemisphere: Latin America's Place in the Postwar Foreign Relations of the United States* (Chicago, 1958), which also includes a number of chapters on U.S. Government ventures in aiding Latin America. Professor Rippy believes that political pressures for transient or personal projects has too often vitiated the gain which might otherwise be expected from government expenditures.

For the most part, pre-World War I statistics compiled for the U.S. Government were fragmentary and of varying unreliability, mostly consisting of on-the-spot estimates by consuls about the situation of the country of their assignment. The first reliable estimate was a truly monumental piece of research and compilation carried out by Frederic M. Halsey and published in 1918 by the U.S. Department of Commerce, Bureau of Foreign and Domestic Trade in its Special Agents Series No. 169 under the title *Investments in Latin America and the British West Indies,* with the exception of Mexico (Washington, D.C., 1918). While not featuring the various tables based on censes and questionnaires of the modern period, Halsey gave in fair detail a physical description of numerous enterprises and their properties, their history, and as much information as could be ascertained concerning their financial status. When the Department of Commerce came under the guidance of Herbert Hoover, Julius Klein was named chief of the Bureau and he directed Halsey to update his study, since conditions had changed and American investment was conservatively set at four billion dollars. Halsey's revision, with the aid of Guillermo B. Sherwell, was so voluminous that it was issued in four parts, which covered only Argentina, Uruguay and Paraguay, Chile, and Bolivia. They were published under the title, *Investments in Latin America,* U.S. Department of Commerce, Bureau of Foreign and Domestic Commerce,

Trade Information Bulletins: Nos. 362 (Argentina), 382 (Uruguay and Paraguay), 426 (Chile), and 466 (Bolivia) (Washington, D.C., 1925–1927). Unfortunately the series was never completed.

The late 1920's also produced two fine private studies: Max Winkler's *Investments of United States Capital in Latin America,* World Peace Foundation Pamphlets, Vol. XI, No. 6 (Boston, 1928), which, despite its title, contains much information concerning other nations, particularly Great Britain; and Robert W. Dunn's *American Foreign Investments* (New York, 1926), a survey of outstanding debts, public and private, presented in a stiffly impartial manner, with samples of contracts between Latin American governments and United States banking houses. The spirit of these studies was carried on in Willy Feuerlein and Elizabeth Hannan's *Dollars in Latin America* (New York, 1941), which emphasized the effects of the Great Depression on portfolio and direct investments.

In 1931, the United States Government began the publication of periodic surveys of private direct investments abroad by U.S. citizens and corporations. The result was a series of definitive studies: Paul D. Dickens, *American Direct Investments Abroad,* U.S. Bureau of Foreign and Domestic Commerce, Trade Information Bulletin No. 731 (Washington, D.C., 1930); Paul D. Dickens, *United States Foreign Investments,* U.S. Bureau of Foreign and Domestic Commerce, Economic Series No. 1 (Washington, D.C., 1938); Robert L. Sammons and M. Abelson, *American Direct Investments in Foreign Countries,* U.S. Bureau of Foreign and Domestic Commerce, Economic Series No. 20 (Washington, D.C., 1942); U.S. Treasury Department, *Census of American Owned Assets in Foreign Countries* (Washington, D.C., 1947); U.S. Department of Commerce, Office of Business Economics, *Direct Private Foreign Investments of the United States, Census of 1950* (Washington, D.C., 1953); U.S. Department of Commerce, Office of Business Economics, *U.S. Investments in the Latin American Economy* (Washington, D.C., 1957); Samuel Pizer and Frederick Cutler, *U.S. Business Investments in Foreign Countries* (Washington, D.C., 1960).

Currently, figures and analyses of United States interests

all over the world are compiled annually and published in detail in one of the fall issues of the *Survey of Current Business* of the U.S. Department of Commerce, often supplemented in other issues by analyses of U.S. investments in manufacturing abroad. A most interesting analysis of recent developments has been done by Leland L. Johnson in an article, "U.S. Private Investment in Latin America Since the Rise of Castro," *IAEA*, Vol. XVIII, No. 3 (Winter, 1964), 53–75.

The best over-all summary of British investments is J. Fred Rippy's *British Investments in Latin America, 1822–1949* (Minneapolis, Minn., 1949). Professor Rippy has not only summarized the major available sources, but he presents numerous figures based on his compilations of statistics in various financial publications. This latter work has been criticized, but it does present the best figures available under the circumstances. Pre-1914 surveys are Irving Stone, "British Capital in Latin America" (unpublished doctoral dissertation, Columbia University, 1962), Alexander K. Cairncross, *Home and Foreign Investments, 1870–1910* (Cambridge, 1953), Albert H. Imlah, *Economic Elements in the Pax Britannica* (Cambridge, 1958), and Leland H. Jenks, *The Migration of British Capital to 1875* (New York, 1938). Recent British activities are covered in a pamphlet of the Federation of British Industries, *British Industry and the Development of Latin America* (London, 1961). The publication in the *Board of Trade Journal* of the study, "United Kingdom Direct Overseas Investment, 1958–1960," Vol. CLXXXI, No. 336 (October 6, 1961), pp. 715–720, lists all transactions on a yearly basis but fails to total them. Hence one knows how much was sent abroad in 1960, but not the total value of British investments in any area as of that date. Probably the best source of running estimates is to be found in the *South American Journal*, published in London, particularly its January issues.

Studies of French and German interests in Latin America are notably scarce, and figures are few outside of United Nations publications, particularly the abovementioned 1955 study of *Foreign Capital in Latin America*. Also see J. P. Guinot, "Les investissements extérieurs de l'Allemagne et de la France," *Observation économique, sociale et financière,*

Vol. CXXXVII (Paris, May, 1959), 3–27. Some historical data can be culled from Professor Rippy's "French Investments in Latin America," *IAEA*, Vol. II, No. 2 (1948), 58–71, and Georges La Fond, *La France en Amérique Latine* (Paris, 1922). German interests are surveyed in Professor Rippy's "German Investments in Latin America," *Journal of Business of the University of Chicago*, Vol. XXI (April, 1948), 63–73, and the anonymous, *Die Deutschen Interessen in Argentinien, Chile, Bolivien und Peru* (Berlin, 1916). The indefatigable Professor Rippy has also surveyed Italian interests in "Italian Immigrants and Investments in Latin America," *IAEA*, Vol. III, No. 2 (1949), 25–37.

Concerning individual Latin American countries, varying amounts of information can be gleaned from a series of studies by the International Bank for Reconstruction and Development published by the Johns Hopkins Press, Baltimore, Maryland, under two uniform titles: *Basis of a Development Program for Colombia* (1952), and *Guatemala* (1951), and *The Economic Development of Jamaica* (1957), *Mexico* (1953), *Nicaragua* (1952), and *Venezuela* (1961).

CASES

The number of studies available covering cases of investment of foreign capital in Latin America and their effects are legion. The following represent only a sample of the incidents and literature available.

For the colonial period, Roland D. Hussey's *The Caracas Company, 1728–1784* (Cambridge, Mass., 1934) and Germán Arciniegas' *Germans in the Conquest of America* (New York, 1943) are excellent introductions to the as yet little explored field of capitalist enterprise in colonial Spanish America. Charles R. Boxer's *The Dutch in Brazil, 1624–1654* (Oxford, 1957) does as much for Portuguese America. John F. Normano's *Brazil; A Study in Economic Types* (Chapel Hill, N.C., 1935), also has excellent material on this period. Perhaps the best general coverage of this era with strong economic emphasis is Bailey W. Diffie's *Latin American Civilization: Colonial Period* (Harrisburg, Pa., 1945).

Early investment was often in government bonds. There is no single work surveying the entire history of those loans, although the lion's share was held by Great Britain up to World War I and is covered in Rippy's *British Investments* and Jenks's *British Capital . . . to 1875*. Some bond issues have been studied by Latin American writers, albeit in an emotional, nationalistic manner. For example, see Octavio Barroso's *Brasil, colonia de banqueiros* (*História dos emprestimos de 1824 a 1934*), 6th ed. (Rio de Janeiro, 1937). Interesting loans are also covered in studies by C. Allen True, "British Loans to the Mexican Government, 1822–1832," *Southwestern Social Science Quarterly*, Vol. XVII (1937), pp. 353–362; Ernesto Pitte, *Historia de un empréstito; La emisión de Buenos Aires de 1824* (Buenos Aires, 1962); César A. Herrera, "El empréstito Harmont" [Dominican Loan of 1869], *Boletín del Archivo general* (Ciudad Trujillo, Dominican Republic), Año X, Vol. X (September–December, 1947), pp. 266–274; Horacio Juan Cuccarese, "El empréstito inglés para obras públicas; Contribución a la historia financiera de la presidencia de Sarmiento," *Humanidades*, Vol. XXXVII, Pt. 2 (La Plata, Argentina, 1961), pp. 235–277. Contrast Pitte with Henry S. Ferns, *Britain and Argentina in the Nineteenth Century* (Oxford, 1960), chaps. 3–5. D. C. M. Platt's study, "British Bondholders in Nineteenth Century Latin America—Injury and Remedy," *IAEA*, Vol. XIV, No. 3 (Winter, 1960), pp. 3–43, is an interesting account for the methods of flotations and vicissitudes of the investors. For problems of American investors in the 1920's and 1930's when the United States became a large buyer of Latin American government securities, see references above.

Foreign investments have spurred many new economic developments. For British capital in Argentina, see Alejandro E. Bunge, *Ferrocarriles argentinos* (Buenos Aires, 1918), and Ferns, above. For Brazil's "new life," see Lincoln Gordon, *U.S. Manufacturing Investment in Brazil* (Cambridge, Mass., 1962). A most interesting story is that of the export of Peruvian guano, told by Jonathan V. Levin in his book, *The Export Economies; Their Pattern of Development in Historical Perspective* (Cambridge, Mass., 1960), pp. 27–123, supplemented by Geraldo Arosemena Garland's *El Coronel José Balta, 1814–1872* (Lima, 1945), which includes the story of the loans floated through the Dreyfus Brothers' guano contract and the public works these funds financed. The banana has probably been the root of more trouble than any other commodity with the possible exception of petroleum. Sharp criticism of the role of the fruit companies has been voiced in Carleton Beals, *Banana Gold* (Philadelphia, Pa., 1932), and the two studies of Charles D. Kepner, *Social Aspects of the Banana Industry* (New York, 1936) and, with J. H. Soothill, *The Banana Empire* (New York, 1935). Alberto Bauer Paíz in his book, *Como opera el capital yanqui en Centro América (El caso de Guatemala)* (Mexico, 1958), denounces the United Fruit Company from the viewpoint of a Guatemalan nationalist. Defenses of the company are to be found in Frederick U. Adams, *Conquest of the Tropics; The Story of the Creative Enterprises Conducted by the United Fruit Company* (New York, 1914); Samuel Crowther, *Rise and Romance of the American Tropics* (New York, 1929); Charles M. Wilson, *Empire in Green and Gold: The Story of the American Banana Trade* (New York, 1947), and the more documented study by Stacy May and Galo Plaza, *The United Fruit Company in Latin America* (Washington, 1958). Foreign investment in petroleum in Venezuela has been the subject of several pro and con controversies. Criticism is voiced by Edwin Lieuwen, *Petroleum in Venezuela* (Berkeley, Calif., 1954) and Rómulo Betancourt, *Venezuela: Política y petróleo* (Mexico, 1956). A sympathetic portrayal of the role of the leading American petroleum company in Venezuela is included in the National Planning Association's series, U.S. Business Performance Abroad, *The Creole Petroleum Corporation in Venezuela* (Washington, 1955), by Wayne C. Taylor and John Lindeman. For a generalized contrapuntal view, see Robert Engler, *The Politics of Oil* (New York, 1961).

Other studies of American capital in Latin America in the N.P.A. series include, *Sears, Roebuck de México, S.A.* (1953) by Richardson Wood and Virginia Keyser; *Casa Grace in Peru* (1954) by Eugene W. Burgess and F. H. Harbison; and *The General Electric Company in Brazil* (1961) by Theodore Geiger and Liesel Goode. Some 15 case studies of joint enterprises in Mexico, Brazil, and Colombia fill over 100 pages of Wolfgang G. Friedman and George Kalmanoff's *Joint International Business Ventures* (New York, 1961).

"The American Mediterranean," as the region of the Gulf of Mexico and the Caribbean Sea has been called, has been the special focus of United States interest. Several interesting studies of the work of foreign capital, particularly American, and its effect on local and hemisphere politics have been made. On the level of general surveys, see first the excellent scholarly studies of Dana G. Munro, *The Five Republics of Central America* (New York, 1918) and *The United States and the Caribbean Area* (Boston, 1934). Then contrast Munro's latest study, *Intervention and Dollar Diplomacy in the Caribbean, 1900–1920* (Princeton, N.J., 1964) with the Marxist-oriented book by Scott Nearing and Joseph Freedman, *Dollar Diplomacy; A Study in American Imperialism* (New York, 1926). For studies of individual countries, see Rafael de Nogales, *The Looting of Nicaragua* (New York, 1928) and Harold N. Denny, *Dollars for Bullets, The Story of American Rule in Nicaragua* (New York, 1929) which contrast with the views of President Coolidge's personal representative, Henry L. Stimson, *American Policy in Nicaragua* (New York, 1927); Melvin M. Knight, *Americans in Santo Domingo* (New York, 1928), Arthur C. Millspaugh, *Haiti Under American Control, 1915–1930* (Boston, 1931); and on Cuba, after the best general study of U.S.–Cuban relations, Russell H. Fitzgibbon's *Cuba and the United States, 1900–1935* (Menasha, Wis., 1935), for critiques of American capital see Leland H. Jenks, *Our Cuban Colony: A Study in Sugar* (New York, 1928); Alberto Arredondo, *Cuba: Tierra Indefensa* (Havana, 1945), and Robert F. Smith, *The United States and Cuba; Business and Diplomacy, 1917–1960* (New York, 1960). A Marxist, Philip S. Foner, presents his interpretations in a four-volume study, *A History of Cuba and Its Relations with the United States* (New York: International Publishers, 1962–   ) of which the first two volumes have already appeared. A more favorable presentation of the United States point of view is by ex-Ambassador Harry F. Guggenheim, *The United States and Cuba: A Study in International Relations* (New York, 1934).

During the late 1920's the American Fund for Public Service Studies in American Investments Abroad was established under the general editorship of Harry Elmer Barnes. Books issued in this series include the aforementioned studies by Knight and Jenks, and Margaret A. Marsh, *Bankers in Bolivia* (New York, 1928), J. Fred Rippy, *Capitalists in Colombia* (New York, 1931), and Bailey W. Diffie, *Puerto Rico; A Broken Pledge* (New York, 1931).

There are a number of interesting biographies of foreign entrepreneurs in Latin America of which only a few can be listed. David Pletcher has collected seven vignettes in *Rails, Mines and Progress; Seven American Promoters in Mexico, 1867–1911* (Ithaca, N.Y., 1958). Charles A. Gauld has written of Percival Farquhar in *The Last Titan* (Stanford, Calif., 1964), a fascinating man who left his stamp on many aspects of Latin American economic life, particularly the Madeira-Mamoré Railway. Watt Stewart has written two noteworthy biographies, *Henry Meiggs, Yankee Pizarro* (Durham, N.C., 1946) on the great railroad builder in Peru in the late nineteenth century, and *Keith and Costa Rica* (Albuquerque, N.M., 1964) on Minor C. Keith, the builder of Central American railways and the modern banana trade. For rather opposite views of one of the great enterprises in Mexico, see Harvey O'Connor, *The Guggenheims* (New York, 1935) and Isaac F. Marcosson, *Metal Magic; The Story of the American Smelting and Refining Company* (New York, 1949).

Expropriation is one of the "facts of life" in the ownership of property abroad: the fear of the investor that an alien government, often for inscrutable reasons, will suddenly deprive an honest businessman of his hard-earned and hard-won property. While the right to expropriate—with compensation—is guaranteed in international law, honestly assessing the value of the property and binding an often unstable government to payments is virtually impossible. Perhaps the most famous case of expropriation concerned Mexican petroleum. The Mexican side of the case is set forth by the Government of Mexico, *The True Facts About the Expropriation of the Oil Companies' Properties in Mexico* (Mexico, 1940), and Jesús Silva Herzog in *Petróleo mexicano* (Mexico, 1941). Merrill Rippy in "El petróleo y la Revolución Mexicana," *Problemas agrícolas é industriales de México*, Vol. VI, No. 3 (1954) makes a presentation to support the Mexican government legally, historically and morally. The oil companies' side is presented by Standard Oil Company (N.J.) in three parts: *Denials of Justice; A Memo-*

randum on the Decision of the Mexican Supreme Court of December 2, 1939 (New York, 1940), *The Reply to Mexico* [Reply to the Mexican document "The True Facts About the Expropriation of the Oil Companies' Properties in Mexico"] (New York, 1940), and *Confiscation or Expropriation? Mexico's Seizure of the Foreign Owned Oil Industry* (New York, 1940); and also in Roscoe Gaither's study, *Expropriation in Mexico: The Facts and the Law* (New York, 1940). Perhaps the most complete statement is Wendell Gordon's *The Expropriation of Foreign-Owned Property in Mexico* (Washington, D.C., 1941). A recent case was the expropriation of the properties of the International Telephone and Telegraph Corporation by the government of the state of Rio Grande do Sul, Brazil. For expositions of both sides of the conflict, see Governo do Estado do Rio Grande do Sul, *Encampação da Compania Telefonica Nacional* (Porto Alegre, 1962), and International Telephone and Telegraph Corporation, *The Expropriation of ITT in Rio Grande do Sul, Brazil; A Threat to the Alliance for Progress* (New York, 1962). For a consideration of the latest trends and materials in this field, see C. Neale Ronning, *Law and Politics in Inter-American Diplomacy* (New York, 1963), esp. chap. 3, "The Treatment of Aliens and Their Property."

ATTITUDES

Men tend to see the world through the lenses of their own values: "the good" is culturally, if not nationally, defined. One man's concept of efficiency is another man's concept of exploitation; one man's rights under international law is another man's intervention. American businessmen and the American government tend to see foreign investment by private corporations as of undeniable value to both the capital-exporting and the host nations in economic development. Latin Americans at best take a "Yes, but . . . ," attitude; at worst they denounce all past acts of foreigners, call for the expropriation of presently-owned properties and bars against future investments.

The best general exposition (in a patriotic vein) of American foreign policy in Latin America up to World War II is Samuel Flagg Bemis' *The Latin American Foreign Policy of the United States* (New York, 1943); the reader is also referred to Graham H. Stuart's *Latin America and the United States,* 5th ed. (New York, 1955). Postwar relations with an emphasis on economic matters is covered by the National Planning Association's monograph, "United States and Latin American Policies Affecting Their Economic Relations," Study No. 5 in 86th Congress, 2d Session, U.S. Senate Doc. No. 125, Subcommittee on American Republic Affairs of the Committee on Foreign Relations, *United States–Latin American Relations; Compilation of Studies* (Washington, D.C., Aug. 31, 1960), pp. 399–537. Dexter Perkins' *History of the Monroe Doctrine* (Boston, 1955), is now regarded as the definitive work on the subject. An interesting new viewpoint of the "dormant period" of American foreign relations is Walter LaFeber's *The New Empire; An Interpretation of American Expansion, 1860–1898* (Ithaca, N.Y., 1963). For a recent view of U.S. foreign policy emphasizing the importance of economic elements in opposition to the "strategic interpretations," see William A. Williams, *The Tragedy of American Diplomacy* (New York, 1959), and also his "Latin America: Laboratory of American Foreign Policy in the Nineteen-Twenties," *IAEA,* Vol. XI, No. 2 (Autumn, 1957), pp. 3–30. For other valuable commentary see Herbert Feis, *The Diplomacy of the Dollar, 1919–1932* (Baltimore, Md., 1950); Joseph Brandes, *Herbert Hoover and Economic Diplomacy; Department of Commerce Policy, 1921–1928* (Pittsburgh, Pa., 1962); Bryce Wood, *The Making of the Good Neighbor Policy* (New York, 1961); and Dexter Perkins, *The United States and Latin America* (Baton Rouge, La., 1961). Valuable source books are James W. Gantenbein, ed., *The Evolution of Our Latin American Policy: A Documentary Record* (New York, 1950); and William A. Williams, *The Shaping of American Foreign Policy* (Chicago, 1956).

For a professional study of the subject of economic development with a discussion of the role of foreign capital, see Howard S. Ellis, ed., *Economic Development for Latin America; Proceedings of a Conference Held by the International Economic Association* (London and New York, 1962); and Institute of International Studies and Overseas

Administration of the University of Oregon, Raymond F. Mikesell, Acting Director, "Problems of Latin American Economic Development," in 86th Congress, 2d Session, U.S. Senate Doc. No. 125, *United States–Latin American Relations,* cited above, pp. 539–684. Albert O. Hirschman in his book, *The Strategy of Economic Development* (New Haven, Conn., 1958) advances a most interesting theory on this subject, drawing upon his extensive work and experience in Latin America.

An excellent scholarly study of U.S. attitudes and problems in relation to private and public investment is the volume edited by Raymond F. Mikesell, who has written extensively on this topic, entitled *U.S. Private and Government Investment Abroad* (Eugene, Ore., 1962). Other studies that give an understanding of the general problem are Raymond F. Mikesell, *Foreign Investments in Latin America,* Economic Research Series, Inter-American Economic and Social Council, Organization of American States (Washington, D.C., 1955); Inter-American Economic and Social Council, Pan-American Union, *The Financing of Economic Development in Latin America* (Washington, D.C., 1958); and a most readable and enlightening evaluation by John Fayerweather, *Facts and Fallacies of International Business* (New York, 1962). Eugene R. Black of the World Bank sees positive values for foreign investment in his essay, *The Diplomacy of Economic Development* (Cambridge, Mass., 1960), *if* the approach of the enlightened, understanding "economic diplomat" is used.

Strong statements of the advantages which could accrue to foreign nations receiving private American aid were made at the Inter-American Investment Conference at New Orleans in February and March 1955, whose *Proceedings* are replete with expositions of how Latin American economic progress would be promoted through greater private capital investment. The U.S. Inter-American Council, whose membership comprises some of the largest American corporations with investments in Latin America, has celebrated its work in a lavishly illustrated brochure, *The Profitable Partnership; The Story of U.S. Private Enterprise in the Economic Development of Latin America* (Washington, D.C., 1957). For strong but not lavish claims, see Clement G. Motten, *et al., Latin America: Development Program-*

ming and U.S. Investments (Philadelphia, 1956) and the Committee for Economic Development, *Economic Development Abroad and the Role of American Foreign Investment* (New York, 1956). The Standard Oil Company (N.J.) notes the reciprocal effects of investments and the stimulation of foreign trade in a pamphlet, *Investments and Trade* (New York, 1940). An official survey of the benefits accruing from U.S. investment was in answer to inferences in the UN study of *Foreign Capital in Latin America* compiled by S. Pizer and F. Cutler, in "The Role of U.S. Investments in the Latin American Economy," *Survey of Current Business* (January, 1957), which was reprinted in their 1957 study, *U.S. Investments in the Latin American Economy,* cited above. Some excellent statements of the United States businessman's position are to be found in two series of Congressional hearings by the Subcommittee on Inter-American Relationships of the Joint Economic Committee: 87 Congress, 2d Session, *Economic Developments in South America,* May 10 and 11, 1962 (Washington, D.C., 1962), and 88th Congress, 2d Session, *Private Investment in Latin America,* January 14, 15, and 16, 1964 (Washington, D.C., 1964). The latter hearing was the basis of a report of the subcommittee to the same session of Congress also entitled *Private Investment in Latin America* (Washington, D.C., 1964), which summarized the benefits to be garnered by the Latin American nations through greater private investment. Similar sentiments are voiced in the report by Hubert H. Humphrey to the 88th Congress, 1st Session, *A Report on the Alliance for Progress, 1963* (Senate Doc. No. 13) (Washington, D.C., April 11, 1963). For strong endorsements of the work of the Alliance for Progress, which assigned half the role of foreign aid to private investment, see John C. Drier, *The Alliance for Progress, Problems and Perspectives* (Baltimore, Md., 1962); Lincoln Gordon, *A New Deal for Latin America; The Alliance for Progress* (Cambridge, Mass., 1963); and the executive branch's annual report to Congress, such as, *The Foreign Assistance Program; Annual Report to the Congress for Fiscal Year 1963* (Washington, D.C., 1964). A strong endorsement of the role of private capital was made by the Agency for International Development's Advisory Committee on Private Enterprise in Foreign Aid in its report *Foreign Aid Through Private Initiative* (Washington, D.C., July 1965).

While the Inter-American Development Bank (IADB), established on December 30, 1959 to promote economic and social progress by loans to Latin American nations, in its *Annual Report* stresses loans to Latin American government agencies to carry out these objectives (only a fraction goes directly to private enterprises), it attempts to involve private capital by selling its own bonds to the general public and to banks, and by a campaign actively encouraging and promoting greater participation by private capital directly. T. Graydon Upton, Vice President of the IADB, reflects this spirit in his addresses published by the Bank in mimeographed form: "Business and Progress in Latin America" (May 16, 1963) and "Private Investment and the Financing of Economic Development in Latin America" (July 29, 1963). A most interesting publication of the IADB is a series of addresses presented at the Third Meeting of the Board of Governors, April 25, 1962, in Buenos Aires, entitled *Round Table on Private Enterprise and the Development of Latin America*. At the same meeting the IADB sponsored another symposium entitled, *Round Table on Europe's Role in Latin American Economic Development*. In addition to the usual summaries of the work of the International Bank for Reconstruction and Development in Latin America presented in its *Annual Report*, a special report on *The World Bank Group in the Americas* (Washington, D.C., June, 1963), summarizes that institution's activities in Latin America as well as those of the International Finance Corporation and the International Development Association. An unusual project is the International Basic Economy Corporation originally sponsored by the Rockefeller family for investment in Latin America. Its many investment activities to stimulate economic growth and social betterment in Latin America and other parts of the world are put forth in its *Annual Report*.

The United States Government liberally extends encouragement to investment in Latin America. One of its activities is a series of studies to acquaint potential investors with the foreign scene issued by the Department of Commerce's Bureau of Foreign Commerce under a uniform title, *Investment in Venezuela, Conditions and Outlook for United States Investors* (Washington, D.C., 1953); *Colombia* (1953); *Mexico* (1955); *Paraguay* (1955); *Central America* (1957); *Ecuador* (1959); and *Chile* (1960). The Department's Office of International Trade has done a fine job of analyzing both the impediments to private investment abroad and business-men's opinion of these impediments in *Factors Limiting U.S. Investment Abroad* (Washington, D.C., 1953). The various types of support offered businessmen interested in investing abroad are summarized in the State Department's Agency for International Development's publication, *Aids to Business (Overseas Investment)* (Washington, D.C., 1963). The growing U.S. Government sponsored program of guarantees is discussed by Marina von Neiman Whitman, *The United States Investment Guaranty Program and Private Foreign Investment,* Princeton Studies in International Finance No. 9 (Princeton, N.J., 1959), while A.A. Fatouros, in *Government Guarantees to Foreign Investors* (New York, 1962), discusses at length the various types of aid and support given by governments to their nationals investing abroad, including traditional means and new programs. The latest information on the U.S. guarantee program is outlined in the U.S. State Department's AID booklet, *Investment Guaranty Handbook . . . U.S. Government Guarantees Available for New American Investments in Less-Developed Countries Under the Specific Risk Investment Guarantee Program* (Washington, D.C., May, 1964). This problem, including the use of tax incentives, is discussed by J. N. Behrman in chap. 8, "U.S. Government Encouragement of Private Direct Investment Abroad," in Mikesell's *U.S. . . . Investment Abroad,* cited above. A recent addition to this literature is Marina von Neumann Whitman's *Government Risk-Sharing in Foreign Investment* (Princeton, 1965).

The problems of taxes and other obstacles to foreign investments in Latin America are treated in Harvard Law School, International Program in Taxation, *United States Tax Incentives to Direct Foreign Investment* (Cambridge, Mass., 1954) and United Nations Secretariat, Economic Affairs Department, *U.S. Income Taxation of Private U.S. Investment in Latin America* (New York, 1953), UN Sales No. 1953.XVI.1. Also see the aforementioned U.S. Department of Commerce study, *Factors Limiting United States Investment Abroad.* For surveys of laws generally regulating the operation of foreign businesses, including tax laws, see Franz M. Joseph and R. U. Koppel, "Planning Subsidiary

Operations in Argentina, Brazil, Chile and the Netherlands Antilles," in *Prentice-Hall Tax Ideas Report* (Englewood Cliffs, N.J., 1963), paragraph 24,003. The problems of operating enterprises with local and foreign capital are surveyed in Friedman and Kalmanoff's *Joint International Business Ventures*, cited above.

A two-volume study edited by Denis de Ricci, *Investissements en l'Amérique Latine; Aspect juridique et fiscal* (Paris, 1955–1957), provides short summaries of the pertinent laws and other economic and fiscal matters for Brazil, Colombia, Ecuador, Peru, Venezuela, Argentina, Bolivia, Chile, Paraguay and Uruguay. The information for each country is summarized by a member of the bar of that nation. Also see Wolfgang Friedmann, ed., *Legal Aspects of Foreign Investment* (Boston, 1959). A short survey is to be found in the above mentioned U.N.–OAS report on *Foreign Private Investments in the Latin American Free Trade Area*, pp. 18–23, which also includes commentary on taxes, and in the U.S. Department of Commerce series *Investments in . . .* , also cited above. Donald R. Shea's research on *The Calvo Clause* (Minneapolis, Minn., 1955) catalogues a number of cases of foreign intervention in support of investors which eventually led to the formulation of the Latin American concept of the Calvo Clause which was designed to circumvent the reasons for such intervention. Also see Ann Van W. and A. J. Thomas, *Non-Intervention: The Law and Its Import in the Americas* (Dallas, Tex., 1956), and the abovementioned C. N. Ronning's *Law and Politics* in *Inter-American Diplomacy*.

Several dissertations have investigated the problem of whether foreign investment has aided Latin America: John R. Moore, "The Impact of Foreign Direct Investment on an Underdeveloped Economy: The Venezuelan Case" (unpublished doctoral dissertation, Cornell University, 1956) —on this topic also see the conflicting review articles by J. Fred Rippy and Virgil Salera of Betancourt's and Lieuwin's studies of Venezuelan petroleum (cited above) in *IAEA*, Vol. XI, No. 3 (Winter, 1957), pp. 73–82; Vol. XI, No. 4 (Spring, 1958), pp. 37–48; Vol. XI, No. 1 (Summer, 1958), pp. 90–95; and also see the aforecited National Planning Association study—Raymond F. Pelissier, "The Contribution of Certain American Business Firms to the Development of Mexico Since World War II" (unpublished doctoral dissertation, American University, 1958); and John C. Rayburn, "Some Aspects of the Impact of Anglo-Saxon Capital and Technology in Venezuela" (unpublished doctoral dissertation, University of Chicago, 1953). Also of interest is Richard A. Lebarge, *Impact of the United Fruit Company on the Economic Development of Guatemala, 1946–1954* (New Orleans, La., Tulane University, 1960).

While it is probably impossible to categorically arrive at a conclusion as to whether foreign investment on the whole is or has been a boon or bane for Latin America, many opinions are advanced. A good introduction to a multiplicity of views is the symposium presided over by Harris G. Warren, "Economic Diplomacy with Latin America," *IAEA*, Vol. IV, No. 4 (Spring, 1951), pp. 3–47, and Fayerweather's *Facts and Fallacies*, cited above. Some good balanced approaches are provided by Clarence H. Haring's short *Inversiones extranjeras en la América Latina; Un exámen retrospectivo* (Mexico, 1949) and Javier Márquez Blasco's very good and well-reasoned commentary, *Inversiones internacionales en América Latina; Problemas y perspectivas*, Informaciones económicas [del Banco de México] No. 3 (Mexico, 1945). Studies which urge intelligent use of U.S. and domestic, private and public capital to fit the circumstances—social and political, as well as economic—are, United Nations, Economic Commission for Latin America, *International Co-operation in Latin American Development Policy* (New York, 1954), Sales No. 1954.II.G.2; Pedro C. M. Teichert, *Economic Policy Revolution and Industrialization in Latin America* (Oxford, Miss., 1959)—a book which cannot be too highly recommended for its wealth of insight, analysis, and data on economic development policies—J. Peter Grace, *It Is Not Too Late in Latin America Now* (New York, 1961 [?]); and two Latin American views, Eduardo Arcila Farías, *El capital extranjero; limitaciones a la inversión de capital extranjero en países americanos* (Caracas, 1950), and the excellent conservative work by Juan Sánchez Navarro, *Ensayo sobre una política de inversiones extranjeras en México* (Mexico, 1955). The latter two works emphasize the thesis that direct foreign investments can be directed into proper channels. Domingo Alberto Rangel, a lieutenant of Rómulo Betancourt in the Venezuelan party Acción Democrática, essayed a difficult task in a book *Una teoría para la revolución democrática* (Caracas, 1958), when he projected a brilliant future for his country and Latin America as a whole based on a quasi-benevolent attitude on the part of the United States. Rangel candidly admits to all the usual accusations leveled against U.S. capital in Latin America and U.S. policies. But he insists that the American people and intellectuals are aware of the scandals, decry them as loudly as the Latin Americans, and sincerely hope for and wish for their government to work for a betterment of Latin America's economic and social life.

For completely divergent views of the effects of private foreign capital see the communist exposition of Alberto Ghiraldo, *Yanquilandia bárbara; la lucha contra el imperialismo* (Madrid, 1929), and Robert W. Dunn, "U.S.A. Imperialist Investments in South America," *Anti-Imperialist Review,* Vol. I (Berlin, 1932), pp. 246–251, and the impassioned defenses of foreign investment by two Latin Americans: Mauricio E. Greffier, *La acción del capital extranjero en el desarrollo económico de la América Latina* (Buenos Aires, 1945), and Filipo Hostos y de Ayala, *Las inversiones de capital privado norteamericano en la América Latina como media de conservar y fomentar el principio de la libertad de empresa* (San Juan, Puerto Rico, 1948).

Most Latin American writers tend to be critical, in varying degrees, of the role of foreign capital, and particularly American capital. William S. Stokes has surveyed this attitude in an article, "Economic Anti-Americanism in Latin America," *IAEA,* Vol. XI, No. 3 (Winter, 1957), pp. 3–22, which is annotated and has an appended bibliography on the subject. While the spiritual progenitor of this Latin American attitude is often cited as José Enríque Rodó's essay *Ariel,* translated by F. J. Stimson (Boston, 1922), today the analysis of Hans W. Singer in his article, "Distribution of Gains Between Investing and Borrowing Countries," American Economic Association, *Proceedings,* Vol. XL (May, 1950), pp. 473–487, is often the inspiration of anti-American polemics. A companion article elucidating the same idea in a more specific application is the work of C. Rollins, "Mineral Development and Economic Growth," *Social Research,* Vol. XXIII (Autumn, 1956), pp. 253–280.

Among the works exhibiting anti-American and anti-foreign feelings in varying degrees the following may be cited: Juan José Arevalo, *The Shark and the Sardines* (New York, 1961), an impassioned indictment of the Yanqui shark preying on the Latin sardines; Clarence H. Haring, *South America Looks at the United States* (New York, 1928), covers Latin American opinion before the Good Neighbor Policy; Carleton Beals, *et al.*, *What the South Americans Think of Us* (New York, 1945), a survey in journalistic style by three Americans of Latin anti-Americanism in the 1930's and 1940's; Octávio Brandão, "O Brasil, explorado e oprimido," *Revista Brasiliense*, Vol. XL (March–April, 1962), pp. 181–193, which damns the power of foreign capital in supporting and corrupting Brazil's economic and political structure; Estevão Leito de Carvalho, *Petroleo; Salvação ou desgraça do Brasil?* (Rio de Janeiro, 1959), passionately defends the necessity of maintaining a public monopoly over Brazilian petroleum; Raúl Díez de Medina (Gaston Nerval, pseudo.), *Autopsy of the Monroe Doctrine* (New York, 1934), gives the views of a Bolivian toward dollar diplomacy and the use of the Monroe Doctrine to help U.S. businessmen and government dominate Latin America; Arturo Frondizi, *Petróleo y política, contribución al estudio de la historia económica argentina* (Buenos Aires, 1954), bewails the effect of British and American capital upon the life of Argentina in particular and Latin America in general; Pablo González Casanova, *La ideologia norteamericana sobre inversiones extranjeras* (Mexico, 1955), excoriates American businessmen from a Marxian point of view and from a nationalist viewpoint suggests offsetting their influence; Salvador Arreola Resendiz, *Inversiones norteamericanas en México y sus consecuencias económicas* (Mexico, 1953) presents a Mexican-nationalist commentary; José E. Rivera, *Los empréstitos extranjeras y la política americana* (La Paz, Bolivia, 1925), for the views of a Bolivian nationalist; Ramón R. Rodríguez, *Latin América, victima del dólar* (Caracas, 1958), is a pure anti-U.S. polemic; Jesús Silva Herzog, *El pensamiento económico en México* (Mexico, 1947) for a summary of Mexican thought; Jorge W. Villacres Moscoso, *La política económica internacional de los estados hispanoamericanos* (Guayaquil, 1955); and a volume edited by the Mexican economist Fernando Zamora, *La intervención del estado en la economía* (Mexico, Universidad Nacional, 1955), has a number of interesting articles including R. Martínez Leclainche, "Ventajas y desventajas de las inversiones extranjeras," and J. L. Ceceña Gamez, "Política en materia de inversión extranjera," which "exposes" American domination of many segments of the Mexican economy.

A number of Latin American economists have put forth, under the editorship of a prominent Harvard Latin Americanist, their standpoints in Raymond Vernon (ed.), *How Latin America Views the U.S. Investor* (New York, 1965).

A NOTE ON THE TYPE

The text of this book is set in Caledonia, a typeface designed by W(illiam) A(ddison) Dwiggins for the Mergenthaler Linotype Company in 1939. Dwiggins chose to call his new typeface Caledonia, the Roman name for Scotland, because it was inspired by the Scotch types cast about 1833 by Alexander Wilson & Son, Glasgow type founders. However, there is a calligraphic quality about this face that is totally lacking in the Wilson types. Dwiggins referred to an even earlier typeface for this "liveliness of action"—one cut around 1790 by William Martin for the printer William Bulmer. Caledonia has more weight than the Martin letters, and the bottom finishing strokes (serifs) of the letters are cut straight across, without brackets, to make sharp angles with the upright stems, thus giving a "modern face" appearance.

W. A. Dwiggins (1880–1956) was born in Martinsville, Ohio, and studied art in Chicago. In 1904 he moved to Hingham, Massachusetts, where he built a solid reputation as a designer of advertisements and as a calligrapher. He began an association with the Mergenthaler Linotype Company in 1929, and over the next twenty-seven years designed a number of book types for that firm. Of special interest are the Metro series, Electra, Caledonia, Eldorado, and Falcon. In 1930, Dwiggins first became interested in marionettes, and through the years made many important contributions to the art of puppetry and the design of marionettes.

Composed by American Book–Stratford Press, Inc.,
New York, N.Y.
Printed and bound by The Colonial Press, Inc.,
Clinton, Mass.